Nicolas Wasser
The Promise of Diversity

Postcolonial Studies | Volume 29

Nicolas Wasser (PhD UFRJ/Brazil) is a member of the Graduiertenkolleg Gender Studies at the University of Basel. His research focuses on affective labor, LGBT issues, precarity, and difference in Latin America.

Nicolas Wasser
The Promise of Diversity
How Brazilian Brand Capitalism Affects Precarious Identities and Work

[transcript]

Doctoral thesis at the Programa de Pós-Graduação em Sociologia e Antropologia (PPGSA), Instituto de Filosofia e Ciências Sociais, Universidade Federal do Rio de Janeiro.

Bibliographic information published by the Deutsche Nationalbibliothek
The Deutsche Nationalbibliothek lists this publication in the Deutsche Nationalbibliografie; detailed bibliographic data are available in the Internet at http://dnb.d-nb.de

© 2017 transcript Verlag, Bielefeld

All rights reserved. No part of this book may be reprinted or reproduced or utilized in any form or by any electronic, mechanical, or other means, now known or hereafter invented, including photocopying and recording, or in any information storage or retrieval system, without permission in writing from the publisher.

Cover concept: Kordula Röckenhaus, Bielefeld
Cover illustration: Nicolas Wasser, Rio de Janeiro, 2016.
Printed in Germany
Print-ISBN 978-3-8376-3754-0
PDF-ISBN 978-3-8394-3754-4

Table of Contents

Acknowledgments | 9

1 Introduction | 13
    1.1 Identity markets and their discontents | 13
    1.2 Culture, hegemony and (sexual) difference | 20
    1.3 Notes on method and research procedure | 23

2 Governing through desires
   Brands, identities and the case of *Visibly Hot* | 29
    2.1 The brand as a mode of conduct | 31
        2.1.1 How commodities obtained a life of their own | 33
        2.1.2 Behavioral science and the shift to the consumer's needs | 36
        2.1.3 Media and the social fabric of the everyday | 39
        2.1.4 The role of lifestyles and political stances | 42
        2.1.5 The corporate brand | 45
        2.1.6 Branding and the body | 48

    2.2 Sexy difference: from product to advertising | 50
        2.2.1 Exploring the product | 51
        2.2.2 Sunglasses are becoming sexy | 54
        2.2.3 Exploiting the sexist gaze | 56
        2.2.4 Enacting feminism and freedom | 63

    2.3 Architectures of the corporate brand | 68
        2.3.1 From Californian rock dreams to brand management | 69
        2.3.2 Style and identity politics | 72
        2.3.3 Up with sales! Spatial, organizational and
            identity expansions | 76
        2.3.4 Conventions and affective bonds | 78

2.4 The search for econo-sexy professionals:
diversity management | 81
   2.4.1 "We don't simply like- we give it a value" | 84
   2.4.2 Diversity, a somewhat different equality | 94
   2.4.3 Inclusion as normalization? | 99

3 Longing to be different | 103
3.1 Identification as government | 105

3.2 Life-work-worlds | 110
   3.2.1 The first employment | 113
   3.2.2 Service and shopping workers | 117
   3.2.3 The artistic improvisers | 121

3.3 "Here I can be who I am", or: authenticity as freedom | 125
   3.3.1 The freedom of style | 128
   3.3.2 The necessity of style | 131
   3.3.3 The malleability of "ser diferente" | 133
   3.3.4 Style as a becoming | 137

3.4 Recognizing and modeling different selves | 140
   3.4.1 Posing in contested differences | 143
   3.4.2 Sexy white girl | 148
   3.4.3 Black beauty and identity | 152
   3.4.4 The gay theme | 157

4 Affective labor | 165
4.1 Emotional work, authenticity, and affects | 167
   4.1.1 Double productivity: sexual labor | 171
   4.1.2 Exuberant sexuality, or, back to affect | 175

4.2 The seductions of retail service work | 181
   4.2.1 "Trabalhar com acessórios é ser apaixonado pela marca" | 183
   4.2.2 Training, individuality, and attitude | 185

    4.2.3 Desires and sticky social bonds | 189
    4.2.4 Compliments and sexual fantasies | 193
    4.2.5 Misadventurous affects | 197

4.3 Ambiguous friendships | 200
    4.3.1 Cordiality, a cultural politics of friendship | 204
    4.3.2 Deprovincializing cordiality | 207
    4.3.3 Recognition at work | 210
    4.3.4 Competitive affects and collectivity | 216

5 (Un)fulfilled promises and different conflicts | 221

5.1 Conditions, submissions and micro revolts in service work | 222
    5.1.1 Capital-competencies and personal growth, a phenomenon across classes? | 224
    5.1.2 Incorporating individual performance and beauty | 229
    5.1.3 Limited freedom, new controls: Pedro's emphatic criticism | 232
    5.1.4 Carol's unbroken passion | 238
    5.1.5 Keeping a safe distance: Juliano | 246

5.2 Precarious recognition in motion | 250
    5.2.1 The fatigue of self-inventions | 257
    5.2.2 *Rolezinhos* and celebrating capitalism – „um tapa na cara da sociedade" | 263

6 Conclusion | 269

7 Bibliography | 277

Acknowledgments

I am grateful to the Coordinator of the *Programa de Pós-Graduação em Sociologia e Antropologia* (PPGSA) of the Federal University of Rio de Janeiro, André Pereira Botelho, as well as to the entire commission and administrative staff of the said institution for their support in writing this thesis in English. Albeit still a rarity within Brazilian social sciences, I hope to encourage more researchers to venture towards such opportunities, creating dialogues and broadening visibility of different research traditions on both sides of the Atlantic. My special thanks go to the examination board, Bila Sorj, José Ricardo Ramalho, Sérgio Costa, Sérgio Carrara and Maria Filomena Gregori, who also made this possible.

First and foremost, the development of the present thesis is thoroughly indebted to the fruitful exchanges and presentations within the *Núcleo de Estudos de Sexualidade e Gênero* (NESEG) at the Federal University of Rio de Janeiro. Therefore, I thank my advisor Bila Sorj for both her wise administration and intellectual dialogue, guiding me safely through this research and continuously contributing with her rich insights. Furthermore, I would like to mention Aparecida Moraes, Carla Gomes, Fabíola Cordeiro, Mani Tebet, Ana Bárbara Araujo as well as the collaborating undergraduate students. Their criticisms of earlier drafts were extremely useful. Beyond the nucleus, I am grateful to the entire faculty of the *Programa de Pós-Graduação em Sociologia e Antropologia* (PPGSA), who always showed a helping hand in the development of this work. Last but not least, I want to emphasize the precious support given by our secretaries, namely Claudia Vianna, Gleidis Maria Corrêa, Angela Maria Dias da Rocha and Verônica Vasconcellos Gomes.

A significant part of this text also resonates the discussions, seminars and workshops in the postgraduate group gender studies at the University of Basel (*Graduiertenkolleg IV: Geschlechterverhältnisse – Normalisierung und Transformation*). I thank my second advisor Andrea Maihofer for her inspiring remarks and critiques, which highly motivated me to "keep on the tracks". Furthermore, I am pleased to thank the members of the research group for their productive commentaries and help, namely Ayşegül Şah Bozdoğan, Laura Eigenmann, Yv Nay, Katrin Meyer, Moni Götsch, Rebecca Mörgen, Nadine Sarfert, Stefanie Schälin, Nathan Schocher, Janina Scholz, Katharina Stöckli, Anika Thym, Barbara Umrath, Fleur Weibel and our excellent coordinator Andrea Zimmermann.

I have been very lucky to have transatlantic mediators between Europe and Brazil, who contributed and assisted me in my venture to the university in Rio de Janeiro. Zinka Ziebell's fundamental instruction in Portuguese, Sérgio Costa's sociological and institutional expertise and Kaciano Gadelha's insightful views on queer and gender studies in the Atlantic encounter were all of essential value. What is more, I thank Bartholomeu Wiese, Márcia Carnaval and Laura Jouve-Villard for their great friendship and intellectual support.

I also want to thank the friends and colleagues who read parts of the manuscript and whose comments were decisive: Laura Kemmer, Rebecca Mörgen, Laura Eigenmann and Ana Teasca. Another debt is owed to all those friends who helped me so profoundly with their revisions and language skills in Portuguese, namely Georgia Pereira, Ana Paula Morel, Guilherme Marcondes, Eleana Salas, Luciana Barraviera, Felipe Magaldi, Guilherme Bezerra and especially Lila Almendra Praça and Elizabeth Harris.

During the preparation of this text, there were a number of local academic encounters that decisively encouraged my research process. I benefited from the expertise of Laura Graziela Gomes and her research group on consumption anthropology, of Ovídio de Abreu Filho's inspiring insights in Deleuzian thought, of Graziella Moraes and Elisa Reis' thorough knowledge of sociological theory, of Eloísa Martín's expertise in academic writing, and of Sérgio Carrara's kind invitation to participate in the monthly colloquiums of the Latin American Center for Sexuality and Human Rights. What is more, I thank the coordinator of the *Núcleo de Estudos em Corpos, Gêneros e Sexualidades Dissidentes*, María Elvira Díaz Benítez, for the opportunity to repeatedly present my research, as well as the group members, namely Everton Rangel, Barbara Pires, Nathalia Gonçales, Carolina Castellitti, Fátima Lima and Nathanael Araújo for their helpful comments and reception.

My appreciation goes further to Gundula Ludwig and Kathi Wiedlack for the stimulating conversations and support at *Queering Paradigms*, Susanne Hofmann's precious peer reading in the context of her book project, Angelo Soares' helpful ideas and literature he provided me at the VII ALAST conference, as well as to Paulo Gajanigo, Rogério Ferreira Souza and Guilhermo André Aderaldo for the inspiring discussions about cultural hegemony and capitalism at the 39° ANPOCS.

I thank all the employees and friends I interviewed during my research, whose names I cannot name here for legal matters, but who were decisive for sharing their experiences, views and self-perceptions. Only their outstanding openness, reception and help gave this research its characteristic contours.

Finally, I am most grateful to my family, who supported me all along the process of this research and writing.

1. Introduction

1.1. IDENTITY MARKETS AND THEIR DISCONTENTS

How does 21st century capitalism act with promises of sexual liberation? What are the probable new constraints and conditions, into which Western economies seduce particularly LGBT people and more generally so-called minority groups? These were some of the questions I had in mind at the early stages of the present thesis. Having moved to Rio de Janeiro at that time, I found the width of both LGBT[1] and, to a minor degree, racial identity-based consumer facilities to be striking. Anthropologists in Brazil have identified this phenomenon as representing an increased segmentation of markets, epitomized by GLS[2] (França 2012; Gregori 2012). The latter includes flourishing tourism around lesbian-gay-friendly beaches, the growth of sex toy industries and shops that responded to presumably all sexual dissidents' tastes, as well as a large offer of nightlife activities.

---

1   As Simões and Carrara (2014: 79) point out, LGBT currently corresponds to the categories of identity used in the political agendas of those social movements in Brazil, which emanated from the national government's program *Brasil Sem Homofobia* in 2004.

2   GLS is the Brazilian acronym for "Gays, Lesbians and Sympathizers", a specific market label to denominate spaces, products and services directed mainly to homosexuals. Since the 1990s, GLS has been widely popular in the country, whereas its use increasingly vanished over the course of the last decade. Several human rights organizations such as the Brazilian national LGBT association (ABLGT) strictly reject the label because they criticize the exclusion of bisexuals, transgender and trans people.

As it seemed at first glance, these sexually directed markets had somewhat ceased to function strictly in terms of niches; they had significantly broadened in number and turnover. Also, their audience was no more continuously represented by or reduced to the exotic other. Given this shift in how LGBT and other minoritized groups appeared to be embraced and eventually normalized in economic terms (see the argument of Engel 2009), the question must arise as to whether the same was true for other cultural spheres, particularly those of rights and everyday life.

As it happens, for someone to think about such different cultural spheres, the first point would be to delimit a more or less clear compass of what is actually meant by referring to the often blurry notions of "the economic", "the market" or capitalism. How, and driven by what economic forces or actors were the logics of sexual norms – as I suppose – about to change? Economic sociologist Zelizer (2005) has argued that the sphere of intimacy had never been as separated from economic activity as most people believed. According to the author, economic transactions such as through gifts or money were but a mode of how people kept alive their intimate ties with others. In general terms, Zelizer endeavors to convince us that "the economic" has always been a consequence of cultural, private, intimate and even sexual motivation between people. Since she is at pains to deny any alienating or destructive effects of late capitalist modernity on social lives, her approach however fails to consider the historical specificities, which mold the very relation of the intimate with the economic. As I will argue with reference to the work of Arvidsson (2006), 20th century entrepreneurial spirits' invention of the brand has profoundly re-engineered the latter relation. Knowledge, practice and power alike, brands are today the bundled governmental tools through which capitalism's market logics are being aligned with people's tastes, lives and aspirations.

Starting from this assumption on the centrality of brands, "the economic" corresponds first and foremost to a complex and always contested cultural sphere, which is specific to contemporary capitalist logics of market growth and neoliberal self-realization. It is complex since a brand's successful operation means that its practices may literally unfold within or in the name of its respective target group. On Valentine's Day 2015, *O Boticário*, Brazil's biggest cosmetic company, launched a television commercial for an allegedly irresistible perfume. The meeting of three amorous couples with chic clothing could be watched: a lesbian, a gay and a heterosexual couple. Although the commercial was neither offensive nor slightly inventive in its forms of gender representation, it generated public controversy. As the media throughout the country reported (Redação/G1 2015), a considerable group of consumers filed a complaint at the National Council for Media Regularization (Conar) and threatened to boycott the brand. Assured by Pentecostal and conservative voices, they said that they saw the Brazilian family disrespected. Open television propaganda, as some specified, was inappropriate to deal with such a delicate topic. But in addition to the homophobic statements, there was also a broad counter-movement expressing solidarity with the spot's idea of "diversity of love". Aside from commentators and consumers, even some other brands of cosmetics and food industry adopted as well as explicitly defended *O Boticário*'s LGBT-friendly attitude in their commercials.[3]

The example of the polemics around *O Boticário* illustrates that the question of how LGBTs are being aligned with market success needs to be seen in the context of ongoing and meanwhile harsh political struggles about preservation or pluralization of the traditional binary gender order[4]. What is recent in these conflicts may be the fact that the agents of heterosexual hegemony see their highness threatened by unsettling initiatives of brands and private enterprises. This again stems from an economic constellation, in which brands are already acting as political forces, participating in identity regimes that decide on the cultural (and eventually existential) legitimacy of an individual's articulation of sexual orientation, sex, race or other social markers. In a certain way similar to political parties, brands do rely on a degree of how people identify with their messages. For identity offers can only work in the desired way if the targeted people accept or take them on as their social places. Marketing sciences have invested a great deal in order to bring into perfection the techniques that strive to weave promising aspirations in brands.

---

3 This was also the case with advertisement of the soft drink enterprise *Mate Leão* that celebrated the "first gay kiss in telenovela" as a welcomed progress.

4 In October 2015, a lower chamber's commission of the Brazilian parliament approved a bill that seeks to further limit access to the morning-after pill, including for rape victims, to which it is restricted under current law. At the same time, another bill plans to criminalize "heterofobia". Former president of the chamber of deputies endorsed both bills.

Martins Filho (2012) points out that new logics of market and media have recently spread throughout Brazil, changing identity offers for black people. As an effect of growing markets specifically directed to Afro-descendants, black people's awareness of their role as potent, self-sufficient consumers had risen. The valorization of the *black way of life* – including own styles of clothing, haircuts, cosmetics, music, and leisure[5] – prevented, as the author argues, from exoticizing non-whites in consumer culture. Once established as an appreciable product, black people and their style were now about to be recognized as equipped with an own economic potential (Martins Filho 2012: 198). But is economic potential, we may then critically ask, equivalent or even the new warranty for one's right to be different, in other words, different to the norm of whiteness or of heterosexuality?

That is just what contends the rhetoric of a Brazilian fashion label, to which I have devoted the central ethnographic case study of the present book. *Visibly Hot*[6] is a Brazilian company specialized in sunglasses and in selling a young and "sexy" lifestyle. First and foremost, its brand is creating a whole architecture of attractive identifications for its own employees, unleashing manifold desires fueled by its slogan and entrepreneurial mission statement: *be different*. As this key slogan seems to bundle a variety of social aspirations, mainly those young people that are affected by lower education profiles as well as by sexual or racial prejudice like to work for *Visibly Hot*. As several salesclerks reported during my study conducted in Rio de Janeiro's shopping centers, they felt a personal bond with the brand's spirit. Unlike common fashion enterprises, they recalled, *Visibly Hot* gave them the sensation of being appreciated as individuals in their own right: "Here I can be who I am", as their common saying goes. The example of Carol – a 20-year-old salesclerk who tattooed the brand's logo

---

5 The author's argument is also close to the theses of Gilroy (1995) on the Black Atlantic diasporic culture, which has been furthered by Costa (2007) with respect to the Brazilian case.

6 Due to copyright concerns, the enterprise's name has been changed. Further evidence has equally been covered in order to guarantee the anonymity of individuals surveyed during this research. Consequently, the web sources that have been consulted, for example, YouTube and Facebook, will not be thoroughly indicated.

on her forearm – seemed to suggest that her affective longing was rooted in her coming of age as a young lesbian, placed between outer threats and inner aspirations for recognition.

More than constituting a question of consumption practices per se, the cases of Carol and other sales employees turned out to point to changes in the field of work. The detection that brands were central to their experiences is an effect of the globally intensifying significance of identity as a resource of retail service labor (Du Gay 1996). *Visibly Hot* is emblematic of this trend. As common in Human Resources policies of other branches too, it adapted tools of so-called *diversity management*, which is aimed at making use of social plurality (Purtschert 2007). In a commercial documentary about its employees, which is primarily shown in training sessions for arriving personnel, *Visibly Hot* communicates its idea of Brazilian diversity as embraced by the brand. The portrayals include four young people, one woman and three men. Each of them comes from a different part of the country, ranging from Pará in the North, Minas Gerais and São Paulo in the Southeast as well as Paraná in the South. But what they have in common is that they are all depicted as struggling for their individual visibility: first, there is the black Rasta and capoeira guy, who lives in a shantytown and has found his first profession as a salesclerk at *Visibly Hot*. Second, we meet a girl from the countryside, who is about to cut manioc roots for lunch and who reports that her father told her to always run after the good things in life. The third portrayal depicts a young, overtly gay *paulistano*[7] who says that the company was like a "family" to him, and that within this "love story" with the brand, he was after personal "growth". Finally fourth, there is a guy from a town in the South, who emphasizes his Pentecostal faith that led him not only to *Visibly Hot*'s ardor for pushing performance but also out of his humble surroundings.

What is striking about this diversity concept is that on the one hand it offers plural and eventually many kinds of identifications, which in other spheres may be adversary and highly conflicting (as is the case with gay and Pentecostal). On the other hand, the portrayed employees' broad agreement on performance, growth and stylization of their selves suggests that their articulations of identity, including the emotional and aspirational content, are unfolding as the main resource of labor, affective labor. In-

---

7   Portuguese term for residents from the city of São Paulo.

spired by Lorenz and Kuster's (2007) approach of emphasizing the powerful role of sexuality and concomitant identity politics in the realm of work, I will show how *Visibly Hot* is inducing an appeal for social recognition within its employees; in other words, how it makes the latters' job sexy and attractive. The brand in question deals with promises that mobilize culturally aspirational identities (of sexual, racial, or other content implying social capital) and turns their articulation into integrated parts of labor. Sales employees are thus confronted with the general demand of playfully experiencing and individually working on their identities. As it will turn out, these demands have not only liberating, but simultaneously precarious effects: firstly, because the employees' work on their identity is virtually unpaid, since it is generally associated to one's will for "personal growth" in life. Secondly, the individual achievement of recognition and beauty (as promised) demands uneven efforts. Paradoxically, those young people who are most addressed by the diversity politics – lesbians, gays, and blacks – need to give proof of additional assets, that is, performing their very difference in fashionable manners, if they want to be embraced by the brand's "family".

Affective labor, by which I also reconsider the notion of emotional work as classically outlined by Hochschild (2003), has gained renewed attention within the debates about the commercialization of feeling. In quantitative terms, this is due to the global expansion of service jobs as one of the basements of post-Fordist relations of production (Hardt and Negri 2000: 285), a process that has lately intensified with even higher velocity in Brazil than in other industrialized countries. Today, the overall service industry represents more than 60% of the country's GDP (MDIC 2014)[8].

---

8   Antunes and Druck (2013) point to a couple of factors, which determine the deep transformation within production and wage labor in Brazil in the recent decades. Above the increased demands with respect to workers' flexibility and cognitive skills, the authors identify widespread outsourcing [*terceirização*] as the country's most devastating changes away from Fordist cycles of production and contracting. It is estimated that about one quarter of all formal wage laborers today are employed under such outsourced conditions. This entrepreneurial withdrawal from social security benefits and workers' rights could then also be described as one of the modes of neoliberal technologies, which unfold in geographically deterritorialized, but globally assembled spaces and logics (Ong

In qualitative terms, there is a strong tendency of "emotionalization" of the tasks of customer care. Even jobs in public administration, which formerly served as symbol for a rationalized and frigidly trained worker identity, are now part of this process (Sauer and Penz 2013). However, there is still a need for more explanation of how identity performances turn into direct resources of affective laborers and profit-oriented endeavors. As Penz and Sauer rightly note, sociological debates on the "entrepreneurial self" often ignore the affective dimensions of these processes and hence the literal "somatization of the conduct of the self and of others" (2013: 126).

I aim to contribute to this debate by discussing the transformation of ordinary service work with the example of Brazilian fashion retail. By stressing the significance of desires stimulated through capitalist incentives to improve workers' self-conduct through tools of *branding* and *diversity management*, I argue that specific sexual and racial selves have turned into something akin to the new raw material of capital. As in the example of *Visibly Hot*, promises for social recognition unfold through excessive (self)identification by its employees, intrinsically linking labor exploitation with the lived aspirations of young salesclerks. Identifying these young people as precarious raises not only the question of salary and social securities, but also and foremost the modes of how they dispose themselves to inhabit such precarious positions. Where are the limits of one's identification with the implied brand's promise of difference? What are the experienced difficulties at work if one is urged to continually articulate both an authentic "sexy" subject and a restless profit motive attitude? And finally, what forms of critique, intended or not, may such unease advance against both the logics of personal growth and the marketed promise of freedom?

2007). Following Antunes and Druck, the main vector of *terceirização* appears as a transfer of responsibility from the enterprise to the individual worker (2007: 221).

1.2 CULTURE, HEGEMONY AND (SEXUAL) DIFFERENCE

Even if the identities in question are being articulated within an entrepreneurial context, their cultural contents are not to be seen as exhaustively determined, as Orthodox Marxism alleged, by means and relations of production. As already the early sociologists of culture like Simmel (1903) claimed, culture needs to be looked at as an analytical and interpretive field in its own right. Starting from such an understanding, Weber (2005[1904)]) famously composed his thesis on the late 19th century spirit of capitalism, which he described as mutually pervaded by the protestant ethic. The latter denominated phenomena like individuals' disciplined and rationalized attitudes to work, but in a broader sense also the mechanisms of capitalist sociation [*Vergesellschaftung*]. Boltanski and Chiapello (2005) have taken up and expanded Weber's approach in order to describe the cultural contours of capitalism at the beginning of the 21st century. The new spirit of capitalism, they hold, refers to project-oriented and individual self-perfecting attitudes as common in marketing and management departments of leading global enterprises. Second, the authors elaborate that this spirit has developed the capacity of incorporating different strands of social critique[9], now using them for its own cause.

Similar to classical sociologists of culture, Boltanski and Chiapello however act on an implicit understanding of culture – and just so of capital's spirit – as corresponding to a consensus, a common of values and meanings, which knits society together. Anglo-Saxon cultural studies[10], by which my work is influenced, vehemently deny this presupposition (Hörning and Winter 1999). Culture may indeed contextually serve to create

---

9   The authors actually distinguish "artistic critique" and "social critique" as motives of indignation, an analytical approach that has been profoundly questioned in the international debate about the contemporary state of critique (Lazzarato 2007; Demirović 2008; Wuggenig 2008).

10 One of the founding institutions of this perspective was the *Birmingham Centre for Contemporary Cultural Studies* (BCCCS) starting in the 1960s, where the focus was initially on analyzing texts form popular culture by using methods from literary criticism. Subsequently, media and subcultures established as their main fields of interdisciplinary investigation (Moebius 2009: 121).

states of commonality, but this does not mean that it is necessarily a process neither of integration desired on all sides nor of consensually shared meaning. Not least in the eye of globalization, new migration regimes and the evolution of communication, it is increasingly clear that former concepts of culture, which were highly thought of within the projects of modern Western nation states, need critical revision. Cultural studies debunk the idea of *one* culture. They insist on the ruptures and social struggles maintained around society's morals, manners and norms. The bourgeois family, whiteness or (hetero)sexuality appear then as hegemonic, that is, as historical constellations of power. As such, they are always contested, representing social arenas of both transforming oppression and resistance.

In their epistemological interest, cultural studies can also be seen in a certain genealogy of critical theory of the Frankfurt School. As Kögler (1999) argues, the former's creative efforts in detecting nonconformist practices not only in sub- and countercultures, but even within spheres of "standardized entertainment items" are a productive extension of the latter's often elitist *kulturkritik* of media and mass culture. For what both theoretical approaches have in common is that they see culture as a mediator of power and subjectivity. In other words, they strive to grasp social processes of how power is anchored in the inner workings of the subject. More specifically, they give insight into the still topical question why individuals identify with disadvantaging and oppressive forms of life[11] (Kögler 1999: 196). Influenced not only by Althusserian structural Marxism, but also by Gramsci as well as poststructuralist thought (Grossberg, 1992), cultural studies see oppression as an effect of dispersed power apparatuses. According to Laclau and Mouffe (1985), former Marxist understandings of ideology are questioned, since they reduced culture to a strictly class-associated phenomenon. In contrast, the significance of gender and race/ethnicity are particularly stressed. Contextually unfolding effects of sexism and racism, the latter two are seen on the one hand as intrinsically entangled with social class, while on the other hand acting in relative autonomy to it.

Based on this critical expansion of the categories, through which the consolidation of hegemony under different social constellations becomes

---

11 Not least, this is also a very central question for the sociology of work, such as for Burawoy's classical study *Manufacturing Consent* (1979).

analyzable, I indicate another central aspect of the present epistemological interest. How do Western, bourgeois modernity marked societies deal with difference? What forces and transforming power relations are involved in defining how or if cultural, corporeal, psychic or other differences of human beings in a society are recognized and sheltered as having equal rights? Feminist scholars have for a long time worked on this topic. On both sides of the Atlantic, difference as referring to the patriarchal inequality between men and women has led to critique and changes in social spheres as diverse as work, political participation, reproductive and sexual rights, the family or domestic violence (Heilborn and Sorj 1999). What is more, radical black and Chicana feminism in the US (Davis 1982; hooks 1994; Anzaldúa 2007) have expounded the problems of the universality of "the woman" as feminism's empiric and epistemic subject, because they saw it reduced to women who were privileged by social class and white race. Postmodern and deconstructionist critique have followed up on these intersecting concerns[12], so that contemporary gender and feminist studies are living ongoing and highly productive debates on (not only gender) difference. According to Maihofer (2013), who defends the concept of difference, claiming recognition of difference must include two aspects: first, a critique of the modern Western idea of equality, which dialectically implies sameness and adaptation; and second, the addressing of any form of discrimination, which is based on otherness (Maihofer 2013: 29).

Demands for difference under global neoliberal governance are facing new risks of cooptation, just because they are often attached to the latter idea of equality, which transposes difference to similarity or sameness. Particularly sexual modes of existence are current examples of how recognition is unfolding in paradoxical ways, including both the normalization and transformation of gender relations. Queer-feminist scholars have detailed such processes with the example of same-sex-marriage (Mesquita

---

12 The concept of intersectionality, as originally suggested by legal scholar Crenshaw (1989), has recently become very popular in social and generally human sciences. Unfortunately, intersectionality ultimately often tends to be operationalized, reducing social exclusion to fixed categories of race, class and gender, thus oversimplifying the historical and regional specificities, in which oppression is embedded. For a critical defense of the concept see Purtschert and Meyer (2010) or Erel et al. (2010).

2011), public images of sexuality (Engel 2009) or the increasing permeation of technology in bodies through pharmaceutical and porn industries (Preciado 2008). On the one hand, both gender and sexuality appear as areas of liberated creative craft, because at first glance they match with neoliberal logics of individualization and self-entrepreneurialism. On the other hand, patient information leaflets for industrialized testosterone, car advertising or legal texts for gay marriage are marked by a dense set of rules and norms, which rearrange rather than undo the normative weight of gender relations. Now the question still arises as to how affected subjects are dealing with these new demands in everyday life. How do individuals participate in molding such normalization through practices of (dis)identification? What is the role of contemporary work relations for young people's lives once it includes identity and emotional work imminently directed towards attractive sexual and racial self-staging? The present book is thus finally an attempt to tackle phenomena of sexual and racial subjectivation under entrepreneurial market conditions as ongoing contradictory processes. In subjects, these processes unfold experiences of precariousness besides solidarity, conformism and cooptation in addition to sporadic liberation and empowerment as well as renewed oppression.

1.3 NOTES ON METHOD AND RESEARCH PROCEDURE

Qualitative research has been proven to give major insight in both subjective views of life and culturally embedded structures (Flick, Kardorff and Steinke 2008: 19). As the social is primarily seen as both structuring and being structured by individuals, the analytical focus is on and around the shape as well as the contents, which people give in order to explain their everyday practices to themselves and to others. Salesclerks' narratives about their identities, their labor at the sales shop or their associations and critiques of the brand in question have thus become the reference point of the present study. For, as Grossberg (1997) puts it, daily practices and their subjective experience may lead us to a closer understanding of, on the one hand, the constraints suffered due to power and, on the other hand, people's efforts to have a livable life.

"Cultural studies is always interested in how power infiltrates, contaminates, limits, and empowers the possibilities that people have to live their lives in dignified and secure ways. For if one wants to change the relations of power, if one wants to move people, even a little bit, one must begin from where people are, from where and how they actually live their lives." (Grossberg 1997: 257)

Ethnographic methods, as mainly applied and for decades self-critically discussed within anthropology (Rabinow 1977; Clifford and Marcus 1986), may be one of the most sensitive approaches to such life-centered, and eventually transformative interest. First and foremost, it provides an adaptable range of tools, including observation, conversation, media, and not least the researcher's self-reflexivity, which integrates the writing process. Due to the latter aspect, it is closer to feminist methodologies, which strive to scrutinize the position and effects of the researcher's knowledge production, especially when it comes to the question of how representation operates in identities (Pillow and Mayo 2007).

Although the allegation of unmethodical procedures against both anthropology and cultural studies may be widespread within "hard" or "exact" social sciences, Gubrium and Holstein (2013) rightly state the opposite. In their view, most qualitative and ethnographic researchers tend to stick too closely to pre-defined procedures, thus "shackling" their imagination as well as causing conceptual-theoretical confinement (2013: 35). Influenced by the basic idea of Grounded Theory (Glaser and Strauss 1967), which insists on theory acting as an ongoing systematic process of re-reading and coding gained data, Gubrium and Holstein call for "analytic inspiration" as a compass for theoretical findings. Qualitative researchers "entertain particular concepts, but they do so provisionally until data collection suggests something different" (Gubrium and Holstein 2013: 36). The authors therefore discuss the example of Abu-Lughod's (1993) feminist study on Egyptian Bedouin life. Observation as well as close attention to people's narratives led the anthropologist to rethinking the common view, which reduces women's place in Arab society to a result of institutions that are uniquely supported or animated by men. The story of an old Bedouin woman revealed not only her direct partake in patrilineal marriage arrangements, but also her personal and situational resistance to it (Gubrium and Holstein 2013: 38).

I see "analytical inspiration" primarily as a fruitful way of how to mutually situate, knit, if not critically reconsider, theory and empiric data. Certainly, this has immediate consequences for both the procedure and choice of research methods. As mentioned above, I started my research with the question of how LGBT people were integrated in new identity markets; a question that guided me through the first steps in "getting to the field", that is, reaching out to the stores and employees of *Visibly Hot*. But as soon as the first interview was conducted, I found that the question of "being different" was narratively commented on in much broader terms than only with regard to sexual orientation or sexual identities. At the same time, I realized the importance people attributed to all channels of the brand's on- and offline campaigns, an aspect that was obviously central to the processes of self-staging and identification I was interested in. There were matters of questions I could not address without working on theoretical-analytical revisions and designing a multiplicity of research methods that would complement spoken language and one-sided perspectives.

The present study comprised nineteen semi-structured interviews, conducted between 2012 and 2015 in five different shopping centers in the city of Rio de Janeiro. They comprised employees of *Visibly Hot*, mainly the "ordinary" salesclerks, but also three team leaders and one supervisor. Conversations focused on their daily tasks in selling products and their strategies as well as their comprehension of their own and the brand's identity. On average, interviews lasted between thirty minutes and one hour. They were however not held *en bloc*, that is, within a short time restricted period of a couple of months or so. This was especially advantageous as I could meet with three salesclerks for a second time, comparing their experiences and subjective evaluations of their employment at two different points in time (two of them had already left the company by the second encounter). What is more, the timely displaced meetings with the salesclerks turned out to be indicators of whether I was still "on the right track". In other words, they helped me to crosscheck if my epistemological interest still accompanied what was actually "at stake" for the sales employees. Technological devices further facilitated this procedure of seeing both data and theories as decidedly co-constructed by the researcher. All interviews were recorded, transcribed and subsequently coded with

MAXqda, which proved to highly contribute to the open analytic approach of theoretical sampling (Thornberg and Charmaz 2013: 155).

Transnationally circulating identity offers have changed the world, and so have the needs and challenges of an ethnographically defined field of sociological inquiry. However, it is still a familiar representation within social and cultural anthropology, that fieldwork

"involves travel away, preferably to a distant locale where the ethnographer will immerse him/herself in personal face-to-face relationships with a variety of natives over an extended period of time." (Amit 2008: 2)

Amit, who challenges such "spatial and social encapsulation" (2008: 5) of anthropology's dominant definitions of fieldwork, sheds light on two main aspects of how "the field" is already being practiced in alternative ways. First, participation as an immersion in social relationships and groups of analytical interest does not necessarily mean a physical presence in space. It can also refer to the researcher's partake in (former or parallel) professional or political contexts. Carrara (2013) shows this quite clearly with the example of anthropology's close relation to the LGBT movement in Brazil. Second, in an ever more digitally entangled world, the encounter with research participants is not in any case best managed as face-to-face meetings or relationships. Phone calls, emails, and maybe more than ever chats and social media can serve as complementary (or even independent) tools for integrating oneself in the social field of inquiry. As Amit emphasizes, it is the circumstance which defines the method "rather than the method defining the circumstance" (2008: 11).

My own relation to the field can be described as at the same time close to people and critically distant to the enterprise's official operations. I got first introduced, in 2012, to a sales team at *Visibly Hot* by being attributed the role of one of their former temporary salesclerk's boyfriend, who was doing a sociological study about work among young Brazilians. From the beginning, access and relationships to the sales staff were thus amicable, to the extent that they once invited me to a barbecue at the house of one of the employees. While making appointments for interviews with the individual salesclerks from this first team was easy due to the their helpful manners, the same was the case in later situations, in which I had no social references, and in which I hoped for spontaneous cooperation as I approached a sales shop. Generally speaking, I was surprised at the salesclerks' drive to tell me about their personal experiences and especially about all they knew of and about the brand. At the one hand, this was due to the fact that I am not Brazilian, for which reason they might make special efforts to share a good and well-explained picture to the "foreigner". On the other hand, my appearance at the sales shops was not different from that of any given consumer, a fan of the brand, or maybe even a salesclerk, as some of them immediately suggested.

The slightly closer relationship to the first sales team in the field entailed that its members sent me friendship requests on Facebook. Rather unintentionally, I got daily insight on how they presented themselves – mainly through pictures and videos, but also through commentaries and other posts – to the public, a type of data which is lately being discussed and used in netnographic analysis (Kozinets, Dolbec et al. 2013). While pictures turned out to be very interesting, additional material on self-staging and singular aspirations for the "different" identity in question, the posts on social media further helped me to track the main sources and links employees referred to when commenting on the brand's latest goals and projects. Books, newspaper articles, videos, party events and TV advertisements were all isolated and sorted by what seemed to be of main attention in the salesclerk's digitally shared information. These sources again did not only allow for tracing the contours of *Visibly Hot*'s "spirit" (this was the critically distancing step), but also for better embedding the employees' experiences within relations of power that both subject and enable them to act. What channel, if not the stage of social media, could better map the relation young people strive to establish with the brand, its managerial discourse and finally the cultural contexts relating to sexuality and race?

Timely displaced interviews and the ongoing follow-up via social media and advertising maintained the research process in a productive tension of, to use the words of Saukko (2003), simultaneously trying to "do justice to the lived experience of people" and "critically analyze discourses, which form the very stuff out of which our experiences are made" (2003: 3). In cultural studies, the often interdisciplinary inspired combination of diverse research methods is thus seen as the key to capture both the "lived and general history" (2003: 7), in which the research is contextually as well as politically embedded. Insisting on the immediate links between people's lived experience and discourse is not least an attempt to overcome a researcher's temptation to see her or himself as the expert. As Rancière (2008) so vividly argues through his reading of Joseph Jacotot (Rancière 1987), we should overcome the idea of passivity or indifference in social actors, challenging the dominant concept of how emancipation is thought to be achieved through hierarchic education and explication. Once we strive to radically promote the equality of intelligences (Rancière 2008: 15), everyday experiences of what is socially effected by heteronormativity, brand capitalism or neoliberal precarity regimes can be recognized as equal constituents of critique. It is in the encounter of intelligences that a "third" knowledge arises, one that cannot be owned and that refuses top-down transmission (Rancière 2008: 21).

2. Governing through desires
Brands, identities, and the case of *Visibly Hot*

This chapter explores the governmental techniques that mold the affective landscape of *Visibly Hot*. Taking this Brazilian fashion enterprise as its example, this section acts on the broader suggestion of the emergence of a specific capitalist conduct that unfolds in branding. As noted by Rose (2004) with and beyond Foucault's work on governmentality[1], 20th century western mass consumption brought about practices and knowledge that have deeply reshaped how people rely on the spheres of both their selves and material goods. Significantly, the branding government that I will analyze here works with logics that are different to the conduct of institutional or state politics. Fostered by advertisers, salesmen, market researchers or fancy entrepreneurs of the format such as Apple's Steve Jobs, the conduct through brands is mainly underpinned by knowledge about people's desires. These are not only encountered but also mobilized or channeled in

---

1   According to Rose, this Foucauldian perspective can be understood as providing a particular "style of analysis" (Rose 2004: 3), where the question of power – over, between and through subjects – is central. On government, the "conduct of conduct" in Foucault's terms (for an overview, see Foucault 1991), Rose writes: "Government, here, refers to all endeavors to shape, guide, direct the conduct of others, whether these be the crew of a ship, the members of a household, the employees of a boss, the children of a family or the inhabitants of a territory. And it also embraces the ways in which one might be urged and educated to bridle one's own passions, to control one's own instincts, to govern oneself" (Rose 2004: 3).

particular directions: social promises for sexual freedom, wealth, individual expression through lifestyles or body cultures, to name a few. According to Arvidsson (2006), this on-going incitement of desires and aspirations is effecting a major dislocation of where both social relations and capitalist production of value emerge: "The brand becomes a hyper-socialized, de-territorialized factory" (Arvidsson 2006: 82).

My critical analysis in this chapter is directed towards the monopolization of both identities and diversity discourse by brand management. Firstly, this perspective is inspired by the work of Boltanski and Chiapello (2005). Capitalism, they hold, had transformed its spirit; the new spirit – evolving from managerial discourse – stood out due to a high ability to incorporating former social critiques that were historically directed against capitalism itself. In other words, it makes continuous movements of normalizing, critique neutralizing inclusion in order to guarantee its survival. Secondly, I hold that sex(uality) and the celebration of diversity is central to contemporary capitalist endeavors, a phenomenon I discuss with the emblematic case of *Visibly Hot*. On the one hand, its marketing strategies such as advertising are aggressively mobilizing sexual desires, picturing female nudity that addresses identifications with both male sexism and re-enacted feminism in a pornographic semiotics. As one could say with Preciado (2008), they affect us with the message of having to fashion ourselves as sexual subjects, thereby exploiting the potential of our bodies in creating sexual pleasure (Preciado 2008: 90). On the other hand, *Visibly Hot* is promoting a corporate brand to its employees that defines a fancy, sexy attitude as its ideal and common of the brand's personality. This managerial discourse calls for "being different" and focuses on the globally circulating rhetoric of diversity, the institutional inclusion of formerly excluded or discriminated social groups. Lesbian, gay and black young people turn into the representatives of this notion of difference, and hence appear at the crossroads of an ambiguous identity politics. While the entrepreneurial strategy of inclusion *de facto* bestows upon them a positive valorization, I show that structural inequalities are being rather reified than decomposed or questioned.

2.1 THE BRAND AS A MODE OF CONDUCT

The term branding (also brand management) refers to the set of strategies raised by the administration of an organization's image, that is, its brand. Refined by large business investments along the second half of the twentieth century, the brand is now about to represent a capitalist institution of its own (Arvidsson 2006) or even the logos of contemporary global economy (Lury 2004). However, its zone of influence transcends any demarcated field of social and political life. As Arvidsson provocatively notes, it is a rather recent phenomenon that to spend "a night in bed talking about Apple products" (Arvidsson 2006: 3) became part of the social fabric of daily life in industrialized countries. At the same time, recent modes of commodity culture led to what the Comaroffs tellingly labeled the "identity industry": occasionally, ethnic groups and individuals tend to "brand their otherness" (Comaroff and Comaroff 2009: 24). As shown by Nahoum (2013) with the example of the Yawanawa from the Brazilian Amazon, identity claims may fluidly transit to market instruments, a process that profoundly remodels former conditions of political imagery and representation.

I argue that brands are playing a crucial role in the movements of a transnationally operating, renewed spirit of capitalism. As suggested by Boltanski and Chiapello (2005), this spirit curiously rose at a moment in which social precariousness increased, but the conventional tactics and language of a systemic criticism of capitalism ceased to be effective. More exactly, today's persuasive power of the capitalist order could be traced back to a peculiar capacity: its high ability to incorporate social arrangements and even its most arduous critics. Since the revolts of 1968, capitalist endeavors would have succeeded in rhetorically adopting the origins of social indignation against itself: the critique of the loss of authenticity and creativity, as well as of capitalism being the originator of poverty, social inequality and opportunism (Boltanski and Chiapello 2005: 37). This incorporative and moving capacity is thus one of the general motors of contemporary capitalist strategies for safeguarding its course.

As already shown by Weber (2005[1904]), capitalism *per se* did not have sufficient appeal so as to convince its followers of its superiority. People needed moral or ethical reasons that would lead them to actively participate in a profit-oriented social order. Weber thus closely linked the emergence of the capitalist spirit to the expressivity of German Protestantism at the turn of the century. In close reference to Weber, Boltanski and Chiapello now describe the renewed spirit as largely detached from the Christian religious mindset. It was managerial discourse that superseded the protestant ethic and constituted the belief in economy as an autonomous and moral-free sphere of thought and action. Consequently, the question of why workers would work for and live in the capitalist system can no longer be explained by ascetical attitudes or the idea of culture-specific vocation. It is rather the new stimulations that irradiate from management and marketing: the announcement of values such as those of self-realization, freedom or emancipation (Boltanski and Chiapello 2005: 13). In more Foucauldian terms, these values are the cornerstones of an economic government in its own right. According to Rose (2004), freedom is an inalienable aspect of conduct. It is only by presupposing and acknowledging the ability to act of the governed that one can utilize it for his or her own purposes of governance (Rose 2004: 4).

The mode of governing that I will describe in what follows is much more than, as Boltanski and Chiapello hold, a new spirit pervading primarily marketing books and managers' modes of justification. The branding conduct, I hold, is shaping a capitalist spirit that fosters liberal (self)governance in potentially all bodily matter and human feeling, thereby relocating and multiplying the production sites of value. First, marketing knowledge proceeds in ways that reconstitute the relation between producers and consumers. Following Arvidsson, brands do enable consumers, "empowering them in particular directions" (Arvidsson 2006: 8). Consent is being assembled by providing the consumer with tools that allow to "act, feel and be in a particular way" (Arvidsson 2006: 8). By the use of Apple products, the logic goes, one can become a creative person, experience a milieu of freedom and relate to artistic social groups. Second, the source of product value is strongly coupled to living forces as well. People creatively 'do things' with the brand, whether expressing and feeling an identity (Comaroff and Comaroff 2009) or remodeling their body through implants or sexually stimulating pharmaceutical supplements (Preciado 2008). Like in the latter case, the brand's machinery of creating surplus incites erotic fantasies, channeling them in often sexist logics that reenact both femininities and masculinities in bodily fragmented, yet (renewed) hierarchized and stereotypical matter.

2.1.1 How commodities obtained a life of their own

Given the often disputed question of what a brand exactly is or means (Manning 2010: 34), tracking its historically decisive appearances, too, can hardly be gathered in its totality. However, there is strong evidence that emerging commercial activities along Western industrialization in the 19th century have paved the way for what we today know as brands. McClintock (1995) demonstrated how early advertising as well as commodity spectacles expanded under the Victorian empire. Imperial commodities such as the soap underwent heavy investments and promoted the civilizing mission of racial purification. In service of the empire, proper professionals – advertisers – started to administrate the signs and systems of the commodity's imagery. Advertising posters and particularly packaging designs of colonial products such as chocolate, coffee or biscuits accessed the homes of millions of people. Soap, as McClintock argues, literally gained "magical, fetish powers" (McClintock 1995: 207). As a technology aimed at social purification, soap advertising imposed the idea of Western superiority by reinventing racial difference and women's invisibility in the capitalist production process as its power basis. Washing away the stigma on the skin of non-white bodies turned into a spectacular, racist promise of regenerating the supposedly threatened middle class values and bodies. In addition, the commercial propaganda indirectly incorporated contemporary social uncertainties. It erased the women in the soap advertisings, since industrial revolution had provoked a major contradiction "between women's paid and unpaid domestic work" for the Victorian notion of middle-class household (McClintock 1995: 216).

For McClintock, the domestic commodity took form of a historical agent. It performed work for the empire, disseminating moral and economic salvation. But another aspect of 19th century commercial changes in Western Europe was of main impact. The emergence of urban shopping houses and the expansion of new consumer groups – especially women – equally contributed to the agency loaned to commodities. By his classic *Au bonheur des Dames* (1980[1883]), Émile Zola created undoubtedly one of the richest documentations on the social history that framed the emergence of the department store. He puts us directly into 19th century Paris, where capitalist ventures of the bourgeois entrepreneurs brought about a revolution not only in terms of merchandise but also related to female gender roles (Nava 1997: 72). At that time, the bourgeois woman had lately been banned to the private realms. But with the urban retailers' investments in pretentious architecture for their stores, the situation changed considerably (Nava 1997: 63). These novel palaces allured with their lucid fashions and smells, thus offering new female pastimes such as autonomous amusement and strolling without any necessary male escort.

Goods such as clothes, silks or lingerie were at the pulsing heart of such early branding efforts (Miller 1981: 25). Alike the *magasins de nouveautés*, Parisian department stores enacted them within a pleasant ambiance. Its purchase should no longer be compulsory and the new consumers could enter the stores for free. Architecture, alongside advertising and striking packaging, started to play a decisive role on how products were presented, made appealing and sold. This was probably also the secret of Boucicaut, the emblematic holder of the Paris' most fancy commercial palaces, the *Bon Marché*. His investments in large-scale and highly illuminated buildings revolutionized former merchandising strategies (Miller 1981: 41) because its architecture contained more than simply visual pleasures for the customers. As historians and annalists agree, the early department stores began to use techniques that produced seductive environments and stimulated people's fantasies (Nava 1997: 66).

The stages of both Victorian commodity advertising and early French shopping architecture contributed to what became the paradigm for marketers and entrepreneurs at the beginning of the 20th century. Products and goods had to be embedded within strictly guided consumer aspirations. As such, they turned into affective instruments that allowed for immediate intervention in social relations, whether these were about the colonial reinvention of white supremacy, the dissemination of the autonomous bourgeois shopping femininity or simply cultural tastes with regards to a specific product. The agents of the early 20th century enterprises were convinced that they could lead social practice (Lury 2004: 16). However, their conviction rose not only due to their economic power. Unlike, for instance, the means of scientific knowledge, commodities could be used to convey messages at much broader levels. The exotic soaps reached households and needy social groups – the masses – that had few or no access to higher education, hence to scientific debates (McClintock 1995: 209).

The commodity interventions grew and especially North American firms advanced their mass guiding marketing techniques. Coca-Cola, the world's most famous American soft drink, owed its rising success around 1900 to advertising of patent medicine, diffused by poster printings. As Pendergrast (2000) puts it,

"Patent medicine makers were the first American businessmen to recognize the power of the catchphrase, the identifiable logo and trademark, the celebrity endorsement, the appeal to social status, the need to keep 'everlastingly at it'. Out of necessity, they were the first to sell image rather than product." (Pendergrast 2000: 11)

Body discomforts such as fatigue and headaches might have been presented as Coca-Cola's medical sales arguments. However, the image sold by the soda pop promised to adopt a far more reaching social mission. In the USA, the transition from a rural farmer nation to an urban society as well as heavy immigration flows had disintegrated people's common practices and expectations. Therefore, Coca-Cola purposefully advertised his soda as being the ordinary drink of the nation: people from all social classes and groups should be able to afford it (Pendergrast 2000: 14). Henceforward, the dark sparkling lemonade became a symbolic ingredient of the American dream.

The following consolidation of commodity imagery in the first half of the twentieth century was accompanied by the technological innovation of modern mass media. Cinemas, newspapers, radio stations and later on television opened new channels for advertising. In 1926, the US-based food corporation General Mills launched one of the first "jingles", a radio song exclusively composed and replayed to market breakfast cereals, the *Wheaties* (Taylor 2012: 84). And Bulova, a New York luxury watch manufacturer, produced public TV's first ad in 1940 (Bischoff, Grzenia and Wollner 2011: 8). These technological changes and their impact on daily and political life were so intense that they became a major concern of contemporary critical intellectuals. Notably influential members of the Frankfurt School equated the consumer business and its artistic marketing instruments with a new rationale of capitalist domination. They argued that people's needs and thoughts were being openly manipulated, controlled and disciplined by the culture industry (Horkheimer and Adorno 1969: 152). Individual resistance or oppositional attitudes would be neutralized because the identifications offered by advertising led to massive aesthetic uniformity and to "one-dimensional behavior" (Marcuse 2004: 32).

Their thoroughly negative perspective on technology[2] as well as the apocalyptic tone of their thesis of cultural decay is hardly useful for contemporary analysis of capitalism's alternating ventures. However, considering these authors as historical commentators of a totalitarian era allows acknowledging several aspects of their argument. Adorno, Horkheimer and Marcuse ascertained that consumer culture had begun to naturalize the mode of how people in Western industrialized countries accessed and experienced subjectivity. The choices of what products to buy or what services to use turned into a considerable factor of social life and identity. Marketers produced commodities that transported attractive social values. And they could often only be accessed or seem close by purchasing that product. People, as Marcuse put it, recognized themselves by means of their surrounding commodities, that is, their car or kitchen equipment (Marcuse 2004: 29). Until the middle of the century, this model of production that in authoritarian ways created new mass consumer needs or steered social aspirations was a key of early branding. Entrepreneurial marketing literally strived to socially engineer, organize "how people think and feel through branded commercial products" (Holt 2002: 71).

2.1.2 Behavioral science and the shift to the consumer's needs

The post-war years introduced a turning-away from former economic receipts in selling commodities. Until the middle of the 20th century, Frederik Taylor's ideals of scientific management of working processes had also dominated marketing. It worked on the basis of making "consumers and producers behave and desire in a certain way" (Arvidsson 2006: 41), quite close to the way Adorno or Marcuse had directed their critique on mass

---

2   Naturally, referring to the Frankfurt School does not necessarily suppose a coherent stance on technology. Especially the work of Walter Benjamin (1996) demonstrated a more differentiated position and complex reasoning about the relation of aesthetics, ideology and technology. Although this author saw the danger of fascism's taking over of technological devices, he equally believed in its potential for social emancipation.

betrayal. With the emergence of a supposedly marketing revolution in the 1960s (Lury 2004: 18), this top-down model lost some territory. Organic marketing intellectuals called for reallocating the focus from the enterprise's needs to the needs of the consumer. "Satisfying the consumer" became the expanding idea that would replace older imposing techniques of merchandising products. This goal could only be attained by knowing more about how ordinary people actually perceived, appropriated and used the products of a given brand (Lury 2004: 20).

Marketing consequently initiated a conglomerate of scientific studies that could facilitate getting closer to the consumers. Behavioral science, mainly psychology, became the most reliable ally of this growing venture. Interviews, group discussions and testing were purposed to create archives of data that gave new insight about consumers' personality and individuality. Both psychologists and advertisers were well aware of what the culture critics deemed at former production's propaganda impositions on consumers. And almost cynically, they conceded a capacity to the consumers that Marcuse had virtually denied them. Customers were no longer looked at in terms of passive beings, but rather as individuals with proper hopes and desires (Miller and Rose 2008: 119). As noted by Miller and Rose, governing such consumers did not mean to conduct them through rough domination or undiscerning manipulation. Beyond the imperatives of profit, marketing techniques produced an assemblage of understandings of human behavior. They located the driving forces of consumers' agency in the psyche particular to specific social groups as well as to sex or age. Accordingly, commodities had to be designed and marketed through diversified, socially discernible promises (Miller and Rose 2008: 139).

These new consumption technologies literally produced new relations between psychological knowledge, consumers and advertising. In the first place, marketing had to go beyond the product's physical, superficial characteristics. How could you sell ice cream in wintertime or convince people of chocolate's beneficial effects? Psychoanalytic approaches seemed to provide new answers. The pleasures of foods in general were attached to early childhood and its expressivity of human drives. Marketing research on ice cream argued that its mode of consumption was attached to the symbol of maternal breasts. Working as a kind of a substitute, licking ice cream could relieve anxiety or depression. Their recommendation to offer ice cream to people in stressful situations was thus directed to institutions ranging from hospitals, cinemas and industrial canteens (Miller and Rose 2008: 123). In a psychoanalytical perspective, food expressed sexual and social wishes – a psychological significance that now had to be addressed by marketers. Advertising chocolate, for instance, needed to tackle people's supposedly unconscious desires and anxieties if it was going to increase the sales. Success hence depended on the marketer's savvy of how to mediate between a product's properties and a message of psychological remedy, imminently acting upon everyday needs of consumers (Miller and Rose 2008: 124).

In many cases, the psychological knowledge acquired in the service of marketing heavily broadened its research focus. Instead of focusing on one specific product and the contiguous consumer's modes of use, especially social psychological studies turned their attention to the general attitudes of certain social groups. Anew, women were of main interest. Emblematically, the British Tavistock Institute for Human Relations (TIHR), an institution that started with marketing research services in the 1950s, operated a case study on marketing home perm. Its aim was defined as to investigate women's overall attitudes and behavior related to their hair (Miller and Rose 2008: 125). The interviews were interpreted by pointing to women's alleged obsessions with hair care, originating from deeper anxieties within the feminine personality that were expressed through fears about hair loss or damage. For the marketing strategies, it was thus recommended to add anxiety relieving smells to the lotion and further to promote the home perm product accompanied by written material that expressed technical, comforting expertise (Miller and Rose 2008: 127).

As Miller and Rose emphasize with their focus on techniques of conduct, the relation of psychological expertise to advertising and production considerably changed the notion of consumer choice (Miller and Rose 2008: 129). Compared to former imperial or totalitarian commodity merchandising, the individual was now understood as having a capacity to create proper psychological meaning. Therefore, it seemed insufficient to influence the customer merely by educative messages or promises of social status – as was the case of Pears Soap or early Coca-Cola advertising. In a first step, consumer choice was to be distinguished from the intended product offer and studied from within a specific social group and in its everyday manifestations. Marketing of vacuum cleaners in the mid-20th century paid much attention to approaching the psychological and physical burden on women caused by housework. Of course, announcing technical advancement for cleaning the home meant the reinvention of a strictly feminine duty, once more naturalizing women's unpaid domestic labor (Glauser 2001: 140). But with regard to the relation of knowledge and product marketing, it is also significant how vacuum cleaners were deeply enmeshed in needs and hopes of ordinary people, including working class women (Giles 2004: 23). Once channeled in the right way, psychologically intelligible desires were used to mobilize demarcated consumer groups, actually reshaping the very subject of consumption (Miller and Rose 2008: 115).

The incorporation of behavioral science affected the relation between consumers and producers: the dominant perspective publicly disseminated by retailers and marketers now projected it as a bilateral process of exchange (Lury 2004: 20). Meaning and value of a commercial product started to be thought of as the outcome of the producer's expanded attention to what was in the minds of consumers. In today's managerial discourse, this defines the so called brand equity, the capacity of a brand to generate value (Arvidsson 2006: 7). In fact, the idea of a brand as an entity of its own, transcending fixed knowledge of both physical characteristics of the product and one-dimensional responses of consumers, emerged in that context. However, the insertion of behavioral science's perspective was not the only agent of that shift. As always, the images and social aspirations attached to a specific commodity were transmitted by technologies of mass media that semantically stimulated the intended consumer groups.

2.1.3 Media and the social fabric of the everyday

Expanding this critical perspective on brands in Marxist terms, I argue with Arvidsson (2006) that first, consumption as well as the consuming subject can be seen as crucial production sites of contemporary capitalist value creation, and second that media culture is an important channel of these undertakings. As mentioned above, critical theorists had already expressed their concern over the alienating effects of media and so called culture industry. People would distance themselves of the allegedly real conditions of their lives, and get virtually caught in a false consciousness. But as Arvidsson concurrently argues, historical change in the 20th century brought about a contemporary situation in which media culture and everyday lives have really been completely integrated. Consequently, rather than trying to analytically separate the two spheres, it would be of importance to grasp media culture as a channel that provides "ambience" (or a series of ambiences) within which life naturally occurs" (Arvidsson 2006: 13). This is certainly not to deny the ongoing significance of profit-oriented discourse that continues to emanate from media such as cinema, television or the Internet. As Illouz has provocatively argued, the ways of how people experience the idea of romantic love would be a result of leisure industry and codified images by mass culture (Illouz 1997).

Post-operaist theorists – although hardly given any attention in debates on branding and consumption – oppose the latter critical perspective in highlighting micro-political potentialities that go hand in hand with new capitalist motors of labor and exploitation. Industrial production processes and Fordist factory work, they hold, have lost their former preeminent role in value creation. Following Hardt and Negri, postmodernization of economy (what they also call "informatization") has changed this era on a global level (2000: 280). It acts in ways that merges the realms of the factory and society. Immaterial labor[3], they argue, is now at the center of capitalist control. Its products are mainly knowledge and communication, but also feelings and social relations (Foltin 2002: 7). Somewhat close to Boltanski and Chiapello, post-operaists act on the assumption that capitalism per se does not possess proper convincing resources. In fact, it depends on the social labor, the creativity and needs of people, their emancipatory aspirations and even political struggles. Labor power then is like a general source of socialities (Hardt 1996: 5), that is, of (eventually spontaneous) collectivities, values and actions between people in the flux of the everyday life that are primary to capitalist control.

Arvidsson (2006) attempts to think about brands in terms of such post-operaist reasoning. For the author, the invention and placement of a brand depend on emotional, aesthetic and social qualities that are not necessarily produced in factories and at worksites, but also generally in the everyday of peoples' practices. Branding is in some way the emblematic representation of capitalism's drive to put to work the socialities needed for its survival. It co-designs and stimulates what post-operaists named the "social

---

3 See the queer and feminist critique of this concept which I discuss in chapter four.

factory" of humanity (Hardt and Negri 2000: 284). Arvidsson even goes as far as to argue that in the reshaped relation of production and consumption in the present "informational" period, consumers would actively contribute their immaterial labor force. With the expansion of electronic media such as the tape recorder, Polaroid photography or video cameras in the 1980s and later on the emergence of social network technology in the 1990s, marketers' anticipated consumer participation intensified. These media interactively multiplied the possible meanings ascribed to certain products, "entering deeper into everyday life and inviting themselves to be deployed productively in new social circumstances" (Arvidsson 2006: 28).

Food and the cooking industry have been an influential example of the interactive attitude disseminated by branding technology. TV-mediatization via cooking programs invited people to take an active role in experimenting, creating exotic or healthy dishes. As also analyzed by Lakoff (2006), discourse around food has turned into a decisive marker of individual and group identity. In the 21st century, the knowledge of supposedly "secret recipes" as well as of adequate vocabulary apparently predicates what "we are" or would like to be (Lakoff 2006: 150). Making use of Arvidsson's approach, such interactively, communicatively assembled identifications appear in the light of opposing effects. The production of value is simultaneously a production of a "common". On one hand, mediated brands serve to subordinate basic qualities of human life. They regenerate capitalist domination by providing a sort of a "biopolitical framework in which life unfolds" (Arvidsson 2006: 13). But on the other hand, brands equally create social overflow, an excess or "ethical surplus" that emanates from the social fabric prior to capitalist control.

Unlike Illouz's (1997) claim of an all-encompassing market industry that reigns on human affections, Arvidsson's approach allows us to consider the productive power of sociality that accompanies branded goods. Affective relations such as friendships or political mobilization are not the natural counterpart of subjectivities that unfold within media and consumer culture. Indeed, within the present production process, there is literally no outside: life is coordinated through a biopolitical context informed by capital goods. However, since consumers "use goods productively" (Arvidsson 2006: 19), a specific market ambience can spontaneously become a critical site of action. Foster (2007) showed how the intervention of a group of photographers in Coca-Cola advertising in India led to unexpected public debates. Their pictures provocatively pointed to the company's aggressive appropriations of water sources, threatening to disrupt the value of the brand (Foster 2007: 726).

Given the unruly ways of how people relate to commodities, marketing invests even more in knowledge about consumer agency. What is known and practiced today as brand management is a bundle of governing strategies that strive to interfere in what people spontaneously or routinely produce as common socialities (Arvidsson 2006: 126). In other words, it is aimed at channeling feeling, making the becoming of subjects and the becoming of value coincide (Arvidsson 2006: 93). Social events such as a child's birthday are scattered as a McDonald experience; aesthetic and social self-confidence turn into an equivalent of using Nike shoes; and Nescafé is affectively positioned within outback camping and landscape (Arvidsson 2006: 82). Brand management is thus engaged with maintaining the brand in a mediating process with the consumers. By this means, the social commons that emanate from peoples' agency are intended to either reproduce or innovate the desired "intentions" of the brand. Monitoring, controlling and enhancing the everyday social productivity of consumers in profit-promising directions are the cornerstones of this mode of managerial conduct. Leaving the common sites of industrial production, "the brand becomes a hypersocialized, de-territorialized factory" (Arvidsson 2006: 82).

2.1.4 The role of lifestyles and political stances

For quite a long time, the historical precursors of brand management used to merchandize products with strictly class-specific profiles. Even if vacuum cleaners, soda pops and cars were heavily dependent on the spending of the working class, their aesthetic point of reference unfolded in bourgeois environment, animating the idea of private homestead bliss and nuclear family. Though with the shift from imposing strategies to consumer interactivity, the branding process diversified. As marketers wanted to know what their customers "became" with the products, they started to engineer new instruments that could "anticipate a certain attitude, mode or feeling" (Arvidsson 2006: 61). With its icons such as the independent cowboy – Marlboro Man – off the 1950s, lifestyles became one of the central focuses of attention in brand management. The projected sovereignty of consumers was to be assembled into particular forms of life that occasionally went beyond specific boundaries of social class. Coolness, youth and subcultures as well as exotic or fancy lifestyles turned into new mediums where brands would be installed and symbolically broadcasted.

Starbucks, an example of a global player, achieved major success by designing its brand around the idea of coffee as a lifestyle. According to Gaudio's (2003) compact insights, this enterprise counts on the conflation of people's supposedly natural conversations with commercialized consumption of coffee. The visit to the coffeehouse is invented as providing the customers with a third space: an ambience that suggests leaving behind both work and home (Gaudio 2003: 676). As its own marketers underline, people needed social interaction on a daily basis and Starbucks offered them the possibility to feel as though they were "out in the world" in a safe and comfortable space. Actually, the coffeehouse brand allures with a whole range of possible activities: chatting with friends, reading in solitude, writing, being creative, listening to "eclectic" background music or consuming the product lines of packaged coffee or CDs (Gaudio 2003: 675). As Gaudio further points out, Starbucks could hardly be successful in a cultural context where coffee was not associated with sociability. In the US and other Western countries where the brand gained ground, conversations and meetings in commercial public spaces were already common. As an effect, Starbucks' coffee conversations became highly naturalized, in a way that presents them not only as if they were a "free activity" but also as a space of cosmopolitan and "egalitarian" social interaction. The obligation to buy coffee, and further, the social exclusion that virtually operates alongside the highly priced hot drinks are affectively hidden within the idea of the "coffee experience" (Gaudio 2003: 683).[4]

---

4   It is worth noting that the social distance and exclusion varies significantly from one country to another. In the Brazilian case, Starbucks' pricing corresponds to the consumer budget of elite classes; the social divide intrinsic of the "coffee experience" may be of more severe nature here than in most of European countries and the US, since most of the attendants at Starbucks could not afford to buy the coffee they serve.

Despite the innumerous techniques of brand management that cannot be described here in detail[5], there is a procedure common to most of them. As in the example of Starbucks, the brand's intended images and aspirations are meant to be spun into existing social interaction – be this of specific social groups, ambiences or spaces. Lifestyle advertising does exactly this. Nike, for example, strategically inserted its brand in urban "ghetto" subculture, represented by rap music and suburban kids. Absolut Vodka, on the other hand, used similar techniques to weave their brand into gay party culture. In general terms, the music industry has been a vanguard in utilizing the creative style of youth movements (Middleton 1990). For marketing discourse, such recycling strategies are seen as highly effective. Once the brand is established within a given subcultural group or style, it is believed that its consumers "act as if one was a part of, or better to act in the style of that universe, by using goods marked with the brand in question" (Arvidsson 2006: 69).

França's (2012) ethnographic studies on homosexuality and consumption in urban São Paulo give insight into such processes. The author discusses the significance of the market label GLS, which is the abbreviation of *Gays, Lésbicas e Simpatizantes* and which denominates a market segment of fashion, tourism agencies, cinema festivals and other commercial product offers aimed at lesbian and gay consumers that emerged in the 1990s. In contrast to the North American acronym *gay friendly*, presupposing a primarily heterosexual ambience where gays are "tolerated", the Brazilian GLS label inversely takes homosexual clientele as its starting point, adding heterosexual "sympathizers" (França 2007: 291). França's research thus focuses specifically gay party locations and nightlife for the production of identities and social markers. *The Week*, a franchised brand of gay disco with local versions in various Brazilian cities, is one of her case studies. Its marketing directed exclusively on consumption needs of gay men tend to anticipate a consensus style, "quality" based offer. International LGBT celebrities, distinguished consumer cards, VIP areas and a

---

5   Some of the more aggressive strategies are named "viral", "guerrilla" or "stealth" marketing. Even more than lifestyle advertising, they use words and brand related topics that are spun into communication channels such as email providers, Facebook or specific social groups that are supposed to spread it to broader social circles (Arvidsson 2006: 69).

diversity of music styles assemble glamorous prestige in duty of the party label (França 2012: 77). Most of the people that frequent *The Week* see it as one of the "world's best gay locations". As França's interlocutors confirmed, the party would have turned into an "object of everybody's desire". And thinking from an entrepreneurial point of view, they reassured that to sell a specific idea of culture, lifestyle and a general way of "how to behave socially" was crucial for *The Week*'s emblematic case (França 2012: 61).

As the same author argued elsewhere (França 2007), the mutual impact of GLS market and LGBT movements would have led to new political and economic vocabularies. The expansion of GLS entrepreneurship coincided with a change in the ways of how the movement defined its identity claims: a leaving of the "ghetto" and victim status towards playful *gay pride*. Leisure markets contributed to promote the visibility of that project to such an extent that entrepreneurs came to look at themselves as political activists, as stimulants of homosexuals' self-esteem and "positive identity" (França 2007: 299). In this case, marketing strategies are quite essentially about appropriating political passions (Arvidsson 2006: 88). Once entwined in a political stance, they work as seemingly "natural" agents of the formation of a collective identity. What is also noticeable in França's examples is that GLS entrepreneurs are apparently rectifying a truth about "being homosexual". They emphasized that their proper identity of being gay was crucial for market success, since heterosexuals did not have similar enthusiasm for that business (França 2007: 301). Indeed, GLS incentives were often of normative nature, since bisexual or trans people rarely entered the contours of their particular lifestyle brands (França 2007: 308).

2.1.5 The corporate brand

Gay branded consumption led by entrepreneurs that self-define as gay is but one example of how the conduct of difference can look like. In general terms, the idea that products and services are best promoted by workers and marketers that represent the same social group or profile as the one of targeted consumers is an already consolidated branding strategy. Fashion labels such as Tommy Hilfiger or Benetton programmatically hire the type of people they intend to sell to. As Arvidsson puts it, they "encourage them to read, travel, go out and otherwise immerse themselves in their peer culture as much as possible, and then make use of their insights in developing new styles and fashions." (Arvidsson 2006: 70)

On the one hand, such direct involvement of workers and consumers in the branding process effects an additional surplus drawn from the "social fabric", since the very distinction between the two groups is being deregulated. On the other hand, these more organic-looking cultural outcomes serve to establish integrity among the company's employees (Arvidsson 2006: 84).

What would come to be known as the corporate brand emerged as an entrepreneurial response to criticism that had unfolded throughout the 20th century. Enterprises were repeatedly accused of being too impersonal, too rationally organized and hence destructive for people's social lives. Initially, Public Relations was the firm's responsible organ to handle the task of creating a positive and convincing corporate image. Now, with the general governmental shift to consumer behavior, management equally invested in knowledge about how employees experienced and acted upon the corporation's imageries. Specialists such as symbol analysts were signed on to mold an enterprise's proper "consciousness" or "soul" (Arvidsson 2006: 83) that should serve to strengthen both well-being and employees' commitment to the company. Not coincidentally, Deleuze took these transforming marketing proceedings as examples of what he commented in the advent of the 1990s: a shift from what Foucault (1977) had called the disciplinary society to control society, a process opened by capitalism's metamorphosis.

"We are taught that corporations have a soul, which is the most terrifying news in the world. The operation of markets is now the instrument of social control and forms the impudent breed of our masters. Control is short-term and of rapid rates of turnover, but also continuous and without limit, while discipline was of long duration, infinite and discontinuous." (Deleuze 1992: 6)

Both high rotation rates and unlimited intervention are crucial characteristics of corporate branding's government. Marketing strives foremost towards blurring the distinctions between work and leisure, thereby increasing its control zone in ever modulating[6] ways. In this logic, employees' work has to be experienced as fun, as participating in a brand project that elates consumers as well as worker's proper life aspirations.

During some decades, the character of the stewardess epitomized the conflation of such subjective workers' lifestyles with the overall branding strategies. As Arlie Hochschild (2003) showed with her classic study on Delta Airlines, the emotional labor performed by female flight attendants served to both externally market images of comfort and internally generate motivational drive among the employees. In Hochschild's words, this mode of capitalist labor led to the phenomenon where "seeming to 'love the job' becomes part of the job" (Hochschild 2003: 6). Delta Airlines made enormous efforts to convince their customers of the genuineness of their stewardesses' smiles. Its employees were therefore instructed by training sessions where they would learn about passenger attendance. As an overall target, the stewardesses were charged for emotionally creating the consumer's sensation of "comfort and well-being" (Hochschild 2003: 10), in other words, producing an affective space in the airplane that reassembled the sensation of a cozy home.

Emotional investment and self-regulation is then to be understood as a driving force of the modulated branding process. It covers the pretended "soul" of Delta Airlines. But as stewardesses are urged on orchestrating both their own and the passengers' feelings, working routine turns nearly into an all-encompassing experience. According to Hochschild's research, flight attendants sometimes suffer from the effects that come along with their smiles. Coming home from a long trip they have major difficulties in finding a way to relax. "It's as if I cant't release myself from an artificially created elation that kept me 'up' on the trip" (Hochschild 2003: 4), as a first year worker related. In a certain way, they feel the repercussion of the same emotional investment they actively produce: the enthusiasm for participating in a glamorous undertaking that is at the same time the airline's corporate effort to stimulate upper-class ideas of freedom. Finally, these

---

6   Deleuze defined the *modulation* as the logical characteristic of the control society, contrasting it to the enclosures that had been significant in disciplinary societies. For Deleuze, the *modulation* is "like a self-deforming cast that will continuously change from one moment to the other, or like a sieve whose mesh will transmute from point to point" (Deleuze 1992: 4).

sensations incited around the airline brand operate as agents that raise the employee's commitment as well as consumer's identification with the brand.

2.1.6 Branding and the body

The stewardess is (or at least was until recently) an emblematic case of corporate branding because she typifies the organizational efforts to encourage its employees to "produce themselves as members of the organization, and thereby produce the organization itself" (Arvidsson 2006: 88). Now, although emotions play a crucial role in this subjectivation under and making of the brand, they are not the only instruments. The stewardess is equally asked to use her body, or better, the visible surface of her body. As feminist research has precisely shown, organizations are not gender neutral. Though often masked, gender difference is actually an embodied substructure that integrates larger control strategies of capitalist endeavors (Acker 1990: 147). In what I introduced above with the social fabric of branding, gender performativity[7] (Butler 1990) is a significant aspect for governing both workers and consumers, since corporeal norms of femininity and masculinity often operate as promises as well as surveillance of subjective becomings.

FARM, amongst the most successful Brazilian retailers for upper class women's fashion, uses the concept of "natural feminine beauty". The body of their salesclerks, ad models and targeted consumer group converge in what it projects as the "carioca zona-sul girl": a tall, slim, slightly tanned white woman in the early twenties. Kátia, co-founder of the brand sees FARM's success as due to its strategy to hire this type of feminine youngsters, the "most beautiful girls". She notes that her salesclerks were their

---

7   According to Butler, gender performativity is related to the materialization of human bodies. "In the first instance", she writes, "performativity must be understood not as a singular or deliberate 'act,' but, rather, as the reiterative and citational practice by which discourse produces the effects that it names. [...]the regulatory norms of 'sex' work in a performative fashion to constitute the materiality of bodies and, more specifically, to materialize the body's sex, to materialize sexual difference in the service of the consolidation of the heterosexual imperative." (Butler 1993: 2)

best showcases, the most important thing to have when a costumer entered the shop. "Hence it is the living product, that communicates who is the brand, to whom it is directed" (Carvalhal 2014: 82). FARM has a very narrowly designed target group. Its "authentic" carioca girl is daughter of Rio de Janeiro's socioeconomic elite who loves to hang out on the beach or ride a fancy electro bike, covered by light and graceful dresses. Her body stands for an unburdened, easygoing lifestyle, a person who studies at "the city's best rated universities and goes out to cool places" (Carvalhal 2014: 85).

Service workers in such an ambience are required to do body work (Wolkowitz 2006). As an extension of Hochschild's focus on emotional labor (2003), Tylor and Hancock (2001) showed that flight attendant's continuous exposure to customer gaze obliged them to tame their bodies in particular ways. They would have to "walk softly" through the cabin's corridors or "always smile" at the passengers (Tyler and Hancock 2001: 31). And in more general terms, these women – like in the example of FARM salesclerks – have to be committed to a feminine aesthetic. As Wolkowitz (2006) accurately holds, unlike men, to women it is not sufficient to look clean and cultivated. Feminine front line service workers are requested to move in sexually attractive manners (Wolkowitz 2006: 82). They mostly have to engage their bodies in accordance to heterosexually coded desires. In this sense, the figure of the stewardess is an incarnated brand that participates in the regulatory regimes of gender. By promoting lipstick and smiles, it engineers culturally intelligible norms of the feminine body.

Queer feminist philosopher Preciado (2008) insists on an even stronger entanglement of contemporary brands and correspondent industries with the sexing of human bodies. Both pharmacy and pornography, she argues, are technologically inciting subjects to simultaneously heighten their sexual and capital capacities. The contraceptive pill, Viagra and Playboy would together form a new postindustrial regime, characteristic for the "pharmacopornographic era" (Preciado 2008: 21). In the patient information leaflet of Testogel, a liquid medication that is aimed at treating "testosterone deficit", Preciado detects the corporeal (gender) identity politics as mediated by medical knowledge directed to the consumer. A recommendation warns the patient from having immediate body contact with other persons after the application. It emphasizes that Testogel use is restricted to adult men and women should not come in contact with it

(Preciado 2008: 43). In the same way as Viagra as a sexual stimulator is reserved for men and the Pill as a means of birth control for women, these high tech pharmaceutical products are imminently turning into ideological agents. Utilizing their molecular as well as semiotic instruments, they actively interfere in the (re)production of gender norms (Preciado 2008: 86).

A central point in Preciado's argumentation is that these identity politics are happening through market incentives. In this way – the *biopolitical* aspect of capitalism – she agrees with post-operaist approaches: life and subjectivity as such are the main target of branding strategies. But at the same time, Preciado criticizes that post-operaists would have ignored sex and the body (Preciado 2008: 34). How could they talk about the importance of desires, of affective labor and instigation without considering the materiality of human bodies? Taking Preciado's examples of how the diffusion of pornographic visual culture and molecular pharmaceutical interventions are molding consumer's subjectivities leads to a better understanding of how somatic capacities are, at least in tendency, subsumed under capital too. Accordingly, I argue that the interactive process that brands strive to maintain with consumers is never gender neutral. On the contrary, as Preciado notes, the "pharmacopornographic" regimes are stimulating the subjects in sexually exciting directions that continually preserve their capacity to turn into "total capital" (Preciado 2008: 44). The social fabric that serves to create profit is then equally a body fabric. Control works less exclusively as an external disciplinary conduct directed on the body. Rather, and as I will equally show with the affective laborers in chapters three and four, control is imminently unfolding within the body (Preciado 2008: 60).

2.2 SEXY DIFFERENCE: FROM PRODUCT TO ADVERTISING

As we have seen, marketing strategies often strive to working above the product's proper materiality. Social groups, experiences, lifestyles and finally the human body are becoming sites of projection, or better, part of the social fabric of brands. They together shape an affective grid that mobilizes subjects to actively participating in the overall branding process, which in turn ensures both compliance and consumer spending. Now, although aspirational and affective flows are massive forces used by brands, we should not all too hastily lose sight of the starting point of marketing: the texture of the product. In many cases, the physical characteristics of the commodity do not cease to be a crucial sales argument. Particularly in such areas as the fashion industry, marketers do concentrate on sophisticated object engineering. Hence, in contrast to food or service, fashion products are usually meant to ornate bodies for a certain while. As such, they are intended to be extensions or plastic tools of a consumer's physical appearance.

In order to elaborate more detailed insight in such material branding, product advertising and associated forms of contemporary capitalist government over bodies and identities, I will henceforth concentrate on the case of *Visibly Hot*. In addition to a few accessory articles (watches, bags, caps), this Brazilian enterprise specializes in sunglasses. And this is a particularly interesting object for thinking about how social difference is being (re)invented through material products. At first, sunglasses are what Kirkham (1996) calls a "gendered object". Their closeness to the human body – as one wears them on her or his nose – makes them an accessory that seems to be perceived as crucially contributing to a sense of social identity. Product designers, advertisers and eventual users are investing cultural meanings of femininity and masculinity both through and onto this object. The gender of sunglasses is decisive for sales because it responds to cultural expectations. More precisely, gender identifications are at the center of what Hartewig (2009) describes as the self-staging aspect of sunglasses. As with clothes, one can use them to perform, to present and change bodily attributions of difference. As cinematically demonstrated by the Blues Brothers or Audrey Hepburn, sunglasses are helping people to elaborate on their beliefs in masculinity or femininity, stressing coolness, glamour and, above all, power.

2.2.1 Exploring the product

Visibly Hot's assortment of sunglasses is wide. Each week, the brand launches ten new models. Initially, the series were partly imported and adapted from foreign designs. With the breakthrough to Latin America's biggest retailer for sunglasses, *Visibly Hot* now engages – similarly to other global fashion brands such as H&M – famous designers that create specific collections and product lines for its brand. At the time of my last consultancy in 2014, the online shop listed up to 4600 different pieces. Navigating through the innumerous pictures and product offers, the customer can opt for refining her or his search keys. As the filter on the website shows (Figure 1), there are two ways[8] of locating the consumer's personalized sunglasses. First, they can be accessed by "style", which is the title for different design tastes of the frame – round, rectangular, classic, sport, handsome, and so on. Second, the consumer can choose his glasses by "type", what refers to the opposition of female and male models. This distinction is further emphasized, as children's sunglasses also exist in either feminine or masculine versions.

Figure 1: The product models

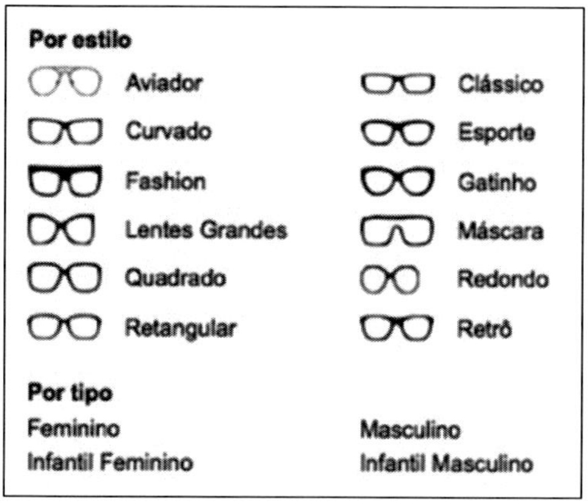

Por estilo			
⌒⌒	Aviador	⌒⌒	Clássico
⌒⌒	Curvado	⌒⌒	Esporte
⌒⌒	Fashion	⌒⌒	Gatinho
⌒⌒	Lentes Grandes	⌒⌒	Máscara
⌒⌒	Quadrado	⌒⌒	Redondo
⌒⌒	Retangular	⌒⌒	Retrô

Por tipo	
Feminino	Masculino
Infantil Feminino	Infantil Masculino

Source: http://loja.chillibeans.com.br/. Last access: 15. nov. 2014, 15:51:29

From a gender perspective, these are clear signs for how commercial products are designed in accordance to cultural notions of sex. They transmit a binary logic, compelling its consumers to fit in intelligible, either female or male subjects. In the managerial discourse of *Visibly Hot* though, gender difference is often downsized to a general aspect of what the company understands as the diversity of its consumers (see 2.4). For

---

8   Further, there are subordinate filtering options that allow the customer to search by material or particular collection.

their marketers, the sunglasses are closely linked to the "democratic" ideal of the brand. First, there is a compact pricing. The costs of the sunglasses range merely between 80 R$ (children's model) and R$ 300 for the most expensive adult glasses. Second, there would be "models for all tastes, ages, genders and styles" (Maia and Araújo 2012: 52), even though this rhetoric already contrasts with the above mentioned product design, which knows but women or men. They further emphasize that it was by the founder's step to abandon the idea of a single target group that consumers could avoid being turned into mere numbers. Consumers could "opt for something that made sense to them" and were thus treated as "individuals with proper and changing personalities" (Maia and Araújo 2012: 52).

In the eyes of *Visibly Hot* marketers, sunglasses are fashion tools. Regardless of age, sex or style, the consumer is invited to use them as a supplement to clothes and hence as a way of stylizing the self. As the head of the brand commented in a recent program about business and entrepreneurship on national Globo TV, *Visibly Hot* would have contributed to a change in people's behavior.

"As pessoas, antigamente, tinham um óculos. Hoje, abrem a gaveta e têm 12 óculos. Que combinam com a roupa, ou homem ou mulher. Então, é mais do que uma marca, eu acho. Acho que a gente mudou o comportamento de consumo de óculos no Brasil e a gente quer agora mudar o consumo no mundo."[9] (Globo TV 2014)

The changes that are declared here as an outcome of branding's successful intervention in consumer behavior also stand in wider cultural contexts. They are not only a result of economic request. For why is it that people in Western countries today consider sunglasses as something that expresses a specifically gendered self? And how did this material object turn into a projective tool for self-staging? I want to tackle these questions with a short excursus on the historical rise of sunglasses in the 20th century, assuming that this is an essential background to how *Visibly Hot* could in-

---

9   "Formerly, people had one pair of sunglasses. Today, people open the drawer and they have 12 pairs. And they combine them with their clothes. Both men and women. So, I think it is more than just a brand. I think we have changed the consumer behavior in Brazil, and now we want to change consumption in the world."

stall its own governmental techniques based on mobilizing and controlling specific modes of desires and subjectivity.

2.2.2 Sunglasses are becoming sexy

At the beginning of the 20th century, tinted lenses were still scarcely popular objects. Mainly, they were produced and designed as protective glasses against dust, heavy incidence of light or wind. They were intended to screen people from nature's unpleasant plagues and hardly bared any glamorous significance. This would only change when automobilists and, above all, aviators moved into the center of public attention. Over the 1920s, aviators stood for a foolhardy, adventurous and successful character and their tinted protective glasses were their crucial trademark (Hartewig 2009: 21). When the US American manufacturer Foster Grant & Co. launched the first cheaply produced pair of sunglasses in 1929, the notion of a rather practical or medically advised tool lost ground quickly. Especially at the time of the Great Depression, sunglasses became one of the objects that cumulated the dreams for glamour and wealth. The message that "they were fun" helped to simulate a lifestyle that was unattainable for large parts of the population (Hartewig 2009: 41).

Besides Italian and French producers, US American fabricators continued to lead the market during the disorders of the war. Their fancy models such as the "aviator" were popular with militarists, politicians and policemen. But the actual breakthrough at a mass level only happened after World War II. The "American way of life" served on both the American continent and in Europe as its patronizing motor. As post-war expectations for a better life were strong, sunglasses interestingly turned into what we could call a "happy object" (Ahmed 2010). Its manufacturers invested in broadening the symbolic attraction and they did this by promoting a range of positive affective value: sunglasses made one feel good and everyone could become happy just by using them. As it is up to today, sunglasses appear as an object that would generate happiness as if it were a natural process. As Ahmed argues, affects are "sticky": it is something that "sustains or preserves the connection between ideas, values, and objects" (Ahmed 2010: 30). At the same time, the feel-good effect is a promise that has to be cultivated in order to keep on sticking. Since happiness is often directed to "what would come after" (Ahmed 2010: 34), a condition that points at somewhere in the fuzzy future, its objects need to be perceived as something that has the power to alter one's state of emotion in such a good or promising direction.

What made sunglasses such an object was the moment when they turned into a tool of playfulness and sexiness. According to Hartewig, the delight of "playful self-staging" (2009: 31) strikingly intensified in the 60s and 70s: fashion and global media stars such as Sophia Loren or Brigitte Bardot transmitted a general "lust for the quick masquerade" (Hartewig 2009: 37). Whereas the former aviator glasses had been designed as unisex objects, the post-war generation sunglasses helped to underline both femininity and masculinity. As an ostentatious tool of consumption, they became finally sexualized: they mediated the emerging cult of the body that belonged to tight swimwear, naked skin and sexiness (Hartewig 2009: 39). And what made the sunglasses particularly seductive and different from other fashion accessories laid in their facility to hide the gaze. One could seemingly become both invisible and visible in a completely different angle. As Hartewig recapitulates, "America taught men and women to feel incognito. The dark glasses became sexy (Hartewig 2009: 51).

In the feminine version, sunglasses were from now on an object of desires. They emblematized a glamorous lifestyle, holidays, and a sexiness that transcended the ideal of romantic monogamy. Whether in the form of the pin-up girl, diva or bad-girl, the sunglasses promised a spontaneous seduction or a hidden persuasion (Hartewig 2009: 58). Significantly, the sexiness seems to be generated by the removal of unfiltered eye contact. Hiding or camouflaging one's eyes intensifies both power and lust: distance, deceit and control grow in a tension of desire. Dark glasses also make one believe to be and look like another person. Drawing on film history, Catherine Deneuve's performance in Luis Buñuel's *Belle de Jour* (1967) is an emblematic example of the incognito-effect. Besides a headscarf, her dark sunglasses are the crucial tool for coating her double life. It permits the wealthy bourgeois madam to mask her daily engagement as a prostitute (Hartewig 2009: 61).

Subsequent to the post-war years, not only femininity but also masculinity is increasingly accentuated by means of sunglasses. "Coolness becomes a duty of men" (Hartewig 2009: 55). Hollywood film stars, musicians as well as despots around the globe make use of them: The Blues Brothers, Miles Davis, Terminator, Charles Taylor or Kim Jong-il. This type of disguise often refers to a rather raw demonstration of power. Just as sexually charged, here the accessory of self-staging mediates male domination. The hidden looks of superiority, anonymous and subject displaced alike, appear as the supplementary counterpart of the feminine coquettish gaze. Following Bourdieu (2002) and his focus on the mostly unconscious and trivial nature of symbolic violence, sunglasses then take on one more part in the "social taxonomy" of looks. They support the gaze as something dependent on schemes of perception and evaluation that, both imposed and tolerated, constitute "the women as symbolic objects, whose being (esse) is a being-perceived (percipi)" (Bourdieu 2002: 94).

2.2.3 Exploiting the sexist gaze

Visibly Hot has launched a range of sexually provocative advertising since its establishment in the mid-1990s. Regularly, thematic campaigns are released that combine printed material with short video clips on television as well as interactive platforms on the brand's internet page. Given the expansive economic success of the enterprise, marketing research has already taken *Visibly Hot* as a role model for latest Brazilian brand positioning. Marketing researchers Souza & Souza Leão (2013), for example, made it their task to analyze the brand's propaganda produced between 1998 and 2010. Studying and grouping the symbolic meanings transmitted by this material, the authors make a pragmatic argument for using myths as a motor for enhancing the mutual identification process of consumer and brand (Souza and Souza Leão 2013: 578). By this, they refer to the idea that the brand was a form of cultural production, destined to communicate consistent histories based on already existing sociocultural narratives or meanings of everyday life.

These histories within *Visibly Hot*, as the marketing researchers' results clearly show, are almost entirely organized around sex. They invoke a normative feminine body (white young beauty), sexist relations impregnated by masculine domination and feminine submission as well as a hedonistic praise of sexually exciting performances. But since Souza & Souza Leão seem to be indebted to market discourse and its profit oriented mission, they completely ignore the symbolic violence that is directed against women. *Visibly Hot*'s advertising is an almost caricatural example of how the feminine body is being projected purely as an object of male desire. As feminist film theorists analyzed since the 1970s, cinematic narrative has for long been a site of constructing women as objects "of the spectator's voyeurist gaze" (De Lauretis 1987: 13) where the female body appears as the emblem of sexuality and visual pleasure. Using de Lauretis' (1987) vocabulary, *Visibly Hot*'s audiovisual branding campaigns are thus not neutral transmitters of cultural myths – as the former authors make us believe – but active "technologies of gender". Its scenes and imageries are constructing specific representations of femininity and masculinity. And these have material effects, inasmuch as they are fabricated for a spectatorship that subjectively absorbs – eventually identifies with – the offered social positions (De Lauretis 1987: 13).

In an earlier campaign stemming from 2005, Visibly Hot laid several semiotic foundations of what accompanies the brand's advertisement until the present. Its title pornochanchada alluded to a genre of popular cinema during the 1970s with the same name, a sort of erotic comedies that were affected by both global movements of sexual liberality and moral censorship imposed by the Brazilian dictatorship. Its story lines followed flirtation, amorous conquests, adultery or the troubles around sexual initiation, visually moderated through indirect insinuation of both sex and feminine nudity (Abreu 2002: 162). Queer theorists also point to the subversive powers that pornochanchada's parodic gender performances at times radiated against the moral order of the political regime (Nogueira and Costa 2016). However, the marketing campaigns of *Visibly Hot* I refer to at this point not only suppress this historical context of pornochanchada, but their aesthetic appropriation also forecloses cinematic arts of deconstruction and parody.

Figure 2: Pornochanchada First Scene

Source: https://www.youtube.com/watch?v=2lwBhgz EWdo.
Last access: 22 nov. 2014, 17:02:30

Figure 3: Pornochanchada Second Scene

Source: https://www.youtube.com/watch?v=-jVFo4gN4Pg.
Last access: 22 nov. 2014, 17:04:03

Figure 4: Pornochanchada Third Scene

Source: https://www.youtube.com/watch?v=1h3qMm Bv_tE.
Last access: 22 nov. 2014, 17:06:22

In the first example (Figure 2), we watch the encounter of a villain with a young girl. The sequence begins with the not announced entrance of a middle-aged Latino into a small single bedroom. Tango music is playing. Following the man's gaze, the camera slides from the doorknob to the bed. There, a young white brunette is about to cover her lower abdomen with a light and airy dress, as though she had been caught in a sexual act. Approaching the bed, the Latino shouts to her: "Why just with the others, hum?! You bitch!" and violently grabs her arm, pulling her close to his moustache that finely rounds off his heavily backwards gelled hair. The girl rather indecisively defends herself. "I don't want to", she says, and only slightly tries to escape his intrusive attempts to kiss her on the mouth. Now aware that she would not – and maybe also would not want to – flee, she puts her hand close to his neck and finishes the scene by exclaiming an instructing "No! Not on the mouth!".

The second example (Figure 3) of the same campaign is suggesting a scene of adultery. There is an approximately 50 year old man with dark sunglasses putting on funky music in the living room of his – presumably proper – house. He wears a white shirt and a red tie that together reinforce the idea that we are looking at the successful head of a family. In the opposing corner of the record player, there is an approximately 20 year old blond girl sitting on the couch. While the man starts to get rid of his sunglasses and loosens his tie, moving his body to the music playing, the girl repeatedly glances at him, soon averting her eyes and communicating her shame and innocent unease to the spectator. The camera focuses on her glossy red lips and her décolletage, and then fades back to the man, who dips his finger in his glass of whisky and then licks it. Then he starts his attack. Animated and in a dancing mood, he approaches the couch and sits down close to the girl. He gently puts his arms around her and his look resembles the way one would use when talking to a small child. She, on the other hand, once again activates her girlish ingénue and insecure comments: "I think I'll go". The scene ends with the man's successful insistence. He orders her to keep silent and to "have one more sip in order to relax". Furtively convinced by the offer, she sips.

In the third and last example (Figure 4) of the *Pornochanchada* campaign that I describe here, the sexual scene is slightly different. Once more, we are in a middle-class house. But this time, the male-female inequality is not only set in scene by age and material power, but also further advanced by race and social class. The dominating character is represented by an older, both white haired and skinned patriarch who is sitting in an armchair. Beneath him and on a ladder of medium height stands a mulatto cleaning lady. It stands out that the statuses as well as occupation of the two are clearly marked by their clothing. While the patriarch is dressed in a light blue suit, the cleaner wears a working uniform with an apron and a fitted white headscarf. Additionally, her uniform is rather tight. When she walks up the ladder in order to remove dust, she skillfully exposes her fine legs. Well attracted by this performance, the patriarch enjoys looking up to her partly stripped waist. All of a sudden, he gets up and furiously commands her to step down from the ladder and put on some trousers. "What have I done?", the cleaning lady whiningly stammers. While she is leaving the living room, the patriarch's gaze fixes the lower parts of her body, in a way as if he was waiting for public endorsement of his sexual appetite.

What unites the three examples is undoubtedly the motif of machismo which is not even superficially questioned through parody, but rather affirmed. Both the gendered characters that appear in the scenes and the way the gaze of the spectator is guided through them are underpinning the fantasy of an unbreakable irresistibility of masculine sexual power. This is first and foremost communicated through the permanent insinuation of feminine nudity that matches a normative body politics. The women in *Visibly Hot*'s ads are invariably subjected to a "beauty dictatorship" (Souza and Souza Leão 2013: 584): they are young, slim, mostly white and always impeccably styled. The men, however, are exempted from such norms. As corresponding to the language of pornochanchada cinema (Gardnier 2001), the characters like the stallion villain (garanhão cafajeste), the tie-wearing pervert (safado engravatado) or the sex-starved old man (velho tarado) do not have to correspond to any beauty ideals. What tends to mediate their male superiority over the sexually objectified women are their higher age as well as attributes of material and symbolic power.

Affectively, the character of the naïve, sometimes helpless, but always sexually willing girl complements the success of the male hetero-sexist seducer. She takes on the role of appealing to moral manners ("Not on the mouth!", "I think I should go") and at the same time discloses her addiction to sex. Secretly or publically, she cannot help but surrender herself to the male command. This relation of domination is at times further accentuated by the distinction of social class and race. In the example of the scene with the housemaid (Figure 4), the male desire is fuelled by a fantasy of the master's power over the non-white subordinate cleaner. As aptly analyzed by Shaw and Dennison (2007), this common sequence in *pornochanchada* cinema draws back to master-slave relations that shaped Brazilian colonial past. It is about "the stereotype of the distinctive charms of the *mulata*" (Shaw and Dennison 2007: 96) within the master's house, a character that stimulated the sexual excitement restrained by moral prohibitions concerning the purity of upper social class and white race.

As a matter of fact, the idea that a specific *brasilidade* (Brazilianness)[10] would lead both the consumers and the enterprise's sex appeal is repeatedly present in *Visibly Hot*'s managerial discourse. Diogo, the brand's founder, publically comments that "as pessoas até falam às vezes que a gente tem uma comunicação sexual. Até tem! Somos brasileiros, a gente é apimentada, é referente"[11] (TV Estadão 2012). Advertisement consequently portrays the brand with the symbol of a red chili pepper, the brand's logo. The narrative of an eminently Brazilian cultural imprint is especially elaborated in the 2010 campaign called "And what if we use some pepper?" (*E se colocar pimenta?*). The promotion clip (Figure 5) initially shows a tropical fairy-tale world full of exuberant flora and fauna where – as the voice-over informs – the chili pepper had originally come from. There is a white girl wearing sunglasses and indigenous feather trimming. The voice-over bridges to another scene, mysteriously whispering that the chili, "as a legitimate [feminine] Brazilian [...] has an intimate relation of love with the sun". Then, the scene changes to a beach with

---

10 Carrara and Simões (2007) are pointing out that the construction of *brasilidade* was both generally referenced to allegedly non-occidental sexuality and specifically salient in anthropological studies of homosexuality. In their critical review of the latter studies, the authors reject the "orientalizing" tendency of this perspective and in contrast underline that sexualities in *brasilidade* should rather be seen as a (singular) variety of thoroughly Western social relations. As further argued by Heilborn (2006), a look at people's everyday sexual practices do highly question the national myths of an explicitly Brazilian sexuality.

11 "sometimes people say that we have a sexual communication. And we really do! We are Brazilians, we are spicy, we are the reference."

palm trees, centered around a young woman lying on a giant chili pepper while being fanned and massaged on the back by two slim guys.

2.2.4 Enacting feminism and freedom

Up to this point, it is clear that sex (and sexism) is a central aspect of present-day branding conduct. *Visibly Hot*'s advertisement deploys the power of desires and sexual fantasies that are objectified in a beauty ideal of a young, mainly white, female body. Its cinematic language makes use of heterosexual pornography, and as described above, of soft-core erotic comedy genres like *pornochanchada*. By this, *Visibly Hot*'s publicity takes part in a transnationally operating iconography of advertising, where hyper-sexualized imagery is believed to gain consumer's attention (Gill 2009: 94). And it also reaffirms Preciado's prophecy of the "pharmacopornographic" era, in which sexual excitation is ever more crucial to capital driven subjectivation (Preciado 2008). But is the objectification of the female body the only strategy of advertising? Gill (2009) and McRobbie (2009) critically reexamined the "current constructions of feminine subjectivities and desires" (Gill 2009: 94). Both authors observe a shift in contemporary representation of women in Western popular and media culture. In many cases, they argue, women's bodies no longer appear in victimized or passive manners. Rather, and especially in the case of young women, they are interpellated as subjects of a new (sexual) freedom and autonomy that paradoxically goes hand in hand with neoconservative values of gender stereotypes (McRobbie 2009: 12) and submission under market control.

Beneath the caricatural campaigns that *Visibly Hot* produced in the previous decade, there is now some evidence of a renewed imagery that grants the female subjects an idea of empowerment. Objectification, the notion previously used for addressing *pornochanchada* video clips, is not an adequate analytical key then, because it cannot gather the complex variety and contradictions of femininities as recently offered by media and advertisement. The most famous example cited by feminist scholars with regard to this representational shift are Eva Herzigová's photographs for Wonderbra in 1994. Different from former advertisement, the model's poses suggested a conscious move to a playful sexual power, imminent in the female body and absorbing the male gaze as a part of the look at the feminine self (Gill 2009: 97). As McRobbie states, Herzigová activates her own gaze on her body, in a way that one could suppose

> "some ironic familiarity with both cultural studies and feminist critiques of advertising (Williams 1978). It was, in a sense, taking feminism into account by showing it to be a thing of the past, by provocatively 'enacting feminism' while at the same time playing with those debates in film theory about women as the object of the gaze." (McRobbie 2009: 16)

Visibly Hot epitomizes this ironic celebration of an autonomous and extrovert feminine sexuality by an advertisement series with two young women in a car (Figure 6). They have long beautiful hair, are blond and brunette, and they are driving a fancy sports car on their own. They are supposedly completely naked – the spectator is being mobilized to imagine what is behind the enclosure of the car's body – they direct their faces up to the air, screaming out in joy. These girls are conscious of their own sexual power. They act in a way that strives to convince both themselves and the spectator that feminine nudity could be lived as an empowering form of freedom. We deal, then, with an ironic incorporation of the "cultural power and energy of feminism" that simultaneously domesticates "its critique of advertising and the media" (Gill 2009: 98).

Compared to the pictorial representations a few decades ago, when women were preferably portrayed within subordinate positions (e.g. in the kitchen) and mostly in displays of a heterosexual family (see the classic study on gender and advertisement of Goffman 1979), the iconic vocabulary of sexually provocative brands such as *Visibly Hot* now include neither the mother nor the sensitive spouse as identification models. Rather, it is the triad of fun, pleasure and power (Gill 2009: 105) that expresses the sexual capital of young women. These are smart, daring, and after all, they are not waiting for a husband that tells them where to go and what to do. *Visibly Hot*'s recent publicity campaigns advance this type of commoditized feminism with an even closer link to commercial sex and pornography. In both *Erotika* (2013) and *Loucura da Nobreza* (2014), the dominatrix, performed by a white young woman, is the leading character. She wears leather and latex and sarcastically cozens the spectator with a whip or whip-like tool (Figure 7). As Gregori (2004) tellingly argues, the commercialization of a "politically correct" pornography, which promises female emancipation, ultimately displaced pornography's obscenity. According to the author, this first and foremost promoted corporeal techniques "aimed at strengthening individual self-esteem" (Gregori 2004). Furthermore, the dissociation of pleasure and danger within this refashioned discourse of pornography bore the question of whether violence was eventually oversimplified, if not ignored.

Explicit pornographic poses and sadomasochistic fantasies have become normalized parts of 21st century advertising (Gill 2009: 94). As is the case with *Visibly Hot*, characters like the dominatrix appear as parodist emblems of feminine autonomy, notably conflating feminine sexual power with economic success. The scenes take place in pompous palaces or brightly polished fantasy worlds where young women consciously mark their mastery. These are no longer helpless 'poor things' but rather actors that renew the dictate of young feminine beauty by mobilizing both sexual desires – they are "forever 'up for it'" (Gill 2009: 98) – and aspirations of individual material wealth. *Visibly Hot* is apparently using a similar language to contemporary pop and media culture. The funk singer Valesca Popozuda, who publicly assumes a feminist stance, also sees her hyper sexualizing performances as emancipatory strategies. "Ser vadia é ser livre"[12], she states and highlights the importance of positively revaluing women's own sexual desires (Oliveira 2014). Media and academic debates are, however, skeptical about the coherence of Popozuda's commercial feminism. As the lyrics in one of her songs insinuate, an intelligent woman could indeed become rich if she knew how to manage the fact that men were sexually mad about her. By this, the lyrics continue, she would not only get jewels and a house, but also silicone, implanted hair and enlarged buttocks (Marinho 2013).

---

12 "To be a slut is to be free"

Figure 5: Pimenta advertisement

Source: https://www.youtube.com/watch?v=8rTbUmvcVLM. Last access: 25 nov. 2014, 19:04:22

Figure 6: 'Sexual autonomy' I

Source: http://www.viewmagazine.com.br/opiniao/entrevista?edition. Last access: 13 dec. 2012, 20:59:01

Figure 7: 'Sexual autonomy' II

Source: https://www.youtube.com/watch? v=KO1YK qJbin8. Last access: 22 nov. 2014, 22:11:40

Popozuda is placed at the often paradoxical crossroads of a newly attributed (mainly sexual) agency to young women and of constraining impositions of the fashion-beauty complex. This "modern kind of freedom" (McRobbie 2009: 9), which is also present in *Visibly Hot*'s latest advertising, conflates a reenacted feminism with a strong endorsement of consumer culture. Young women appear as the entitled subjects of economic productivity. Their obligation to be free, to use Rose's terms, are operating a success oriented regime of the self (Rose 2004: 87) that often renews heterosexual desire as well as cultural norms of femininity (McRobbie 2009: 63). As McRobbie accentuates, the obligations of body maintenance and feminine identity are emanating from a new government of self-production. Rather than being externally forced by a physically present male spectator or counterpart, advertising and media culture ironically engineer them as self-imposed. Popozuda, for example, publicly calls for a sexy handling of the female body, ambiguously enmeshing aspirations of freedom with hedonistic desire of consumption and submission under men's material domination. It is on this basis that she mediates the sensation of self-acting, of being able to live individual aspirations – a crucial aspect of what Rose named a government without need to govern society (Rose 2004: 88). Once the addressed subjects perceive their individual responsibility, it affects compliance with commodity freedom and apparently renews sexist attributions to the female body.

2.3 ARCHITECTURES OF THE CORPORATE BRAND

> "[A] consolidação de um dos mais reconhecidos e agressivos empreendimentos de varejo em todo o planeta"[13]
> (Maia and Araújo 2012: 16)

Within less than two decades, *Visibly Hot* ascended to Latin America's largest brand for sunglasses and accessories. Today, the enterprise is maintaining above 600 sale locations in Brazil, corresponding to a presence in most of the country's commercial shopping centers. Together with its expansion both regional (Colombia, Peru) and global (US, Kuwait, Angola, Portugal, Israel), the retailer reaches an annual turnover of about 500 million Reais (Redação/Terra 2014). Hardly surprising, there is a growing interest by a large business audience striving to grasp the secret of *Visibly Hot*'s apparent key to entrepreneurial success. Diogo, who launched the brand at the end of the 90s, is constantly being invited to give a speech in administration or marketing schools as well as in business related TV shows. Also, he co-authored the book *E se colocar pimenta?* (What about adding some pepper?), intended to tell the true history of the brand (Maia and Araújo 2012). First and foremost, the book reads like a marketing manual. As the authors underline in the preface, it is thus directed to students, admirers of the products, their own salesclerks, businessmen looking for innovation, and finally academics with interest in economic growth.

---

13 "[the] consolidation of one of the most recognized and aggressive retail ventures all over the planet"

Regarding our present inquiry of economic governmental techniques, these public reports of *Visibly Hot* are very rich sources for analysis. They can be looked at as constitutive narratives, meticulously designed components of what symbolically bundles both the enterprise's commercialization strategies and its efforts to shape a far-reaching corporate identity. What follows in the next sections is thus a critical, focused account of the above-mentioned book, complemented by additional media sources about *Visibly Hot* as well as its surrounding events. It is directed to the question of how the enterprise's self-portrayal and public appearance are expanding massive identity politics as a way of pushing compliance within its followers (employees, franchisees as well as present and future consumers). According to my thesis, the "democratic sensuality" (*sensualidade democrática*) promised by *Visibly Hot* is re-enacting contemporary (sub)cultural values and projects of subjectivity that simultaneously celebrate and renormalize capitalist relations of work and consumption.

2.3.1 From Californian rock dreams to brand management

"Mas tudo isso só se tornou possível devido ao empreendedor visionário, apaixonado e incansável, que 'contamina' todos à sua volta, disseminando a cultura da empresa que fez desenvolver. [Diogo] é assim, um empreendedor brasileiro que superou vários desafios até chegar ao sucesso e que não se cansa de querer cada vez mais. Sua história se confunde com a da empresa apimentada que criou e mostra que é possível sonhar e realizar, apesar das várias adversidades que se apresentam diariamente àqueles que querem empreender no Brasil."[14] (Maia and Araújo 2012: 11)

---

[14] "But all this only became possible due to the visionary entrepreneur, who is passionate and tireless, yet 'contaminates' everyone around him; disseminating the enterprise's culture that he developed. [Diogo] is like that, a Brazilian entrepreneur who mastered several challenges before finally reaching success and who doesn't tire in wanting more and more. His history is entirely mixed up with the history of the spicy enterprise he created and it shows the possibilities of dreaming and realizing, even under the hindering circumstances that those who wish to do business in Brazil encounter on a daily basis."

Right at the beginning of the book, the reader is being informed that the enterprise's overwhelming success is due to its visionary founder. The preface, written by marketing guru José Dornelas, is leaving no doubt of Diogo's almost miraculous entrepreneurial skills. Diogo, grown up in middle class São Paulo and trained in prestigious colleges, quickly started travelling to the United States. According to his own account, he started to develop his deep passion with rock music and instruments, when he was a teenager of about 14 years of age. At the same time, he started his first trading activities: buying instruments in the US and reselling them afterwards in Brazil. But also his concerns with both his body and identity stem from that period. "Sempre fui gordinho, mas um gordo ágil, descolado, gente boa."[15] At age 18, he started doing exercises and suddenly lost weight, "e isso é muito importante para um garoto dessa idade, para sua autoconfiança."[16] (Maia and Araújo 2012: 18). According to this narrative, Diogo not only developed his disciplined ambitions, but also his ability of changing identities:

"[Diogo] viajou como 'gordinho gente boa' e retornou absolutamente transformado, tanto que recebeu diversos convites para ser modelo e começou a trabalhar na área. Essa capacidade de se reinventar baseada na garra e na vontade de fazer acontecer foi o elemento propulsor de seu espírito empreendedor."[17] (Maia and Araújo 2012 : 18)

In the early nineties, Diogo spent most of the time in Miami but repeatedly returned to Brazil, as he was still dreaming about his musical career as a drummer within his friends' band. However, he did not surrender his own version of the American Dream. In order to sustain his fashionable lifestyle close to celebrities of the American cultural industry, he used to make business by selling magazines. Again travelling to and returning

---

15 "I always was chubby, but an agile, cool, good guy."
16 "and that is very important for a boy of that age, for his self-confidence"
17 "[Diogo] travelled as a 'chubby good guy' and returned [to Brazil] absolutely transformed, to the extent that he got numerous invitations for being a model and started working in that area. This capacity to reinvent himself, based on his given natural will to make things happen, was the driving element of his entrepreneurial spirit."

from Brazil, it was only in Venice Beach, Los Angeles, where Diogo got the idea of entering the trade with sunglasses. At times, there was a street vendor that sold dark glasses at the boardwalk. Deeply impressed by the mixture of "executivos, comerciantes, advogados, médicos, [...] tatuados, roqueiros, clubbers"[18] who all made part of the street vendor's consumers, Diogo decided to adopt this concept of a heterogeneous audience (Maia and Araújo 2012: 23). He was convinced that there was no such thing in Brazil yet. Promptly, he negotiated with the street vendor, bought 200 pieces of sunglasses, boxed them in his suitcase and resold them among his friends in São Paulo. This was the early model of the one-man-business later called *Visibly Hot*.

"Com as malas vazias, [Diogo] cumpria a insana rotina de embarcar às terças-feiras principalmente para Los Angeles e Nova York. Chegava ao destino na manhã seguinte, enchia a bagagem com as peças, tomava um rápido banho no aeroporto, comia por US$4 em um restaurante chinês dos menos indicados e retornava a São Paulo."[19] (Maia and Araújo 2012: 24)

His trades started off well. Several shopping center based fashion brands became interested in his imported sunglasses. But Diogo lacked organizational skills. In 1996, only two years after its launch, his first enterprise ceased to exist. This was a moment of major impact, for Diogo at the same time underwent his ultimate attempts aimed at becoming a rock star, ending this time with definite failure (Maia and Araújo 2012: 31).

1997 was actually the year when *Visibly Hot* was invented as a brand. Diogo mounted a small stand at the *Mercado Mundo Mix* in São Paulo. At times, the latter was a fashion fair, where young designers, artists and DJs were selling their oeuvres. Once installed there, Diogo very much appreciated the circulation of "performers, drag queens, punks, entre outros indi-

---

18 "executives, merchants, lawyers, physicians, [...] tattooed people, rockers, clubbers"
19 "With empty suitcases, [Diogo] put up with the insane routine of boarding on Tuesdays, primarily to Los Angeles and New York. He arrived at the destination the other morning, filled his baggage with the pieces, took a short bath at the airport, had a 4 dollar meal at one of the least recommended Chinese restaurants and returned to São Paulo."

víduos e tribos"[20] in order to re-launch his enterprise (Maia and Araújo 2012: 28). He hosted performances with similar characters and finally promoted his brand's symbol, the red pepper, that remains as the enterprise's logo until the present. But soon, the stand at the fashion fair could not keep step with the growing number of consumers, already because the *Mundo Mix* only happened once a month. So Diogo found a shop in the *Galeria Ouro Fino*, a shopping gallery run by emergent fancy fashion labels and located in one of São Paulo's central commercial areas around Rua Augusta. In his memoirs he comments:

"Enquanto os demais corredores da galeria estavam vazios, a loja [*Visibly Hot*] estava abarrotada, com filas imensas, música alta – um oásis de loucura em meio a uma decadência – por que não? – elegante."[21] (Maia and Araújo 2012: 32)

As the selling rates continued to turn out high and "os pais da classe média alta ainda não permitiam que seus filhos frequentassem ambientes como o da Ouro Fino"[22] (Maia and Araújo 2012: 32), the step towards broader consumer access was but the next one to take. In 2000, *Visibly Hot* opened its first stand in a shopping center in São Paulo.

2.3.2 Style and identity politics

"Ao ser acessível no preço, flexível na estética e democrática na abordagem, a [*Visibly Hot*] faz todo o sentido em um mundo no qual ser alternativo é cada vez menos uma exceção, pois – de sinônimo de underground – passa a ser a tradução de 'ter vários estilos'."[23] (Maia and Araújo 2012: 191)

---

20 "performers, drag queens, punks, above other individuals and urban tribes"
21 "While the rest of the corridors remained empty, the [*Visibly Hot*] store overflowed, with enormous queues, loud music – an oasis of craziness in the middle of – why not? – elegant decadence"
22 "the parents of higher middle class did not yet allow their children to go to such establishments such as *Ouro Fino* by themselves"
23 "With its accessible prices, flexible aesthetics and democratic attendance, [*Visibly Hot*] makes very much sense in a world in which being alternative is less and less an exception, because – as synonymous to underground – it turns into the translation of 'having various styles'."

What marketing discourse calls the "brand positioning" refers to what I previously mentioned about how brands are being designed to be woven into existing social groups or communities (Arvidsson 2006: 69). Especially from alternative, subcultural or dissident groups, as Arvidsson argues, brands draw and capitalize an "ethical surplus": values that mobilize a different common – e.g. through a political identity – and thus are attractive for capitalist market strategies. As we just saw with the initial stage of *Visibly Hot*, first Diogo's background with US-American rock music and second, his breakthrough within the São Paulo's *Mundo Mix* art fair, were decisive cornerstones of the kind of lifestyle intended to be sold to the consumers. From the beginning, the central idea was obviously one that proposed to transcend mainstream culture. Discursively, this mainstream included even the aspect of mass commercialization: the first *Visibly Hot* shop in a shopping gallery is portrayed as crazy "oasis", something that would not naturally match the commercial center and promise something beyond conventional goods. This concept was further personified by Diogo's first generation employees:

"O vendedor dos primórdios da Ouro Fino era [Stan]. Com visual absolutamente assustador para os mais conservadores – cabelos brancos e uma tatuagem com as três letras de seu apelido gravada nos dedos de uma das mãos –, era mestre em convencer as pessoas de que elas precisavam de um, dois, três, quatro óculos."[24] (Maia and Araújo 2012: 32)

The exotic or monstrous appearance of this salesclerk is one emblematic part of how *Visibly Hot* lays out its own economic success. It is about the rhetoric figure that it was: an authentic, different, and unadapted lifestyle that constituted the brand's sales crew and its spirit (see my detailed discussion in sections 3.3 and 3.4). These were "descolados, informais e próximos"[25] and therefore stood for a new generation that superseded formal, white-collar employees (Maia and Araújo 2012: 34). Diogo's auto-

---

24 "The seller of the early days of Ouro Fino was [Stan]. With his absolutely scary appearance in the eyes of conservative people – white hair and a tattoo with three letters of his nickname on his fingers –, he was a master at convincing people that they needed one, two, three, four sunglasses."
25 "cool, informal and close"

narrative about his biography further sustains this discourse. It transmits the spirit of a cosmopolitan, bohemian, and constantly changing artistic conduct of life (remember his career as a rock musician in California as well as his creative, quasi-impromptu entrepreneurship).

Sexuality and sexual identities, too, play a considerable role in this propagandized "island of style". The *Mercado Mundo Mix*, the art fair through which Diogo succeeded in launching his brand, was a prominent locus of the processes of market segmentation along the 1990s. By this term, several authors (França 2006; Gregori 2006; Braz 2014) name the emergence of a proper GLS market (*mercado GLS*), meaning an ensemble of products, magazines, party and leisure culture directed at "Gays, Lesbians and Sympathizers" (*Gays, Lésbicas e Simpatizantes*). Diogo relates that, at times, he sold his sunglasses in the middle of "drag queens" and other sexual dissidents. Also, he states that two *travestis* helped him out for product propaganda within the *Mundo Mix*. Although Diogo never used a discourse that would precisely defend LGBT-rights[26], he economically emerged within this market niche, in which self-esteem and the establishment of a positive loaded gay/lesbian identity was core for both profit and political visibility. As França emphasizes, GLS entrepreneurs often defined themselves in terms of representatives of a political mission that would enhance the process of outstripping marginalization (França 2006: 147). At the same time, the relation between consumption and citizenship remained a contested terrain within the LGBT movements. On the symbolical level, as Braz indicates, GLS market incentives simultaneously represented a "glamourization" of gay identities, often attaching older and depoliticized stereotypes of both party culture and excessive consumer practices (Braz 2014: 291).

The identity styles spread by Diogo and his sales crew repeatedly raise concerns in broader public. Blogs and fan pages show a very opposed course of opinion. On the one hand, there is curiosity of whether *Visibly*

---

26 In another public interview, Diogo states that he would have been expecting a female clientele when he was at *Mundo Mix*, but then who came was a "male and gay public" (Source: http://mundochillibeans. blogspot.ch/2010/ 10/jo-soares-entrevista-caito-maia.html. Last access: 14.12.2014, 16:02:05)

Hot and his founder "are" gay[27]. The brand's style and fashions are seen as cool "although" it is "all homo". And the marketing manual is keen on emphasizing that *Visibly Hot* is not only about gay style. A democratic spirit, so goes the rhetoric, would guide the formation of the sales crew. Felipe, an intimate associate partner of Diogo, rectifies:

"Sempre fomos ligados ao mundo GLS e à música eletrônica. Não somos apenas uma marca estilo gay. Estamos abertos a todos os modos de vida. […] Começamos a trabalhar com pessoas guerreiras, sem medo, ousadas. E elas perceberam que poderiam ganhar junto conosco esse jogo. E aí passamos a orientar esse trabalho para formar as pessoas."[28] (Maia and Araújo 2012: 181)

The immanent discomfort of seeing the brand reduced to a "gay style" undergoes a turnaround by accentuating *Visibly Hot*'s character of diversity (see later 2.4), an allegedly win-win situation for both employees and the brand. This positive and promising attribution is further evident in different LGBT discussion platforms. In a humorous speech, one page for example lists the ten advantages of "being gay". On position six, it promotes: "Assuma sua homossexualidade e ganhe desconto nos óculos da [*Visibly Hot*]"[29]. And another public GLS humour-Facebook-Group vividly discusses the question: "Porque todo vendedor da [*Visibly Hot*] é lésbica ou gay?"[30]

---

27 Source: http://forum.jogos.uol.com.br/esse-dono-da-chilli-beans-e-simpatico-e-bonitinho-ate_t_2174551. Last access: 14 dec. 2014, 15:01:07.

28 "We always had a link to the GLS market and to electronic music. We are not simply a gay style brand. We are open to all modes of life. […] We started working with militant people, who were without fear, daring. And they realized that they could win this game together with us. And so we began to guide this work in order to train our people."

29 "Assume your homosexuality, and you will get a special discount on [*Visibly Hot*] sunglasses." (Source: http://www.canudoscoloridos.com/2011/10/10-vantagens-que-poucos-comentam-sobre.html. Last access: 14 dec. 2014, 15:05:34)

30 "Why are all [*Visibly Hot*] salesclerks lesbian or gay?" (Source: https://pt-br.facebook.com/ humorgls.lgbt/ posts/ 388901201210732. Last access: 14 dez. 2014, 15:10:18)

2.3.3 Up with sales! Spatial, organizational and identity expansions

"Começou uma nova fase no crescimento da [*Visibly Hot*]. [Diogo] já não era mais um 'vendedor alternativo', mas um empreendedor que começava a ser reconhecido pelo mercado."[31] (Maia and Araújo 2012: 103)

Diogo's step away from the *Mercado Mundo Mix* to the shopping center industry was decisive in many respects. As the internal managerial discourse suggests, he lost his specific "alternative" role, the former "underground" stance that was initially so central to his entrepreneurial endeavor. But in economic terms, this dislocation was even more far-reaching. What is hardly mentioned in the marketing manual is the fact that *Visibly Hot*'s "miraculous" growth coincided with an enormous expansion of Brazilian consumer markets in the recent past. As the numbers of the Brazilian Development Bank show, overall retail trade nationally increased 75,5% in the period between 2002 to 2011, including not only essential goods but also clothing, cosmetics and electronics (Gonçalves et al. 2012). And the people that sustain this development are emerging social groups, a supposedly "new middle class" (Neri 2008), as the economic and state discourse goes.

While in other Western countries due to economic recession, mass consumption and shopping centers have somewhat lost their showcase role for capitalist modernity, the Brazilian situation was – until recently – living an opposing trend. The current expansion of shopping malls is still a very lucrative business for investors (Economia Baiana 2012). Contrary to popular belief in sociological studies (see particularly Padilha 2006), I argue that these business governments are not based on the exclusion of lower and formerly marginalized classes, but on an aggressive inclusionary strategy of the same. Following neoliberal logics of widening markets into full society, poor and socially emerging people are seen as the new motor of Brazilian economy. Already a quick glance at investment trends is sufficient to grasp this logic. Illustrious investors such as Elias Tergilene

---

31 "A new chapter in [*Visibly Hot*]'s growth began. [Diogo] was no longer an 'alternative vendor' but now an entrepreneur who was about to be recognized within the market."

now focus on society's most needy population. His project *Favela Shopping* is aimed at constructing "Brazil's first mall in a favela" (Nogueira 2013), an endeavor in which brands like *Visibly Hot* immediately showed interest, for the favela population, countrywide comprising 12 million people, made it to one of the economically most "interesting" groups (Redação/WSCOM 2013).

However, the rapid growth of *Visibly Hot* as a commercial brand could not only be accomplished by a widening of consumer groups. Together with the expansion into the realm of shopping centers, Diogo had been advised to organizationally bank on franchising (Maia and Araújo 2012: 41). This booming business concept – especially in Brazil (Gomes 2012) – is based on collaboration between franchiser and franchisee. While the franchiser provides the overall organizational framework (the brand or trademark, including the product segments from the supplier, design, as well as operational procedures such as staff trainings and supervision) and receives payment, the franchisee can benefit from the already asserted concept, which can possibly minimize risks of entrepreneurial failure. Globally, Subway and McDonald's are amongst the biggest franchisers, while in Brazil enterprises like O Boticário lead the franchising market. In the case of *Visibly Hot*, Diogo directly owns only 9 stores. As the internal marketing manual remembers, franchising was key to the early expansions of the brand in the beginning of the 2000s.

"No início, o modelo de franquias também se mostrava altamente lucrativo. A marca conseguiu garantir margem suficiente para que os empreendedores vendessem os produtos a um preço competitivo e, assim, demandassem rapidamente mais unidades. Dessa forma, a atualização seminal de coleções era garantida, de maneira sustentável, também com os franqueados."[32] (Maia and Araújo 2012: 53)

The wide network of franchisees is then one more part of the strategic tools that serve to accelerate, multiply and spread the brand. Consequently,

---

32 "At the beginning, the franchise model proved to be highly profitable, too. The brand succeeded in guaranteeing sufficient margin, so that entrepreneurs would sell the products at a competitive price and, by that, promptly ask for more units. Thus, the weekly update of collections was guaranteed in sustainable ways, also through the franchisees."

Diogo sees himself less in terms of the exclusive tenant and more as the heart of "development brand" (Dornelas 2013). Metamorphosed from the front-line and stand-alone vendor to the "spiritual" leader of *Visibly Hot*, he is engaged in maintaining the "offensive" and "dynamic" style of his trademark. Regarding the selection criteria for his franchisee, Diogo stresses that he did not want to discriminate anyone but in order to become one of his partners, "você tem que ter um espírito jovem"[33] (Dornelas 2013).

2.3.4 Conventions and affective bonds

This "young spirit" is what encompasses the enterprise's tireless efforts to set the stage for a dazzling corporate brand. Business partners, franchisees, and front-line salesclerks are periodically called on to participate in bigger commercial events. In 2012, Diogo launched the first edition of the now annually happening so called conventions that take place on especially rented cruise liners or islands in Brazil's Southeast. As a franchisee of *Visibly Hot* commented during a popular Brazilian TV-show:

"A [*Visibly Hot*] tem uma tradição de convenção, [...] ela tem o diferencial de trazer os colaboradores para essa reunião. É um momento de festa anual, todos os anos a [*Visibly Hot*] tem que se superado. Esse ano, ela realmente quer botar para quebrar, um navio exclusivo da [*Visibly Hot*]. Está lotado, têm 3000 pessoas. Têm muitos colaboradores, e é isso, o DNA da marca é injetado, com força, nessa galera. Então, eles voltam para suas operações mais diversas no Brasil, com esse DNA, entendendo o que é que a marca quer para o ano, entendendo como que foi o nosso crescimento, aonde a gente quer chegar. Então, é uma reunião que alinha tudo, e, na verdade, é festa. São 36 horas de festa, 17 atrações, DJs."[34] (Programa Expressão 2012)

---

33 "you need to have a young spirit"
34 "[*Visibly Hot*] has a tradition of conventions, [...] the enterprise has the distinction of bringing the employees to this meeting. It is a moment of annual party, every year [*Visibly Hot*] has to surpass itself. This time, it will really exceed all present dimensions, there is an exclusive [*Visibly Hot*] cruise ship. It's full, there are 3000 people. There are many employees, and that's it, the brand's DNA is being injected, with force, into the crew. So they will return to their

The term and concept of the "convention" seems to be inspired by the fan conventions, a genre of public reunions that emerged at the end of the 1960s. With upcoming US science fiction series such as Star Trek, fan groups then organized broader events that were aimed at exchanges with the actors, public viewings and speeches as well as fashion parades of the series' characteristic uniforms and alien species (Coppa 2006). This idea of party events, themed around a commercial spectacle, around a common identification medium (whether it is about an enthusiasm about science fiction and starships or a celebration of youth and coolness) is vividly enacted by *Visibly Hot*. As the franchisee above explicitly reveals, the conventions that comprise up to 3000 people and last about three days would be able to "align everything". They are intended to direct the brand's fan and collaborator crowd: those should be "forcibly" injected a "DNA", a bundle of the enterprise's success stories and future mission targets. By this, as the franchisee also tells us, even the labor force in geographically most distant regions would return to their homes with a literally incorporated ideal of the brand's aspirations.

Many informal and amateur videos on YouTube record the happenings at the conventions. In 2013, once the fan crowd was arranged at the cruising ship the convention started with a multimedia show. There, the audience watched the enterprise's annual financial statement and the latest advertising films while dancers, rock bands and finally the founder Diogo got on the stage. As soon as the show reached the peak of the crowd's ecstasy, Diogo shouted: "Abram os seus corações! Recarreguem as suas baterias! Temperem as suas vidas! Porque, a pimenta vai arder!"[35]. And with thunderous applause, the party would continue with the next attractions. As Diogo stated elswhere, his area could be compared to a football match. "Sou animador de torcida da minha equipe, sabe"[36] (Tavares 2013). This image is important to his general style of leadership. In contrast to signal-

---

different operations all over Brazil with this DNA, understanding what the brand wants for this year, understanding how was our growth, and where we want to go. So, it's about a meeting that aligns everything, and actually it's a party. 36 hours of partying, 17 acts, DJs."

35 "Open your hearts! Reload your batteries! Flavor your lives! Because the pepper will burn!"
36 "I am my team's cheerleader, you know"

ing any idea of hierarchy or exclusiveness of his position within the enterprise, he is ostensibly concerned with emphasizing his close and personal relationship with his shop vendors and franchisees. For instance, he says that the salesclerks were his main inspiration for why he would not need any prescribed manuals to tell him how to proceed in new commercial strategies (Dornelas 2013). It is not surprising then that the *Visibly Hot* corporate brand is portrayed as a "big family", a rhetoric figure that foregrounds the affective and egalitarian bonds within the enterprise.

For sure, this anti-authoritarian entrepreneurial government is not specific of *Visibly Hot*. Already the global management literature of the 1990s had highly recommended to supersede old hierarchical structures in corporate leadership. According to the analysis of Boltanski and Chiapello (2005), management discourse recommended their followers to create a "vision". To be monitored by a a few leaders and coaches, this would first bear the advantage that former executive cadres or top-of-the top bosses could be replaced. Second, a "vision" is there seen as a more powerful way to guarantee the engagement, or say devotion, of both employees and stakeholders, and even more: it does so without the use of force (Boltanski and Chiapello 2005: 97). Now, with the growing importance of emotional ties that are reminiscent in this analysis, Boltanski and Chiapello advised in a direction that is additionally enforced within *Visibly Hot*'s managerial speech. The family, but also the propagated value of trust, are seen as affective surplus benefits that helped in reducing costs of administration and excessive control mechanisms (Maia and Araújo 2012: 199). This centrality of positive affects[37], always refreshed by the conventions, also appears in the managerial re-evaluation of the brand's development:

"A afetividade, quando genuína, encurta caminhos, cria laços mais fortes e engaja os públicos de forma consistente. Prova disso, na [*Visibly Hot*], é a intensidade dos participantes da convenção anual. Envolvidos em um ambiente vibrante, demonstram que viver uma cultura de marca extrapola a retórica e influencia, efetivamente,

---

37 In section 4.3, I discuss Brazil's singular relation with affectivity, with the figure of the *homem cordial* (cordial man).

os hábitos e comportamentos individuais e interpessoais."[38] (Maia and Araújo 2012: 212)

Control and conduct of employees are apparently seen as based on affection, in other words, employees are seen as conducible and transformable by promising them positive emotions. The party events such as the conventions are not only crucial tools of corporate branding. As mentioned in the cited paragraph of the *Visibly Hot* marketing book above, these events are also meant to transcend brand culture into the affective experiences of real individual lives. Such interlocking of brands and social experiences unfolds precarious effects of which Arvidsson (2006: 10) advises us: once branding is successful, it is getting more and more difficult to disentangle individual hopes and affectivities from market interests.

2.4 THE SEARCH FOR ECONO-SEXY PROFESSIONALS: DIVERSITY MANAGEMENT

"Esta é a porta de entrada para o mundo da pimenta. Um universo democrático, afetivo, louco, cheio de desejos, ódios, tropeços, recomeços, e, principalmente, sucesso. Uma cultura ousada, seminua, transparente, superlativa e construída diariamente com intensidade e amor. […] Esqueça os milhões de gráficos e dogmas. A [*Visibly Hot*] é feita de histórias traçadas por pessoas dos mais diferentes perfis e naturezas que se uniram em torno de um ideal comum e fazem desse empreendimento um dos símbolos de um Brasil diferente, globalizado, aberto e sério. São milhares de jovens – e outros nem tanto – responsáveis pela vitalidade de uma marca que aprendeu a ser forte desde o início. […] A [*Visibly Hot*], em vez de seguir formulas, criou um jeito próprio de fazer negócios baseado, principalmente, na

---

38 "Affectivity, if it is genuine, shortens distances, creates stronger ties, and engages the public in more consistent ways. Proof of it, at [*Visibly Hot*], is the intensity of the annual convention's participants. Involved in a vibrant ambience, they demonstrate that living a brand culture goes beyond the rhetoric and actually influences the individual and interpersonal habits and behaviors."

igualdade entre as pessoas. Sua grande virtude: nesta história, todos os personagens têm o mesmo peso."[39] (Maia and Araújo 2012: 13)

In these opening words to the 2012 book about *Visibly Hot*'s story, we find once more a close link that is being made between economic profit and affective desires, the latter ranging from love, nudity and, without pausing, values of democracy and equality. Similar to the sex(ist) imagery of the brand's advertising, but now more than just an identification model directed to consumers, the supposedly true history about the enterprise conveys the message that its audacious, spicy and sex appealing corporate identity is the central key to its overall success. With reference to a non-bureaucratic and non-dogmatic spirit, it sticks the meanders of sexual freedom – crazy and startlingly untamed – to the idea of a democratic and inclusive corporation, one that hires young people of all kinds of personalities. And this is at the same time the nodal point where affectivity meets diversity. Thus, above the sexual content, this second rhetoric agent (which I analyze in sections 2.4.2 and 2.4.3) is intrinsically built along the conviction that economic success is guaranteed by the appreciation of singular identities and bodies (they call it 'profiles' and 'natures') that converge in an ideology of equality within its employees.

As already argued with Arvidsson (2006), branding as a mode of conduct has decades ago exceeded the realm of product advertising. Designing a corporate spirit with regard to the employees has turned into another crucial point of the managerial agenda. In public interviews given to fash-

---

39 "This is the gateway to the world of red pepper. A democratic, affective, crazy universe, full of desires, animosities, stumbles, restarts, and primarily success. A daring culture, half naked, transparent, superlative, and daily created with intensity and love. […] Forget the millions of charts and dogmas. [*Visibly Hot*] is made of histories drawn by people of most different profiles and natures, who have come together around a common ideal, and they are a symbol of a different Brazil through this enterprise, a globalized, open and serious one. It is about thousands of young people – and others not so much – responsible for the vitality of a brand, which learned to be strong from the beginning. […] Instead of following formulas, [*Visibly Hot*] created an own way of making business, mainly based on the equality of people. Its great virtue: in this history, all characters are equally important."

ion magazines and marketing professionals, *Visibly Hot*'s founder Diogo always underlines that he is not interested in money. Rather, as he says, his performance is about "growing" in his specific role as the brand's creator, a kind of young mindedness that affected him and that he would like to pass on to his team. Because, as he puts it in an interview with a marketing specialist, one should not let the atmosphere turn into something robot-like. On the contrary, one had to "respect every person exactly how she is and lead her to the heart" (Dornelas 2013). Actually, people would create a personality within his endeavor and in turn enrich the company with that.

Visibly Hot draws its persuasive power not merely because it melts down the actual distinction between its staff and its consumers. "Be different" (*ser diferente*) and "spice up your life" (*apimente sua vida*) are its central slogans used to unleash a generic longing for the expression of an identity, uncommitted to specific social promises and hence rhetorically open for enthusiasts as much and diversified as possible. Once the staff is recognized as taking a necessary part in the branding process, the collective spirit calls for a more active, and mostly flexible subjectivity. In contrast to highly normative fashion brands such as the US American retailer Abercrombie & Fitch, where consumers as well as the workforce are addressed in uniformity[40], the workforce of *Visibly Hot* is constantly encouraged to autonomously create new associations of (and for) the brand. This hungry request for subjectivity reminds us of the shifting of business responsibilities toward the individual worker in terms of a creative "self-monitoring" subject (Boltanski and Chiapello 2005: 114). But are these individual, multiple identity constructs synonymous to unbound free expression? Does the alleged pluralization of the employees' legitimate bodies and desires within the company correspond to a notion of equality that

---

40 One of the more recent spot advertisements of Abercrombie & Fitch (Abercrombie & Fitch 2013) portrays, for example, a noticeable homogeneous group of young men, white and with trained bodies, having a conversation about their joint football team. "Great personality", "lifestyle" and "really cool" are some of the buzzwords of how they characterize their own spirit. And finally, one of the men states: "We found amazing how similar we are". Abercrombie & Fitch's strategy is committed to a very singled out subject – each in its male and female version – of brand identification.

turns the concern of exclusionary norms into an obsolete question? Or are there rather other processes of in- and exclusion at work? And finally, what exactly means difference or to be different in this example of managerial discourse?

2.4.1 "We don't simply like- we give it a value"

At the beginning of my first interviews, Marina, cashier at a *Visibly Hot* kiosk, asked me perplexed: "But what is the profile of that person? Do you think that I fit in?" She was curious to know why I had chosen precisely her as an interlocutor of my research. Actually, as it turned out later, until the moment when she handed in her CV, Marina thought that she would not "have the style for *Visibly Hot*". And her doubts apparently caught up with her when she felt obligated to speak on behalf of her teammates. Marina's insecurity stems from what we questioned above as the possible twilight of what the present brand offers as all-inclusive identity politics. While promising the valorization of the most "different" personalities, the company's personal management must apparently keep alive a certain guideline or number of model-identities. If there were a real absence of such an envisaged ideal employee with reference to personality, Marina would probably not have to feel unease about representing or speaking in the name of *Visibly Hot* employees.

As we have seen throughout the present chapter, there is a range of possible identifications that are offered to the employees. But first and foremost, *Visibly Hot* declares that associate partners, franchisees and general collaborators until the sales staff need to be "young minded". In recruitment praxis of salesclerks, this means a physical age restricted to a period of one's life reaching from 18 to 23 years. It is on the basis of this youngness that the brand is acting upon the multiplicity of young people's aspirations. For those who are interested in a fashionable identity, there are the projected images of coolness, of a sexually provocative femininity, of rock music and alternative lifestyle, of party culture, as well as of non-heterosexual desires. As portrayed by the "monstrous" appearance of the first generation salesclerks – it relates of tattoos and eccentric hair – along the brand's history, *Visibly Hot* seems to at least partially rely on physical moldings or expressivity of these singular personalities – in other words, on representatives of what this sexy "different" subject could look like.

However, the conception of a physically determined ideal type does not match with the managerial discourse. When I spoke to the supervisor Ana, I directed my inquiry in this direction, requesting her to compare *Visibly Hot*'s specificity of style with other fashion labels she had previously worked for. Significantly, Ana highlighted the retailer's benevolence with regard to its identity and body politics:

"A *Visibly Hot* é diferente das outras marcas. Porque o vendedor, o funcionário, ele é mais aceito como ele é. Eu acho que isso é uma grande diferença positiva, né? Eu trabalhei em lojas femininas onde a gente não contratava negros; a gente não contratava gente gordinha. Eu já fui desclassificada por lojas femininas por causa da minha altura, porque eu sou baixinha e eu ouvi claramente dizendo que não, que eles estavam procurando um perfil de passarela mesmo. E isso é muito complicado, você saber que tem um profissional de uma característica física, mas para aquela loja, a característica física, ela vem até antes mesmo da capacidade. Na *Visibly Hot* não. A gente contrata- eu não falo que a gente contrata qualquer pessoa, porque a gente tenta contratar profissionais com excelência. A gente contrata qualquer perfil. A gente não olha se essa pessoa é bonita, feia, gorda, magra, se é gay, qual a opção sexual da pessoa, qual o tipo de vida que ela leva, isso a gente não, não discrimina."[41] (Ana, 34, sales supervisor at *Visibly Hot*)

Ana recalled her own experiences within the fashion branch in which she had worked for about the last 15 years. She complains here about the fashion stores' open racism against black people and similarly about their

---

41 "*Visibly Hot* is different from other brands. For the salesclerk, the employee, he is more accepted as he is. I think this is a very positive difference, huh. I've worked in shops where we would not hire black people; we would not hire chubby people. I've been disqualified by female fashion brands because of my height, because I'm small and I heard clearly saying no, that they were really looking for a catwalk profile. And this is very complicated, to know that there is a professional with a certain physical characteristic, but for that store the physical characteristic comes even before the candidate's capacity. Not at *Visibly Hot*. We hire- I don't say that we hire anyone, because we try to hire professionals with excellence. But we hire any profile. We do not look if that person is pretty, ugly, fat, thin, if gay, what's the sexual orientation of the person, what kind of life she leads, this- we don't- we do not discriminate."

beauty imperative regarding the female body. Since she had also repeatedly been rejected because of her height, she now sees the central, positive differential in *Visibly Hot*'s inclusive politics, where specific body mass indexes or catwalk profiles were not the pivotal preconditions. Ana subsequently contrasts the physical appearance with the economic idea of capacity. This would come first at *Visibly Hot*. In the focus were excellent professionals, but on the basis of an anti-discriminatory stance that dismissed an interference in the candidate's lifestyle or physical appearance. All profiles were welcome, as long as they did their job in a way that met her expectations. As Ana further points out, her salesclerk teams included both the "cara evangélico" (pentecostal guy) and "aquele cara completamente psicodélico" (that completely psychedelic guy). As long as they would do their job with dedication, both would have equal opportunities at *Visibly Hot*.

Ana's role as a supervisor is especially interesting here because she is both taking part in the final evaluation of whether a salesclerk candidate will be recruited or not and having to monitor the daily workflows as well as behaviors of the sales crew. Beyond the anti-racist and anti-homophobic position of the brand, she relates that she would draw her proper motivation from the relations that she had to establish with the salesclerks.

"Eu tenho os meus clientes. Os meus clientes são os meus vendedores, são os meus gerentes, né? Só o que eu tenho que vender hoje não é um produto, mas uma idéia, de padrão, de normas, de postura, de atitude, né? Eu também continuo vendendo, que era uma coisa que eu gostava muito, mas em vez de vender um produto em si, eu vendo a marca, eu vendo conceito, eu vendo uma atitude profissional. Isso eu acho que é muito prazeroso."[42] (Ana, sales supervisor at *Visibly Hot*)

Providing a comparison to her former jobs as a trained retail saleswoman, Ana points here to the analogies that her position as a supervisor features. Even though she is no longer in direct contact with the consumers, she re-

---

42 "I do have my customers. My customers are my salesclerks, my branch managers, right? Just, what I have to sell today is not a product, but an idea, a standard ideal, of norms, stances, an attitude, right? I am also selling, something I liked a lot, but instead of selling a product I am selling a brand, I am selling a concept, a professional attitude. I think that's very pleasurable."

defines her sales team as her immediate customers. To them, she conveys, she had to sell the brand's idea or concept, that is, a bundle of norms, postures, and as she sums up, a professional attitude. The attitude – that will also concern us further in the self-perception of the salesclerks in chapter three – turns out as a decisive category, because it apparently mediates what *Visibly Hot* normatively expects of its employees. Thereby, it bears the affective contours of how the brand strives to engineer and convince its followers of the promises, its fashionable identities and experiences. Rather than being organized around normatively charged bodies, the brand demands an affective effort and devotion from the candidates. This also became clear at the end of the conversation with Ana, when she stressed that *Visibly Hot* would also engage people with a more conventional profile. Once hired, she would never ask that "normal" person to alter her or his style but definitely to "change her behavior". What counted in the end was "the salesclerk's attitude". Andrea, branch manager of a *Visibly Hot* sales point in Rio de Janeiro, also confirms that she demanded "conviction" in the recruitment interview, the candidate's persuasive power "of what she wants".

Returning to the former example of salesclerk Marina, the category attitude and its inherent, ambiguous requests of style and worker identity can apparently provoke a kind of disorientation. Although Marina stated that she felt uneasy at the beginning but later on would have understood that more "common" profiles like her own would also be included, she had difficulties to resume or put into words what characterizes the dominant style of *Visibly Hot*. As I encountered such difficulties in other conversations too, I decided to include a sequence of four pictures as part of my methodical instruments for the interviews[43]. They all portrayed people that had to do with *Visibly Hot*, but not all of them revealed an obvious message as to whether they were consumers, employees or simply fans of the brand. My own selection criteria for the photos I had found on different

---

43 The inspiration for this additional research tool draws back to Collier & Collier's classic work on visual anthropology and photography (Collier and Collier 1986). As they show in their chapter on projective interviewing, photographs are a very rich source for grasping the informant's imageries, that is, her or his proper perceptions of what the image portrays or depicts (Collier and Collier 1986: 118).

webpages followed the aspects that I had previously registered in *Visibly Hot*'s media associations: first, I included the sexually provocative white woman; second, three fashionably dressed black girls who were eventually involved in drag performance[44]; third, a group of girls with rather inconspicuous appearance; and fourth, a young fashionably styled guy that I supposed to be identified as gay by the spectators. During the interviews, I would consequently ask the informants to tell me about their own image interpretation, focusing the question on whether they thought that the portrayed people could or could not work at *Visibly Hot*.

---

44 It was only after one of my informants called my attention to the fact that the person in the middle of this group (Figure 9) was probably the US American hip hop musician Big Freedia, famous for his male-to-female gender performance.

Figure 8: Cruiser advertisement

Source: http://www.zinecultural.com/
blog/da_redacao/navio-chilli-beans-reune-
18-atracoes-em-cruzeiro-pela-costa-
brasileira-passando-por-santos-e-angra-dos.
Last access: 27 nov. 2012, 15:20:21

Figure 9: Black musician group

Source: http://guestofaguest.com/los-angeles/sponsored-
post/youre-invited-chilli-beans-hollywood-flagship-grand-
opening-party. Last access: 5 dez. 2012, 21:05:43

Figure 10: Group at shopping center

Source: http://mundochillibeans.blogspot.com.br/2010_09_01_archive.html. Last access: 4 dec. 2012, 11:07:38

Figure 11: Fashion guy

¨Source: http://chillibeans.com.br/virus_2011/. Last access: 3 dec. 2012, 10:41:22

The analysis made by supervisor Ana is particularly revealing, because she constantly associated the portrayed people with – or at least in dependence of – the category of attitude. Regarding the first photo (Figure 8), she noted:

"Eu acho que ela exprime muito bem o que é realmente [*Visibly Hot*], porque a gente é atitude – eu acho que a foto transmite isso. Eu acho que a marca defende isso. É exótico porque é uma marca de óculos. Onde que está com uma propaganda, você tem uma mulher com o que ela mostra, uma pegada sensual, que eu acho, também tem a ver com a questão da nossa identificação, né, da [pimenta]. [...] Esse modelo com certeza poderia trabalhar na [*Visibly Hot*], porque ele é lindo, né [sorriso][...] Tem essa atitude [*Visibly Hot*]."[45] (Ana, 34, sales supervisor at *Visibly Hot*)

In this first consideration, Ana reiterates what I have discussed above with regard to *Visibly Hot*'s advertising. Attitude hence means the "exotic", the sexual, sensual pleasures that the female subject literally incorporates and communicates to the spectators. Further, Ana reads the young woman's sensuality in terms of an unashamed behavior that she equates with the brand's identification with the sexual symbolism of the hot pepper. Subsequently, she renews this perspective of attitude as a resolute way of self-relation when she evaluates the second picture (Figure 9). This time, she gets back to the problem of racial prejudice present in both fashion industry and society in general, in order to emphasize *Visibly Hot*'s exceptional benevolence towards black people.

"Eles não seriam aceitos em muitas marcas. Mas a gente não só gosta, mas a gente valoriza. Principalmente, porque eles são negros com atitudes que valorizam a raça: o cabelo é bacana. Eles não tentam forçar e fugir desse padrão. Então, de novo, eu

---

45 "I think that she expresses very well what [*Visibly Hot*] really is, because we are attitude – I think that the picture conveys this. I think that's what the brand defends. It's exotic because it's a sunglasses brand. Where you have an advertisement, there is a woman who is showing what she's got, a sensual vein, what I think has to do with our identification, right, with the [red pepper]. [...] This model could certainly work for [*Visibly Hot*], because she is marvelous, right? [laughs][...] She has this [*Visibly Hot*] attitude."

vou falar da palavra atitude. Eu acho que eles estariam plenamente classificados para trabalharem na [*Visibly Hot*]."[46] (Ana, 34, sales supervisor at *Visibly Hot*)

According to Ana's account, being black could be an advantageous resource of a sales candidate as long as she or he is presenting a behavior towards the self that stresses black race. With reference to the cool hair style of the portrayed group, she once more underlines the brand's valuation of attitude, which here takes shape in terms of an affirmative, individual handling of a specifically styled blackness. The racial authenticity Ana evokes here then means equally a distancing of those people that do not display such a style, namely those that would try to "flee" from their allegedly assigned racial otherness. As shown by regionally focused studies (Gomes 2003), hair is commonly negotiated as a decisive social marker for de/valuing race, since thicker and curly hair conventionally stood at the bottom of feminine beauty ideals. According to Gomes, styling of curly hair has now equally turned into a transformative symbol of black pride, interfering in the aesthetic imperatives that stem from the colonial past (Gomes 2003: 8).

The apparent search for the not all too mainstream-looking salesclerks also appears in Ana's evaluation of the third picture (Figure 10). She concedes that this portrayed group of young people would be "um pouco mais séria, um pouco mais formal do que a gente busca no mercado"[47]. But in general, Ana continued, everybody could work at *Visibly Hot*, subject to the condition that one had already an affinity with the brand. Based on this, the candidate would enter a learning process on behavior.

"Da gente, ela poderia receber um pouco da nossa pimenta. [...] O que é bacana, é assim, se a gente fosse contratar qualquer uma dessas moças, a gente não pediria de nenhuma delas para mudarem suas aparências, a gente pediria para elas mudassem

---

46 "They wouldn't be accepted by many brands. But we don't simply like it, we give it a value. Mainly because they are black and because they have attitudes that valorize race: their hair is cool. They're not factitious and they don't try to escape from this pattern. So, once again, I will use the word attitude. I think they would be fully rated as being able to work for [*Visibly Hot*]."

47 "a little more serious, more formal than we are looking for in the market"

um pouco o comportamento. O que seria mais atitude."[48] (Ana, sales supervisor at *Visibly Hot*)

Ana finally sums up her understanding of attitude and difference when she examines the fourth and last picture (Figure 11) of the serial.

"Eu vejo nitidamente um vendedor [*Visibly Hot*], sabe. É um cara exótico, mesmo, usando óculos super atual, está com relógio. É uma foto que mostra- não sei, assim, o que eu sei, ele parece ser, não sei qual a opção sexual dele, mas me parece homossexual. Se não, uma pessoa que está aberta a se fotografar dessa forma. E, o meu marido, por exemplo, não tiraria uma foto com essa postura, dessa atitude, por isso que eu tive essa visão, parece um pouco preconceituoso, mas não é. Eu acho que ele tem tudo a ver com a marca. Ele tem uma tatuagem, sabe. E eu acho que eu resumiria aqui-[...] A gente define que a marca trabalha com pessoas diferentes. Então, se eu só trabalhar com negros, se eu só trabalhar com brancos, se eu só trabalhar com homossexuais, a gente vai estar, de certa forma, excluindo algumas pessoas. Então, a gente trabalha sem este sentido de exclusão. Como eu te falei, vai desde a pessoa mais formal, que a gente dá uma pimentadinha, até aquela destrambelhada que a gente dá uma seguradinha."[49] (Ana, 34, sales supervisor at *Visibly Hot*)

---

48 "From us, she could get some of our red pepper. [...] What's cool, you know, if we were to hire any of these girls, we would not ask any of them to change their appearance, we would ask them to change a little bit their behavior. What would be the thing of attitude."

49 "I see clearly a [*Visibly Hot*] salesclerk, you know. It's an exotic guy, really, he's wearing super trendy sunglasses, a watch. It's a picture, which shows- I don't' know, like, what I know is that he looks like, I don't know what's his sexual option [orientation], but he looks like homosexual. Or at least like a person who's open to being photographed like that. My husband, for example, would not take any picture with this pose, this attitude, that's why I had this impression, it seems like somewhat prejudiced, but it isn't. I think that he really incorporates the brand. He has a tattoo, you know. And I think I'd summarize here-[...] We define that the brand works with different people. So, if I only work with blacks, if I only work with whites, if I only work with homosexuals, in a certain way we will exclude some people. So, we work without this kind of exclusion. As I told you, this starts with the most formal person, to which we

Similar to the character of the sexy white girl and the black styled group above, the portrayed young person in figure 11 is subsumed under the category of the fancy exotic. On the one hand, Ana associates the portrayed as an ideal model of *Visibly Hot* because of his fashion accessories such as the watch, the sunglasses and the tattoo. And on the other hand, it is also because she classifies him as homosexual, an interpretation that she draws from his pose, contrasting it to her husband's distaste for this kind of photography. What Ana eventually recapitulates about the brand's spirit shows that it is aimed at selling the idea of diversity ("the brand works with different people"), which means here a rhetorical concept referring to an inclusionary equality between differently styled young people. What unifies them is less their fancy physical appearance, since more "formal" people can also access the world of *Visibly Hot*. Rather, they are all invoked to "love" the brand and – if they do not already have one – to develop and work out their attitude.

2.4.2 Diversity, a somewhat different equality

When Ana speaks about the breadth of the profiles hired by *Visibly Hot*, she situates the brand's strategy at the center of one of the contemporary paradigms of human resources: *diversity management*. This matter actually emerged in US American organizations of the 1980s when the prospect of including historically discriminated minority groups promised to improve the working environment and thus the company's performance. According to Fleury (2000), enterprises in Brazil lasted two more decades until the topic of diversity was gradually integrated, and the local vanguards continue to be represented by subsidiaries of US-American companies. Fleury, a sociological researcher in business administration, traces this back to cultural factors, which separate the Brazilian from the US-context, namely the "non-acceptance of prejudice and racial discrimination" in Brazil's self-image. To this she writes:

"Os brasileiros valorizam sua origem diversificada, incluindo raízes africanas, presentes na música, na alimentação, no sincretismo religioso; gostam de se imagi-

pass on some red pepper, and goes on to that stage hog, which we calm down a little bit."

nar como uma sociedade sem preconceitos de raça ou cor. Mas, por outro lado, é uma sociedade estratificada, em que o acesso às oportunidades educacionais e às posições de prestígio no mercado de trabalho é definido pelas origens econômica e racial."[50] (Fleury 2000: 19)

According to Fleury, this cultural aversion to diversity politics had to stand back as of 1996, when Brazilian federal programs of Human Rights responded to the demands of the International Labour Organization (ILO). Although diversity has since turned into a buzzword in general institutional policies, the concepts and entrepreneurial practices widely diverge. In Fleury's early evaluation, most enterprises do not see the topic as referring to human rights. As also observed on an international level, the "competitive advantage" for investors and consumers is first priority (Krell and Sieben 2007: 236). Furthermore, the early focus of diversity in Brazilian entrepreneurialism was on women, while black people were only reservedly addressed and other minority groups did not appear (Fleury 2000: 24). However, the strengthening of institutionalized social movements, such as within the state secretaries for racial equality (SEPPIR), for women (SPM) and for Human Rights with special agencies for LGBT rights, has had major impact in Brazilian enterprises. Besides women, black as well as mainly homosexuals are the typically addressed social groups. The dominant business discourse anticipates that the hiring of such "different" employees both stimulated creativity at work and responded better to the diversified demands of customers (Saraiva and Irigaray 2009: 339).

Due to the fact that large parts of this entrepreneurial discourse are promoting their corporate brand strategies through rhetoric endorsement of equality and equality opportunities for minority groups, they also became a target of broad critique. Purtschert (2007), for instance, asks if diversity management was really to be seen as the implementation of a better world or rather as a way of prestige advertising. For these recent inclusionary models based on the logic of economic profit are evidently altering not on-

---

50 "Brazilians are valuing their diverse origins, including the African roots as present in music, food and religious syncretism; they like to imagine their society as free of prejudice both of race and skin color. But on the other hand, it is a stratified society, where educational opportunities and prestigious positions in the labor market is defined by economic and racial backgrounds."

ly the cultural valuation of selected subjects but also the very notion of what equality and difference may denote. Critical perspectives on diversity management – within which I situate my present inquiry – broadly indicate a process of individualization of difference that results in concealing structural inequalities (Ahmed 2012: 53). Indeed, more recent empirical studies within enterprises in Rio de Janeiro and São Paulo (Saraiva and Irigaray 2009) showed that openly homophobic and racist discourse within the employees can go hand in hand with official diversity rhetoric.

In the case of *Visibly Hot,* what produces the specific meaning of equality? First and foremost, it is the engineering of a common spirit – an affective bond as well as a belief in the brand as representing a cool and fancy youngness: a lifestyle. However, and maybe rather surprisingly, this common spirit is not being established by a mass conforming or assimilatory synchronization, but by a procedure that both stimulates and tames difference. Whether someone can actively take part in this endeavor or not depends on the degree of how she or he emotionally – and second, eventually also physically – affirms or expresses the expected attitude. According to the managerial discourse demonstrated by supervisor Ana, the latter means an active, authentic relation to the self: a convincing behavior that sticks to one of the brand's most cherished attributes. Beneath them are the noticeable utterance of sexual desires, whether hetero- or non-heterosexual, the allusion to an alternative or subcultural sociality, and the stylization of black race. As Ana's enthusiasm about these attributes suggests, these showpieces of "being different" are referred to as *Visibly Hot*'s anti-discriminatory and anti-exclusionary commitment.

As convincing as this stance may be at the very first moment, it equally bears some problematic conceptual contractions when it comes to its understanding of difference. As with diversity management in general, it is an almost ingenious "trick" that the promise for more justice and inclusion comes together with the guarantee for more sales (Purtschert 2007: 91). However, as we have seen with the category of attitude, is not literally everyone who could be included into the *Visibly Hot*'s "family". There is obviously a filtering of those subjects that are really promising in economic terms. According to the images and its associations made by Ana, being "different" from the managerial point of view can be the term that equates to the sexually or racially "exotic". These are young people that bear the prospect of offering a kind of affective outbreak from the monotony of everyday life to the customer public. It is a diversity that can securely be consumed, celebrated and it even has the surplus, to use Ahmed's terms, to function as a "feel good" politics (Ahmed 2012: 69). More explicitly, *Visibly Hot*'s anti-discriminatory stance towards black, gay and lesbian people succeeds in evoking a positive emotion of victory over discrimination and exclusion.

In her book on how diversity and racism are handled by and within institutions (her ethnographic example is the university), Ahmed locates a specific language of diversity, a form of institutional speech and strategy that unfolds within what she calls a "new equality regime" (Ahmed 2012: 8): a discursive redefinition of "equality as a positive duty", working as a mobile and transnationally circulating bundle of policies. Similar to the argument of Purtschert (2007), Ahmed points to the tendency that such equality regimes are not necessarily aimed at deconstructing, let alone overcoming, inequalities. Paradoxically, the premature invocation of an all-encompassing difference amongst humans can camouflage and even re-legitimate historically grown relations of power and inequality[51]. In this line of argumentation, Rodrigues and Abramowicz (2013) are expounding the problems of state driven promotion of diversity in Brazilian education and public policies. The often imprecise and capital-driven rhetoric, they hold, may "be restricted to a simple praise of differences, pluralities and diversities, turning into both a conceptual trap and political strategy of emptying and/or appeasement of differences and inequalities" (Rodrigues and Abramowicz 2013: 17).

The present Brazilian example of inquiry is framed in a context where – as mentioned above with the argument of Fleury (2000) – cultural or racial difference is seen as central to the nation's sense of self. Since the founding of the modern state in the 1930s, the discourse of a harmonious racial mixture has turned into a kind of common Brazilian vocabulary, a "widely prevailing national narrative" (Costa 2007: 148). Mainly influenced by the writings of Gilberto Freyre (1900-1987), it understands the nation as a *mestiçagem*, a successful amalgamation of three racial groups, namely the white Portuguese colonizers, the indigenous Americans and the

---

51 As Purtschert tellingly provokes related to the Western European context, the boss of a transnational enterprise would then appear "as different" as the migrant cleaning lady (Purtschert 2007: 90).

black Africans. *Mestiçagem* means a positively connoted unity in diversity[52], where each of these three groups had equally – albeit in quite diverging ways – contributed to the building of society. Politically and culturally, these ideas continue to have importance up to contemporary conflictive negotiations of difference and otherness amongst diverse social groups. For in a similar manner to the transnational diversity language, the idea of *mestiçagem* sticks to a discourse about difference that disciplines actual heterogeneity (Costa 2007: 153). As was the case during the Vargas era, only very specific cultural expressions such as samba and capoeira have been officially chosen as parts of the "national spirit", while, for example, a whole range of indigenous cultures never found any entrance into national symbols.

So, despite its inclusionary proceedings and politics of positively valorizing (racial) difference, the aspired Brazilianness (*brasilidade*) led to a synchronizing of culture that ultimately domesticates and partly does away with difference as such. Though in present time this image of a society made of a harmonious mixture is being attacked by several social movements and political actors that criticize it for its blindness for discrimination and inequalities[53], it is still being used as the dominating argument for national self-affirmation. Now, my contention is that the transnationally circulating regimes of diversity have encountered a fertile ground here. Even if the latter are not historically grown in the Latin American context – most authors locate the emergence of diversity discourse in US American management (Ahmed 2012: 52) – there are striking analogies in how difference is being both perceived and controlled. In both cases, there is a foregrounded celebration of difference – cultural, racial as well as sexual[54]. And in both cases, this celebration acts in ways that specify and disci-

---

52 Historically, this positive valuation of racial mixture was a crucial anti-racist statement that Freyre had been elaborating against scientific racism, until then the prevailing position of the national elite (Costa 2007: 150).

53 Costa (2007) refers mainly to different black movements, but also music styles such as baile funk in Rio de Janeiro or hip hop in São Paulo as cultural expressions that strive for "valorizing difference" (Costa 2007: 175).

54 As Lopes (2003) argues, the up-to-day discourse of permissiveness and sexual promiscuity as something specifically Brazilian has its roots in Gilberto Freyre's work on the Nation's formation.

pline heterogeneity. Diversity can then be understood as a strategy of coping with conflicting notions of difference, a way of tackling them by "managing its more troublesome constituents" (Ahmed 2012: 53).

Visibly Hot is selling this strategy in terms of a proof for its globally oriented, self-confident, and different image of Brazil (see Maia and Araújo 2012: 13). Beyond the emphasis on his most different employees, the enterprise hires celebrities from the national cultural industry that are equally intended to represent the brand's diversity concept. Carlinhos Brown, famous Bahian and black musician whose success includes both the national and international stages, loaned his name to a special collection of the brand's sunglasses. He further takes part in the conventions and advertises the *Visibly Hot* sunglasses in his role as a jury member of the TV casting show *The Voice Brasil*. Brown faithfully serves the brand's proceeding, since, as the anthropologist Lima notes, he "didn't develop the experience of the militant black" (Lima 2002: 229). Even though the percussionist and songwriter Brown is consciously addressing both local and global aesthetics of black culture, touching the contours of black alterity within a dominant Western context of white supremacy, he does not use a tone of accusation. According to Lima, his social critique is indeed not racially based (Lima 2002: 230). Rather, his music and personality stand for a playful handling with history and religion that finally reifies the discourse of *mestiçagem*, effecting but positive affects and the kind of celebration of diversity that turns out to be useful for the market.

2.4.3 Inclusion as normalization?

Speaking the language of diversity, contemporary institutions and enterprises do often mean a very specific handling of difference. As we have seen with the example of *Visibly Hot*, personal management that sticks to an aggressive corporate branding is fostering both an aesthetic style and affective self-control of his employees and consumers. The brand's concepts and (re)production agencies of difference are thus passed on to wider social spheres. Concomitantly, describing the brand's tactics merely as a matter of aesthetics and style might reduce the complexity of this government. As the promises for anti-discriminatory policies with regard to recruitment of its salesclerks suggest, *Visibly Hot* evokes racial and sexual difference that are potentially troubling. Troubling, in the sense of Butler, as something that disturbs (and eventually rearranges) the cultural norms of how subjects are given legitimacy to come into being. Since the brand does not exclude, but rather exhibit black, gay and lesbian people as representatives of its political (and aesthetic) guidelines, its proper version of the diversity regime is in fact softening former regulatory norms of the fashion industry. However, what continues to matter from a critical perspective is the question on whether these newly integrated different subjects are automatically provided with a gain in rights or at least with a collective emancipatory moment, that is to say, on whether difference as such is not reduced to a matter of individual aesthetics; to something cautiously separated from power relations and hence eventually preventing awareness of structural inequality.

Queer theorist Engel (2009) deals with this question when she reflects on the inclusion of gay and lesbian subjects within the image world of both commercial advertising and state diversity discourse in Germany. Formerly excluded, she argues, the latter were now addressed in order to participating in new alliances with the ruling order of neoliberal economy. Lesbians and gays would even have advanced into "image bearers" of neoliberal concepts (Engel 2009: 56). Engel finds evidence for this phenomenon neither by presupposing that gay or lesbian people were the more decadent consumers nor by affirming that the same had turned into cultural prototypes. Rather, her diagnosis draws on how lesbians and gays were used to represent a contemporary concept of subjectivity: the image of the managing self, that is, as emblematic posters of how the contemporary subject was getting by with social difference and mechanisms of exclusion, and a specific way of transforming such experiences into cultural capital. Governing the newly included thus means a "seduction towards the privatized responsibility" (Engel 2009: 67). It prompts the sexually invoked subject to managing existential problems of its own accord.

Actually, Engel is interested in understanding how individualistic concepts of difference are woven into relations of power as articulated through images. In one of her examples, a car advertisement for Ford, she calls attention to the ambiguous offers made by what she calls "projective integration", a contemporary form of normalizing difference. On one hand, the Ford advertising touts with its engagement for the LGBT parade in Cologne, promoting its enterprise as an open-minded brand by using a "language of tolerance" that can easily be absorbed by cultural hegemony of heterosexuality: as long as the sexually deviant subjects are portrayed in terms of partnership and love, they are not painfully disturbing. On the other hand, the same ad allows for a reading specifically directed to a LGBT public. Here, both consumers and employees can in fact enjoy the surplus of diversity management, a gain in recognition that operates despite, or better, simultaneously with its capitalist exploitation. As Engel provocatively notes, Ford as a longtime patron of the Christopher Street Day in Cologne can celebrate "together" in the "name of love – and of increase in sales" (Engel 2009: 145). Contrary to the first reading, she argues, this second does not operate in terms of a strict dividing rule of tolerance that separated the self from the other. Ford is using a language of "us" that does not treat the LGBT public as something outside, as something that had to be monitored or tamed. It is rather a kind of a specifically "chosen difference", invited to move into the enterprise's self.

Engel seeks to prove that sharp contrasts between homo/hetero, black/white, foreigner/native and so on have lost their all-encompassing significance in late capitalism. Hegemony, the condition for the subject's approval to an economic, social and political order, could be generated through a consensus that is heterogeneous in itself (Engel 2009: 60). New alliances, as in the example of the Ford advertising, are supporting the rule of profit, where rigid norms would give way to a playful assortment of elected sexual subjectivities and forms of life. I argue that *Visibly Hot*'s strategies are directed in a similar way. Although the brand's advertising is not showing gay or lesbian characters and neither wants to be reduced to being a gay brand, it seems to offer an alliance between the sexy pin-up girl and the not heterosexually oriented. Inter alia, the already discussed ideal worker's attitude comprises the promise for a liberating and highly profitable force that would spread by – whatsoever – utterance of sexual desire. Broadly speaking, consent is being established by valuing sexual diversity, simultaneously integrating and neutralizing dissension or contradiction (Engel 2009: 61). Furthermore, racial difference, as attributed to the black body, is subsumed under the same logic. Once reenacted under the aesthetics of a stylish working resource, it turns into one more site of economic celebration.

It seems more than obvious that downsizing norms and inhibiting exclusion are more conducive to contemporary capitalist endeavors. It is the mentioned "ingenious trick" (Purtschert 2007) of strategies such as diversity management that combine economic profit with promises for social justice. However, such rhetoric of integration or pluralization is not automatically synonymous with equal rights or status. Rightly, Hark and Laufenberg (2013) are questioning Engel's claim that gays would literally "be figured" as ideal types of the neoliberal concept of citizenship and consumer capitalism (see Engel 2009: 43). Although the authors equally detect a pluralization and hedonization of integrated sexual forms of life, they are insisting on the tenacity of heteronormativity[55] as a structural agent. To them, it is not only capitalism that is dynamic but also the latter principle of how heterosexuality, the binary gender divide and monogamy are together sorting genders, bodies and desires. Consequently, they see the integration of homosexual or transgender subjects into heteronormative arrangements not as subversive but rather as stabilizing phenomena of the present order (Hark and Laufenberg 2013: 233). Hark and Laufenberg allude to the paradox that minorities could be partially integrated into mainstream society, but still treated as unequals: sexuality means "the sexuality of the others", and as I would equally add with Ahmed (2012): race remains the race of the others.

The managerial discourse found in *Visibly Hot* echoes the transnationally circulating rhetoric of diversity, addressing specifically lesbian, gay and black young people. As an interim conclusion, we thus found that the propagated sexual and racial emancipation through the brand – the intended positive valorization of difference in one's attitude – is rather (re)normalizing than undoing structural inequalities. Why and how one is incorporated in the brand's alliance of "different" styles and identities, to name the assumption up to this point, depends thoroughly on one's sales-oriented capacity in creatively extending and stylizing her or his sexual or racial difference in highly fashionable manners.

---

55 The concept of heteronormativity goes back to Michael Warner (1993). According to his definition, heteronormativity analytically addresses the power relations that organize genders, bodies and desire in accordance with norms of heterosexuality, binary gender arrangements and monogamy. Not only restricted to institutional levels, these norms equally act through social practices in daily life; they are thus both structuring and structured forms of life (Warner 1993: 53).

3. Longing to be different

Brands and their related managerial strategies, I argued through the last chapter, are a crucial aspect of contemporary capitalist governmentality. Advancing the tactics of weaving in manifold desires of young[1] people in their business projects – such as for emancipation and self-realization – brands assemble an auspicious regime for individuals to "act, feel and be in a particular way" (Arvidsson 2006: 8). In my case study on the Brazilian fashion label *Visibly Hot*, such desires unfold through the promise of "being different", that is, a playfully rhetoric, inclusionary strategy of socially disadvantaged groups, namely lesbians, gays and blacks. The enterprise's salesclerks, who are the main target of this diversity management, usually get excited about this promise. As it generally became clear in my empirical inquiry about their perception of the brand was that they are enthusiastically moved by the idea of incorporating a "different", authentic, cool and stylish identity. They "love" the brand, as they say, because they individually identified with it.

This chapter discusses the salesclerks' singular understandings of what it means to "be different" through *Visibly Hot*. Regarding the question of the branding government, I theoretically presuppose that processes of

---

[1] I use here the term young primarily as a discursive category, referring to cultural valorization of youngness or young-mindedness as common in contemporary cultural industry.

identification are the points of "suture" (Hall 1996): feelings, practices and modes of thought that effect the conduct of others through a conduct of the self. On this basis, I proceed with some short portrayals of the social and professional backgrounds of the company's employees I spoke with, accentuating the specific value they want the brand to occupy in their biographical narratives. Although different in dimension and reference, most of the salesclerks agree on an idea of both freedom and professional opportunities attached to *Visibly Hot*. According to their perspective, they maintain a symbiotic-like relation with the brand: they are given the opportunity to be authentic, to "be who they are" and express their individual styles, allegedly creating a win-win situation that responds to their individual aspirations as well as to the company's branding endeavor.

Further developing the critical questioning of the brand's diversity politics in the precedent chapter, this section addresses processes of symbolic constitution of social difference as salient in everyday knowledge of ordinary sales staff. I asserted before with Engel (2009) that capitalism has recently been both downsizing and pluralizing norms of heterosexuality in favor of "projective integration". Now, the empiric insight in the salesclerks' perceptions contrasts this discursive condition of normativity: the question here is less about who is inside and who is outside the norms of the brand. Rather, the analysis of the employees' stylizing efforts in incorporating the "different" is pointing to the individual processes of how people invest in aspired positions even if they probably never fully get there. With a special emphasis, I discuss three social groups historically embraced by diversity rhetoric in Brazilian entrepreneurialism (see Fleury 2000), namely women, blacks and homosexuals. In the case of *Visibly Hot*, they are again addressed by "being different": through the figure of the sexy white girl, the aspirations around black beauty and identity, and finally through the more intricate attributions to gay and lesbian identities. In general terms, there seems to unfold a multiplication of both beauty and style ideals, although the content of these ideals remains as highly contested terrain. While the employees' individual identifications may grant them a certain scope of recognition, the alignment of new identity content with retail marketability, as my argument finally contends, does not dissolve, but often rather reenacts heteronormativity and whiteness.

3.1 IDENTIFICATION AS GOVERNMENT

The ways in which *Visibly Hot* governs its brand have extensive effects on how both consumers and employees feel and behave. Sociologist du Gay (1996) turned his attention to such processes when he analyzed how the expansion of consumer society and neoliberalism in the UK had captured the inner logics of organizations. More exactly, he provoked the argument that retail was playing a central role in shaping the cultural contours of contemporary social life. Since this sector was eminently interested to establish closer and more immediate relationships to the consumers (the process that subsequently severed with what I previously described with the branding conduct), the question of identities and identification became increasingly important to the entrepreneurial strategies. How could the targeted emotional proximity to consumers best be ensured? Corresponding with du Gay, the intermediation of sales employees turned into an important instrument to this endeavor. Lifestyle marketing, the author distinguishes, assured its quality and performance paradoxically through the "very commitment and motivation which is required from staff" (du Gay 1996: 115).

Looking at the subjective meanings given to *Visibly Hot* by ordinary salesclerks –which is going to be the focus of this chapter – the question is to what extent and by what channels identification works as the nodal point of the branding process. Identities, to use Hall's words, can here be seen as points of "suture",

"between on the one hand the discourses and practices which attempt to 'interpellate', speak to us or hail us into place as the social subjects of particular discourses, and on the other hand, the processes which produce subjectivities, which construct us as subjects which can be 'spoken'." (Hall 1996: 6)

Hall is pointing here to the double-sided process of how identities are joining discursively imposed self-relations[2] with individually mobilized entry

---

2   Hall is referring here to Althusser's (1976) model of "interpellation": the argument that an individual becomes a subject only at the moment she/he affirmatively reacts to the communicated invocation. Famously, Althusser outlined his notion by the example of the policeman who shouts at a person on the

points in the same subject offer. As du Gay also notes with reference to Foucault's late work on governmentality (Foucault 1991), subjectivation is a necessary tool for a government to be able to function. So, indeed, "particular rationalities of government involve the construction of specific ways for people to be" (du Gay 1996: 54). What salesclerks tell us about their experience within *Visibly Hot*, then, reflects in a certain way as to how the brand discourse succeeded (or not) in fulfilling its mission.

However, there is a second aspect in Hall's argument. The author rightly refers to the deficient explanation in Foucault of how individuals actually relate to the norms and lifestyles as imposed from above. It is Hall's point referring to theory of ideology. Identities, he holds, are positions that the subject becomes obliged to take on. But he adds that this subject was always at least potentially aware that the summoned representations were nor fully complete nor adequate, hence really "identical" with her/his identity aspirations. Thus, he concludes that a better understanding of identification is also needed to consider how "the subject invests in the position", not only how it is "hailed" (Hall 1996: 6). The term Hall proposes to think about the relation of the subject and the imposing discourse is "articulation": a notion that, beyond the (dis)identifications of individuals with summoned positions, reflects how these individuals

"fashion, stylize, produce and 'perform' these positions, and why they never do so completely, for once and all time, and some never do, or are in a constant agonistic process of struggling with, resisting, negotiating and accommodating the normative or regulative rules with which they confront and regulate themselves." (Hall 1996: 14)

According to Hall, identification is a process that is not happening unconsciously. Rather, the subject that finds herself/himself in an imposed position is (consciously) contributing to that position. It articulates invest-

---

street. The very moment of that person turning around, he holds, means that she/he turns herself to a subject (which is, in the authors focus, the subject of state control). Althusser's notion has been very influential, since also Judith Butler (1990; 1993) accessed it for her argument of how bodies were discursively materialized according to compulsory, binary gender identity.

ments, though incomplete, but always both of consent and resistance to the stipulated identity.

However, as I will argue with this chapter, the emphasis on individual resistance within the branding context should not be overrated, let alone presupposed. Identities at the workplace, such as those of *Visibly Hot* salesclerks, are never located outside of the branding discourse. Similar to what du Gay asserts with his empirical studies in British retail companies, "staff were not acting autonomously of official norms but always in relation to them" (du Gay 1996: 171). The employees, although creatively doing things with the technologies and representations they are subjected to, can never "keep a distance" from these regulatory forces. Finally, they do everything but effecting a failure of the discourse of the enterprise (du Gay 1996: 174). As I will hold with the case of *Visibly Hot*, it seems that the company is even recycling these individual investments, because they are contributing to the branding process, stimulating both the individual and the enterprise's aspirations.

Du Gay had stated in the mid-nineties that the question of work identities was far from common theoretical engagement within the tradition of the study of work and organizations (du Gay 1996: 5). Actually, two decades later this situation has hardly changed. Apart from recently growing investigation sites on emotional and affective work (that I will discuss in chapter four), a solid body of studies continues to treat the profound changes in capitalist organizational policies and its impacts on employees' lives as being reduced to a problematic of social class. Workers from the Brazilian service industry, such as from telemarketing, may aptly be analyzed as the new (sub)proletariat (Braga 2012; Singer 2012), since most of them are struggling with new precarity regimes that include more flexible working hours and poor payment. But problematically, these workers are also presupposed to identify – and even act politically – as such, as individuals. In other words, most of these studies implicitly assume that these workers feel like workers and that this would be their all-encompassing identification. Today, such analytical presuppositions are rather surprising, considering the fact that neither in common sense nor in most areas of social inquiry does the idea of an enclosed, one-sided or stable identity at the workplace remain tenable. This is because, first, general approaches to identity have been influenced by post-structuralist thought that deeply questioned the truth and essence of identity discourse (Butler 1990; Anderson 1991; Hall 1996). Second, it lies in the very transformations within work in industrialized countries that the role of the worker's identity has suffered the loss of its supposed natural stability.[3]

How, then, can identifications be addressed within contemporary entrepreneurial endeavors? I believe that the first step lies in overcoming what has been mentioned above with Hall's critique of the orthodoxly Foucauldian line of analysis. Most studies of organizations, including those with a feminist, anti-racist and intersectional claim (as an example, Acker 2006) tend to set their focus on the discursive and regulative mechanisms from above (such as institutions, laws, the state and so on), whereas they often lack in giving extensive accounts of the lived experience, if not contribution, by individuals. This is a critique that has been formulated in similar ways to dominant perspectives about the notion of difference in gender studies. It is mainly in the consequences of the social constructivist turn where Maihofer (2013) locates a one sided concentration on the question of *how* individuals were compulsorily made women or men. What was often missing, however, would be an account of what was actually happening *inside* the individuals. The fact that they "became" women or men would mean that, "to a certain degree, they then really 'are'" (Maihofer 2013: 36). They "existed" in these roles, aligning their feelings, thoughts and actions.

This is a decisive point because it leads us back to the question of how branding as a specific mode of (self-)conduct is able to exercise and spread its dominion. Social relations of power, Maihofer insists, are not only operating from outside, but also literally from inside the individuals. Norbert Elias (1978) exemplarily showed this with the feeling of shame. As eating with the fork – an etiquette historically invented by European nobility – turned into a social norm of bourgeois lifestyle, everyone that would or

---

3   Both du Gay (1996) and Dubar (2005) are referring to that transformation in terms of a "crisis of identity". As a consequence of major structural changes in British and French economies, they show that the model of the white male breadwinner with a stable employment situation has been replaced by highly flexible and changing working conditions. Consequently, employees were confronted with self-optimizing regimes (see also Bröckling 2013) that forced them to constantly be flexible, adapting their proper identifications regarding the organizational targets and values.

could not use it reacted, as though by compulsion, with embarrassment. Only this singular, individual feeling could finally guarantee the consolidation of bourgeois social order. Du Gay (1996) also uses this argumentation scheme when he analyses the basis of normative regulation in the entrepreneurial setting. This regulation, he holds, rested upon "an identification between the individual employee and the goals and objectives of his or her employing organization" (du Gay 1996: 115). Consequently, this means that the government of retail enterprises was less interested in direct control of its employees. Rather, it would have "come to operate through the 'soul' of the individual employee" (du Gay 1996: 115).

This chapter takes individual identification as the starting point. Whereas Dubar (2005) focused the question on whether and how identification between an individual employee and the enterprise was possible, I describe the fact that virtually all employees in my case study on *Visibly Hot* highly identified with the enterprise. During the research, their constantly repeated statement "here I can be who I am" turned into a central question of my inquiry. What did they mean and what did they refer to by this affirmation? In organizational studies influenced by Foucauldian thought, sociological analysis mostly strives to grasp such phenomena in terms of the "entrepreneurial self" (Bröckling 2013): self-relations at work appear to be subjected to neoliberal values of creativity, empowerment and heightened individual responsibility. However, my contribution lies in arguing that the individual identifications that can be found in contemporary retail employment do not only refer to strict, and sometimes abstract market values. Additionally, they are articulations of singular, but very concrete identities that young people project for themselves and that suture not only their relation to the enterprise, but also their relation to broader social constraints. What is striking with the salesclerk's subjective meanings given to *Visibly Hot* is that they are explicitly negotiating social discourse about alternative lifestyles, race, sexuality and youth. Both their aesthetic of the body (tattoos, body ornaments and clothes) and their emotional relation to the brand can be seen as intertwined with their proper biographical narratives. In other words, the salesclerks' articulations are more than responses to the positions they are hailed to: they reflect multiple aspirations and singular desires.

3.2 LIFE-WORK-WORLDS

I cannot emphasize enough that the focus group of this study embraces young people. At first sight, this even means "real" numbers. Apart from only one exception, the age amongst salesclerks that have been interviewed, ranges from 18 to 24 years. However, my discussion of identification processes does not suggest psychosomatic specificities[4], but rather foregrounds the social contours that give meaning to that period of life. The *Visibly Hot* workforce is a generational group characterized by its socially demanded efforts for their integration into the formal labor market. Since the 1990s, service jobs in retail or other commercial settings represent a remarkable percentage in Brazil's landscape of employment opportunities for young people of both sexes. At the same time, it is also one of the sectors that is most marked by unstable and short-term engagements. As the 23-year-old branch manager Jéssica commented, retail was a very difficult branch because the work with young people implied an extremely high labor turnover. "Cara, a gente trabalha com jovens. Jovem se cansa cada três meses de uma coisa"[5]. Actually, high labor turnover is the diagnosis economists made already in the 90s. Gonzaga (1998) once argued that Brazil's structural market problems were not due to a lack of job creation, but rather of "low job quality" that made workers hop from one contract to another.[6] The same author also held that basic education was a cru-

---

4   As Almeida and Tracy (2003) tellingly hold, studies on adolescence often presuppose somewhat unfinished identities, because they act on the assumption of a linear psychic development that would be common to all humans. In contrast, studies influenced by French medievalist Philip Ariès (1960) strive to denaturalize such understandings of age and identity. Ariès had famously provoked the argument that the feeling of childhood, as diametrically opposed to that of adulthood, did not exist as such in medieval society. Children were, for instance, commonly mistaken for adults and consequently had to work like them.

5   "We are working with young people, you know. Young people are getting tired of things like every three months."

6   Exactly this context led Ulrich Beck (1999) to formulate his metaphor of the "Brazilianization of the West" at the end of the nineties: "Brazilianization means the irruption of the precarious, the discontinuous, the flocking, the informal in the Western bastions of full employment societies. Within the center

cial factor for altering the lacking labor productivity. But to this day, the relation between education level and labor market has slightly changed. Souza (2012) shows that increased democratization of schooling has brought about a new situation for young people from lower social ranks. Although most of them finish high school (*segundo grau* or *ensino médio*) today, their job options remain trapped in precarious conditions. New job regimes, such as those installed in telemarketing or other commercial services, are taking advantage of their aspirations. This, so Souza's main argument goes, was one of the characteristics of the emerging social groups: they are battling for social advancement, fueled by hopes for better life and work conditions, but their expected social standards – job and health security, better salaries and so on – are hardly available to them.

Visibly Hot employees from Rio de Janeiro astonishingly fit in this category as outlined by Souza's sociological perspective. All of them finished their *segundo grau*. Most of them – and this almost automatically – mentioned their interest in getting higher education. Some already tried, but did not succeed in passing the entrance examination. Others emphasized that it was merely impossible to study and work at the shopping center at the same time. They all attended specialization courses in their secondary schools, ranging from fashion, tourism, physical education, and computer science. Still, their early occupational careers show that they barely manage to enter their envisaged tracks. Mostly, they encounter a series of structural difficulties that make them stay much longer in jobs within the commercial service-sector than they had intended before. As Souza (2012) similarly argued with young employees in telemarketing, they even tend to internalize market ideals they are subjected to. They would often explain their failure in reaching other jobs as due to a lack of their own individual efforts, and not as a consequence of structural problems within the labor market. Yet the employees adapted the entrepreneurial jargon ("management of life", "professional growth"), turning them into their own worldviews and parameters of what generally defined leading a "good life" (Souza 2012: 78). In other words, their affective internalization of market values led them to experience both private and professional ethics

---

of the West, a socio-structural patchwork is spreading, that is: the diversity, unpredictability, complexity and insecurity of forms of labor, biography and life in the South." (Beck 1999: 7)

as emerging from their personal will and not as subjected to dominating forces imposed by their employer or by broader economic regimes.[7]

Visibly Hot's workforce is thus not only among the – somewhat spongy – social group of youth, but also among a group of lower social class. Without getting into the ongoing debates on whether we have to deal with younger representatives of a new middle class (Neri 2008), a new (sub)proletariat (Braga 2012; Singer 2012) or simply a newly struggling working class (Souza 2012), I suggest describing the employees in question, quite broadly, as something like the *scouts* of an emerging – still lower class – social group: scouts that paradoxically find themselves both given new ascending aspirations and denied effective opportunities. They neither count with the social securities of the established Brazilian middle classes nor are they situated amongst the lowest ranks, where juvenile unemployment predominates (Cardoso 2013: 296). Almost all of them live at their parent's houses, located in Rio's urban districts that belong to either low middle class or to the urban poor. With their completed *segundo grau*, several have higher schooling than their parents, and it is not uncommon, too, that *Visibly Hot* employees strategically distance themselves from their actual domicile when they go to the job interview. As salesclerk Letícia explained, she didn't want the enterprise to know that she lived in Nova Iguaçu, a district more distant to the urban centers in the South Zone. Instead, she officially indicated the address of a friend who lived closer to that area, thinking that this would give her more chances to getting the job.

In what follows, I subdivided the individual cases of interviewed people into three groups. Methodologically, these were not seen as relevant in terms of describing different intensity grades of the employee's identification with the brand. Rather, the groups should somewhat summarize three main modes of salesclerks' orientation within their narratives about their own professional situation. These were analytically isolated according to approaches stemming from grounded theory, that is, through careful reading and coding of the interview material (Thornberg and Charmaz 2013: 157). The three groups – *the first employment, service and shopping work-*

---

7   Souza even goes as far as to argue that these incorporated values would shed light on how "capitalism operates in people of flesh and blood" (Souza 2012: 63).

ers, and *the artistic improvisers* – thus correspond to different modes of how the young salesclerks situate and orient themselves not only within their biographical past and future, but also within the fields of their professional (im)possibilities and aspirations.

3.2.1 The first employment

Marina is 19 years old. During our conversation, she seems somewhat shy, a little insecure. She further underlines this by her girlish smiles that decorate her slightly bronzed face. She lives in Madureira, North zone of Rio de Janeiro, where she also went through secondary school. Her specific training in computer science gave her some insight into the world of business, but her first job contract she got as a cashier at *Visibly Hot*. As she comments, it was not the thing she ever wanted. She knew little about the brand before, although she enthusiastically adds: "Eu lembrava o marketing da [*Visibly Hot*], a pimenta e tal, eu achava super legal"[8]. But the idea to work for this company was rather one ad hoc. Hanging around the shopping mall in Rio's hot summer days, she decided to hand in her CV at the shop. "Eu terminei o meu terceiro ano, não tem nada para fazer, vou tentar arranjar empreguinho"[9], she told herself. Hence some of her friends had ended up in staying at home, their parents' house, and for quite a long time, doing nothing. "É um saco[10]". When she got the call from *Visibly Hot*'s human resources, it first led to anxiety at her house. As she was supposed to work in Recreio, located about a distance of 25 km, both her grandmother and her father thought this was too dangerous, because there were several *morros*[11] on the way. Already sad about having to cancel this job opportunity, she got a second call and was offered her actual position at the shopping Nova América that is but a short hop from her house.

---

8   "I remembered *Visibly Hot*'s marketing, the red pepper and so on, I thought it was very cool."
9   "I finished my last year of high school, I have nothing to do, I will try to get a little job"
10 "It sucks"
11 With *morros*, literally hills, Marina points to Rio's characteristic urban favelas, commonly perceived as highly violent areas and where young girls of her age should not walk around by their own.

Bruna, of the same age as Marina, marks a somewhat more independent and resolute impression. Her voice is secure and her natural behavior expresses a professional training in customer service. In little more than one year at *Visibly Hot*, she made it to a VR, the term for "Responsible Salesclerk". Different from "normal" salesclerks, she is the substitute of the branch manager, which means that she has to work 8h instead of 6h a day. Above sales, she is also responsible for smaller supervising tasks. Commenting on her integration into the company, she says: "Eles sempre contratam, assim, para primeiro emprego. Eles dão bastante oportunidades"[12]. In her own case, she took this opportunity in order to save some money that will help her prepare for the Vestibular. Literature, she already knows, will be her course at the university. Consequently, she would leave the shop soon. But still, this was not a reason to break up with the brand. When she came to *Visibly Hot*, she had already felt an attraction to it:

"Eu conhecia a marca, sempre gostei dos produtos. Sempre me identifiquei com as armações para graus, óculos, sempre gostei bastante. Então, por me identificar com a marca, eu dei preferência para tentar trabalhar aqui."[13] (Bruna, 19, salesclerk at *Visibly Hot*)

Bruna is maybe the only salesclerk I encountered during my field study that would (probably) succeed in getting higher education at a public university in the near future. She seemed to having things under control, to being satisfied with what she got from the enterprise to that point, since she did not show any interest in more sales bonuses or opportunities within the company.

Conversely, this leads us to the example of João. He is 18 years old and, in this, he sees a special advantage in climbing within the brand:

---

12 "They always give contracts, you know, to first job engagements. They give you lots of opportunities."
13 "I knew the brand, I always liked the products. I always identified with the glasses' spectacle frames, I always liked it a lot. So, as I identified with the brand, I preferred to try working here."

"Minha meta agora é, realmente, é virar um gerente de ponto de venda. Assim, como eu ainda sou muito novo, tenho apenas 18 anos, eu tenho ainda muita chance de crescer na marca."[14] (João, 18, salesclerk at *Visibly Hot*)

After having finished his *segundo grau* with a special course in computer science at the age of 17, João started to work at the *Visibly Hot* administration office. As he lives in Jacarépaguá, West zone of Rio de Janeiro, he soon realized that heading to the Zona Sul every day was way too tiring. He quit the office. But he could not afford to stay unemployed since he has a little son to care for. He asked for relocation to the sales point at Barrashopping, where he has actually been working since 10 months ago when I met him.

"Desde que eu comecei trabalhar- eu comecei trabalhar com marca e vista, cheguei no arquivo morto da [*Visibly Hot*] [Eu: o que é isso?] Arquivo morto: eu pegava tipo contratos, recibos, de cinco anos atrás, e jogava fora. Então, eu fiz uma limpeza naquele local, diariamente. E dali, eu entrei em contato com as pessoas da venda e falei assim, cara, que energia que eles têm, é sensacional! Isso é muito gostoso. E acabei me apaixonando e tal, e quando encerraram o meu contrato, foi aquilo- eu não posso ficar sem trabalhar. Eu vou arriscar. Eu nunca trabalhei com venda. É que a minha área é informática. Falei, ô- vamos ver o que acontece. E vai fazer um ano já na marca. E tô- eu amo a marca."[15] (João, 18, salesclerk at *Visibly Hot*)

---

14 "My target is now really to become the branch manager of a sales point. You know, as I am still very young, I am 18 years old, I still have a lot of chances to grow within the brand."

15 "Since I started working- I started working with brand and visuals, I worked in the dead archives of [*Visibly Hot*] [Me: what is that?] Dead archives: I picked out contracts, receipts, five years old, and threw them away. So, I cleaned up that place, day after day. From there, I got in touch with the salespeople, and I said, wow, what an energy they've got, that's sensational! This is very nice. And I became passionate about it and so on, and when they terminated my contract, it was that thing- I cannot become unemployed. I will risk something. I had never worked with sales before. Because computer science is my domain. I said, oh- let's see what happens. And now I will complete one year with the brand. I am- I love the brand."

With his experience of changing from one position to another within the enterprise, he obviously agrees with Bruna's positive evaluation regarding the professional prospects within *Visibly Hot*. What is more, he signals a specific moment of having been affected by the salesforce's positive energy – like something contagious that made him "love the brand". The learning process he already went through at *Visibly Hot* turned him – he is convinced – into a sought-after candidate on the service job market. C&A as well as other shops had personally asked him if he would not want to work for them. But as they pay the same salary, he saw no reason for leaving the brand he identifies with.

"Loving" the brand is something many of the salesclerks reported. Though Carol, captivated since the first time she saw a *Visibly Hot* store at the age of 17, might be one of the most passionate examples. Trained in physical education during her *segundo grau*, she had her first contact with the professional world as an animator trainee in a holiday resort. But she never thought of continuing in that area. Because, as she reports, when she discovered the *Visibly Hot* sales point at a mall of her hometown Belo Horizonte, she got completely "into it". She loved it because she met there with a "more alternative crowd". By buying a range of fashion accessories, she eventually made friends with the salesclerks. Consequently, when she turned 18, getting a job at *Visibly Hot* seemed to be the best option for her. Carol said to herself that "they will accept me the way I am, with my style, with my sexual orientation." In fact, many employees echo the link she makes between *Visibly Hot* and lesbian/gay identities. As outlined in chapter two, this is due to the prominent strategy of *diversity management* that literally stimulates different lifestyles in order to benefit from its economic outputs. Carol's coming of age is linked first, to having a job at age 18, and second, to be recognized as an alternatively styled young lesbian. Working for *Visibly Hot* allows her to live and construct this identity through a daily practice – even if it is ultimately dedicated to the public realm of merchandise and consumption.

Also for Leidiane, 23 years old, her position as a cashier at *Visibly Hot* is her first "real" job. She grew up in the neighborhoods of Rocinha, one of Brazil's largest urban favelas, and she did several informal jobs like being a babysitter or distributing newspapers. Unlike Carol, she didn't know the brand before, but she came to like it shortly after her initiation at work.

"Eu- tava querendo emprego, aí eu perguntei para um amigo meu, pelo Facebook, na época, assim- poxa, você sabe de alguma coisa? Ele, pô, tem uma vaga na [*Visibly Hot*], na caixa, você se interessa? Falei, pô, claro! Mas, o que é isso? E ele: é de óculos. Aí, tá, eu vim no dia seguinte aqui, fiz a entrevista com o gerente, e ele me entrevistou e me mandou para o escritório."[16] (Leidiane, 23, cashier at *Visibly Hot*)

For Leidiane, the everyday life at *Visibly Hot* turned into a sphere where she encountered a form of social recognition that had been previously denied to her. As she reported, several customers told her that she was "stylish", something that she had never thought of herself. The experience at the shop made her like the brand's style. "Adoro isso. É muito inovador, adoro isso. Exclusividade, sabe"[17]. But what concerns her work as a cashier, she also emphasized that a possible change to active sales would pose her a challenge. "Eu me acho muito na defensiva"[18], she added, thinking that she lacked the right behavior most of the girls in sales already had.

3.2.2 Service and shopping workers

Leidiane's hint to the other salesclerks' selling skills takes us to another group within the *Visibly Hot*'s workforce: young people whose contract at the company is not the first one in their careers. They already worked for other fashion companies or, at least, held positions within the service industry. To them, being engaged at *Visibly Hot* corresponds to an opportunity with special features. Juliano, 21, has worked in telemarketing before. "Pessoas ligaram para mim. Era atender- problemas das pessoas para ouvir e resolver. Só problemas"[19]. He got tired of it and was looking for

---

16 "I- wanted a job, so I asked a friend of mine, via Facebook, back then, like- hey, have you heard of something? He was like, man, there is a position at [*Visibly Hot*], as a cashier, are you interested? I said, man, for sure! But what is that? And he: it is about sunglasses. So, ok, I came here one day after, had an interview with the branch manager, he interviewed me and sent me to the office."

17 "I love this. It is very innovative, I adore it. Exclusiveness, you know."

18 "I find myself very defensive"

19 "People called me. It was all about operating- listening to people's problems and solving them. Only problems."

another job in the field of commercial services. As he already used sunglasses from *Visibly Hot* and thought that the brand suited him, he handed in his CV. Comparing his actual employment to his former job in telemarketing, he assesses:

"Gosto bem mais daqui. A gente vê pessoas o tempo todo, é incrível, cara- a gente tem que lidar com um público muito imenso. Em um dia, a gente fala com pessoas pobres e com gente, sabe, que é formal- você não pode brincar. Tem que lidar com todo mundo aqui. Isso é ótimo. Lá era formal, não podia brincar, era formal, você ficava preso em uma sala."[20] (Juliano, 21, cashier at *Visibly Hot*)

In Juliano's case, the feature of *Visibly Hot* consists in his perception of the daily labor as being less formal, a place where one can "joke" and that is more lively than a sterile office room. Furthermore, he likes the aspect of interacting with customers from very distinct social backgrounds.[21]

For Diogo, 23, his sales activities at *Visibly Hot* are more like a continuation of former contracts. For five years, he has worked in shopping centers, most of the time for a label specialized in surfer's fashion. His parents had died when he was young, urging him to organize his independent life a lot earlier than most of his colleagues. He also started studying at a private university in Jacarepaguá, close to where he actually lives. But he had to suspend his studies because his financial situation was too difficult. He has got a little daughter and, at the moment of our interview, his girlfriend was pregnant with another baby. This background of having a young family at home is what he thinks that most influenced his motivation to work and continue working at *Visibly Hot*. Initially introduced by one of his best friends who, as he says, "went crazy about the brand", he

---

20 "I like it a lot more here. We see people all day long, it's incredible, man- we have to deal with an enormous clientele. In one day, we chat with poor people and with people, you know, that are formal- [with whom] you cannot joke. You have to deal with everybody here. This is great. There [in telemarketing], it was formal, you could not joke, it was formal, you were trapped in an office."

21 This may be a very specific characteristic of the shopping mall Juliano works in. Also João, who works at Barrashopping, called my attention to the fact that the Nova América was a mall with consumers that were "less formal", more relaxed and not that demanding, as it was the case in the Barra Shopping.

also got to like it, notably because he identifies with his team mates and highly respects his brand manager's personal frankness.

"Eu entrei aqui com o objetivo de crescer na empresa, para que eu possa retomar outros planos da minha vida. Infelizmente, hoje o dinheiro move o mundo e a gente precisa de dinheiro. Então, eu crescendo aqui, ganhando mais dinheiro- e assim, eu conseguiria dar continuação aos meus planejamentos. O que seria voltar para faculdade; já moro sozinho, tenho uma filha. [...] Então, eu venho trabalhar com a maior responsabilidade, coisa que eu não tinha- que tinha que criar com o tempo."[22] (Diogo, 23, salesclerk at *Visibly Hot*)

While Diogo pragmatically links his motivation to the aspiration of getting a better economic position, allowing him both higher education and other professional opportunities in the near future, others posit themselves as being more loyal to the enterprise.

Andrea is 22 years old and has already been working as the branch manager of a sales point for two years. After some initial experiences at a newspaper kiosk, she started her career in the commercial area with a contract at C&A at the age of 18. She stayed three months and gave up because she didn't identify enough with the enterprise. From there, she came directly to *Visibly Hot*; initially, as a cashier, then as a responsible vendor and as a vice branch manager. After only one month doing the latter job, she was offered her current position as a branch manager. The supervisors, as Andrea relates, were no longer satisfied with the performance of her precursor, "mas gostaram do meu trabalho e eu tô aqui até hoje"[23]. In our conversation, she emphasizes her talent for sales.

"Eu trabalhei um ano e meio como caixa. Até quando eu era caixa, sempre entrava no atendimento, sempre fui muito boa de venda. [...] Adoro venda. Adoro lidar com

---

22 "I entered here with the objective of growing within the enterprise in order to be able to resume other plans for my life. Unfortunately, today it is money that runs the world and we need money. So, growing here, making more money- I could continue my planning. That would be to go back to university; I already live by my own, I have a daughter. [...] So, I come to work with the highest responsibility, something I didn't have before- I had to learn it over time."

23 "but they liked my performance and I' m here until today"

público, adoro conversar, adoro desenrolar, eu gosto muito disso aí mesmo."[24] (Andrea, 22, branch manager at *Visibly Hot*)

What is more, she thinks that, compared to other enterprises, *Visibly Hot* is giving extraordinary opportunities to its workforce. Especially the conventions or the staff trainings were more than exceptional.

"Eu fui na convenção, foi muito bom. [...] Eu amei. Por isso eu falo, cara, essa empresa é foda de trabalhar. Uma excelente empresa, uma empresa que sempre está dando treinamento, a todo mês acaba promovendo treinamento, de motivação, incentivo, fazendo corridas, e fazendo uma convenção assim, essa empresa é show de bola!"[25] (Andrea, 22, branch manager at *Visibly Hot*)

For Andrea, as it seems, her contract at *Visibly Hot* could not be any better. She draws her enthusiasm for the brand from both her personal addiction to sales interaction and the entrepreneurial strategies aimed at increasing workers' motivation.

Such a kind of motivational drive helps getting through the years in the commercial area. Supervisor Ana, in her mid-thirties, looks back to a sales career since she is 18 years old. Similarly to Andrea, she has passed through all of the different stages, accumulating, as she says, a "bagagem de varejo" – retail luggage. Within the area of women's fashion, she worked as a salesclerk, then several years as a branch manager and finally as a supervisor. She has always liked to work with people. When she was younger, she was into selling, attending, and "gaining" customers. In the last years, she managed to find a similar meaning in relating to the people she was supervising.

---

24 "I worked one and a half years as a cashier. Even when I was a cashier, I interfered in sales, I was always very good at sales. [...] I love sales. I love to deal with customers, I love to chat, to unwind [sales], I really like that stuff a lot."
25 "I went to the convention, it was very good. [...] I loved it. That's why I say, man, this enterprise is fucking great to work for. An excellent enterprise, an enterprise that is always offering training, every month they are promoting training, of motivation, incentives, races, doing things like a convention, this enterprise is awesome!"

"Assim que ficou, de novo, prazeroso para mim. [...] Eu tenho os meus clientes. Os meus clientes são os meus vendedores, são os meus gerentes, né? Só o que eu tenho que vender hoje não é um produto, mas uma ideia- de padrão, de normas, de postura, de atitude, né. Eu também continuo vendendo, que era uma coisa que eu gostava muito, mas em vez de vender um produto em si, eu vendo a marca, eu vendo conceito, eu vendo uma atitude profissional. Isso eu acho que é muito prazeroso."[26] (Ana, 34, supervisor at *Visibly Hot*)

Just like Andrea, Ana points out that she has an ardor for sales. But as she has no more direct contact with customers, she managed to reinterpret the supervisor's role as a branding agent on a higher level. Selling an idea, both a concept and the professional behavior of *Visibly Hot*, is her personal motivation.

3.2.3 The artistic improvisers

For sure, not all members of the *Visibly Hot* sales force are travelling on a path through the world of work that straightforwardly. As scouts, many of them may be looking for something specific when they come to the brand, having explored different areas, but not always encountering the places they had previously and mentally mapped out. There are paths breaking off, changing their surface, and demanding patience for zigzag courses and strategies of improvisation. Letícia, 26 years old and from the Baixada Fluminense, has been through such experiences. Already, her *segundo grau* demanded some detours; as she had difficulties in the regular course, she only finished it later through night courses. Professionally, she passed several years as an independent cultural producer. She collaborated in several theater productions, while at the same time working in a vegetarian restaurant. Furthermore, she adds "eu entrei no movimento das mulheres, e

---

26 "Like that, it was again pleasurable to me. [...] I've got my customers. My customers are my salesclerks, my branch managers, right? It is only that today I don't have to sell a product, but an idea- of role model, of norms, of posture, of attitude, right? I also continue to sell, something I liked a lot, but instead of selling a product as such, I sell the brand, I sell a concept, I sell a professional attitude. I think this is it what it makes it very pleasurable."

fiz militância LGBT. Trabalho era militância"[27]. Getting to university continued to be one of her aspirations, too. She tried for mathematics and dancing, but she didn't achieve the demanded scores. That was a difficult moment for her, as she notes, because she also didn't want to continue as an independent. She handed in her CV in the commercial area close to culture and arts, primarily in bookstores, but always got stranded in the job interviews.

Her situation changed slightly when she got together with her former girlfriend. This girl ran a self-service restaurant, where Letícia could immediately start to work.

"Eu trabalhei desde faxineira, caixa, a porteira. Trabalhei- eu fiz também a parte das saladas- de tudo. De tudo que você pudesse- contabilidade- tudo que você pudesse imaginar, eu fiz ali dentro."[28] (Letícia, 26, salesclerk at *Visibly Hot*)

After that experience as a maid-of-all-work, she had an engagement in a cinema's bookstore, where she was discharged after two months. She had to move back to her mother's house in Nova Iguaçu. She gave it some more tries in cinema projects and photography, but her money came from informal sources such as reselling concert tickets. She finally got to *Visibly Hot*, because she was looking for a short service job during the Christmas sales season. So, she applied for a series of fashion brands that she thought fitted her own style. This excluded companies such as Mr. Cat, "uma loja que não tem nada a ver comigo"[29], since she saw herself as somebody with style and refined fashion taste. Actually, this is also where she localized her personal match regarding *Visibly Hot*. For the second stage of the job interview, she says,

---

27 "I joined the women's movement, I did LGBT activism. Work was activism"
28 "I worked [everything] from cleaning lady, cashier, to doorman. I worked- I also did the part of the salads- of everything. Everything you could- accounting- everything you could imagine, I did in there."
29 "a shop that has nothing to do with me"

"eu fui de galocha, já fiquei mais à vontade. Essa calça preta. Um vestido verde. E o meu blazer vermelho. Mas não tinha aquela questão de preparo."[30] (Letícia, 26, salesclerk at *Visibly Hot*)

Since she realized that she fitted in the brand's ideology, she would not have to use a special dress or make-up. When she mentions that *Visibly Hot* recently started to hire also people "without style", she makes it clear she ranks among the more genuine and legitimate employees.

The question of style is also crucial for Pedro, 21 years old and from the neighborhood of Olaria. He worked as a showcase designer for C&A before, due to his former training in fashion that led him to this area. However, there he felt somewhat constrained in being able to express his personal and artistic streak for the style. Besides mentioning the favorable salaries one could earn at *Visibly Hot*, he compares:

"E também é uma empresa que te dá muita liberdade. Você pode ser quem você é. Uma coisa que na C&A, vamos supor, eu não pod- sei lá, eu tinha que trabalhar de uniforme que achei muito brega. Apesar de ter que usar esse uniforme aqui, esse uniforme é mais despojado, uma coisa mais descolada. Não é uma coisa tão séria como na C&A. E muda de três em três meses, eu acho."[31] (Pedro, 21, salesclerk at *Visibly Hot*)

Similar to how other salesclerks related to the brand, Pedro is passionate about the company's informal and relaxed handling of working dress code. Like his colleague Letícia, he enthusiastically reports on the details of how he had introduced himself at the job interview.

---

30 "I went there using overshoes, I felt already more comfortable. These black trousers. A green dress. And my red blazer. But I didn't care about that part of dressing."

31 "And it is also an enterprise that gives you a lot of freedom. You can be who you are. Something that at C&A, let's suppose, I couldn- I don't know, I had to wear a uniform I found very cheesy. In spite of having to wear this uniform here, this uniform here is more easy-going, something more casual. It is not that serious as at C&A. And it changes every three months, I think."

"Eu fui louco p'a caralho- não, não- eu estava com uma bermudinha toda rasgada, enfiada. Tava com sapato meu que tenho da Adidas que é todo listrado de preto e branco. Coloquei um blusa minha que é muito diferente. E um óculos. E botei um óculos tipo anos 80."[32] (Pedro, 21, salesclerk at *Visibly Hot*)

For Pedro, his style also closes the circle with other activities he follows up at weekends, like partying, DJing, or frequenting events that have to do with the arts. When he finally left the company after two years of employment[33], he concentrated on performance art and started teaching theater for a small NGO-driven project in his home neighborhood.

Also Jéssica, 23, is proud of her style. During our interview, I find striking her fast and sophisticated speech as well as her superior tone. Especially the way she reports on her biography dispels all doubt that she is a highly self-confident and professional young woman. She has already gained experience as a fashion designer, she says, in addition to (private) university where she coursed Computer Science and English language. Her dream was to become a fashion designer for FARM, one of the most successful Brazilian brands for female upper class fashion at the moment. Therefore, she was not that passionate about *Visibly Hot* from the first moment, but rather came into it due to her quick professional success.

"Eu terminei faculdade, eu não queria trabalhar no varejo, eu queria trabalhar na minha área. [...] Fui designer de moda. [...] E aí- eu não queria trabalhar no varejo, mas eu estava precisando dinheiro para fazer os cursos que eu queria. Todos os cursos custavam uns 300, 400 Reais. E aí, eu precisava da grana. Aí, a [*Visibly Hot*] me ligou e me chamou para trabalhar com ela. A princípio, eu não queria me envolver de novo com varejo. Mas eu entrei, e logo já fui uma das melhores vendedoras do ponto de venda. Então, isso meio que me animou."[34] (Jéssica, 23, branch manager at *Visibly Hot*)

---

32 "I went there like fucking crazy- no, no, I wore some shorts that are completely ripped, skinny. And I wore some pair of shoes I've got from Adidas, which are all striped in black and white. I put on one of my shirts that is very different. And sunglasses. I put on sunglasses like 80s style."

33 I present and analyze further Pedro's case in chapter five.

34 "I finished college, I didn't want to work in retail, I wanted to work in my area. [...] I was a fashion designer. [...] So- I didn't want to work in retail, but I

According to Jéssica, she only returned to a retail job because she lacked money for her further studies. Furthermore, a friend of hers left his position as a salesclerk at *Visibly Hot*, advocating her as a substitute. Once in that position, she advanced very quickly. After one year as a salesclerk, she was promoted to branch manager of a sales point. Premiums, like for being the "salesclerk of the month" of Rio de Janeiro, were things she gained repeatedly. This gave her a good part of the motivational drive she has got today. Nevertheless, she remains committed to her former aspirations for the future. Although she can imagine continuing at *Visibly Hot*, it had to be at the design factory in São Paulo or at one of the special job offers abroad, like training new salesclerks in shops recently opened in the US.

3.3 "HERE I CAN BE WHO I AM", OR: AUTHENTICITY AS FREEDOM

The portrayal of professional phases as lived through by young Cariocas[35] reveals quite clearly that these phases develop very differently. For some, the sales job at *Visibly Hot* is but a first arrival point in the workforce. Still exploring both the possibilities and limitations of their employment, their aspirations range from aiming at a career in the company to preparing plans for studies at a university. For others, their contract is but one more step within a fluctuating series of service employments. They are pondering, mostly rather pragmatically, aspects of salary and career opportunities; furthermore, they are comparing the brand's specific benefits to their previous experiences. Now, what is striking about the narratives of all my interlocutors is that although the integrated picture of their singular moti-

---

needed the money in order to continue with the courses I liked. All the courses cost 300, 400 reais. Really, I needed the bucks. So, [*Visibly Hot*] called me and asked me to work for them. At first, I didn't want to get involved with retail again. But I did, and soon I was among the best sellers of the sales point. So, this kind of cheered me up."

35 *carioca* is the Portuguese term for the inhabitants of Rio de Janeiro.

vational sets unfolds in a multiplicity[36], they are all attached to the same affective field. What I mean by this is that the narratives bear an emotional consensus on what the employees believe the brand is offering to them: an ideal of individual freedom as assured once one identifies with; in the salesclerks' words, the benefit of being able to "be who you are". Larissa, for example, put it in a nutshell:

"Assim, o [Diogo] que é o dono da marca, diz: 'Eu sou isso que sou hoje só por causa dos vendedores.' Então, ele tem- cara, ele é muito genioso, esse cara. Eu o admiro p'a caramba. É lógico que é a gente. Porque a gente só faz o que faz porque ele dá o espaço para a gente fazer do nosso jeito, ser quem a gente é. Eu acho que é por isso que eu gosto mesmo. Porque é um trabalho, mas acaba sendo gostoso de fazer: você estar num lugar onde não tem preconceito de nada, se você é estranha, eles vão te aceitar, se você é gay, eles vão te aceitar, entendeu? É tipo uma família. A gente passa mais tempo aqui do que na própria família, então, acaba se tornando a nossa família mesmo, entendeu?"[37] (Larissa, 21, salesclerk at *Visibly Hot*)

Larissa emphasizes the room for individuality provided by *Visibly Hot*' s founder and highest manager. He would let his employees work in their

---

36 I refer here to the understanding of Gilles Deleuze and Félix Guattari (1980). To theses authors, multiplicity means an alternative figure of thought to embracing (fictive) wholes or unities of a given phenomenon. Multiplicities are rhizome-like, "there are only lines" (Deleuze and Guattari 1980: 15) but no fixed points or positions that could be traced back to a common root. As an image for measurement, it also stresses the dynamic and constantly changing character of its dimensions, unfolding like a musical performance that turns points into lines.

37 "So, [Diogo] who is the brand's owner, says: 'I am what I am today because of my salesclerks.' Actually, he ha- man, this guy is a genius. I totally admire him. It's obvious that it's us. Because we only do what we do because he gives us that space to do the things in our way, to be who we are. I think that's why I really like it here. Because it's work, but it turns out to be gratifying doing it: you are in a place without any prejudice, if you are strange, they will accept you, if you are gay, they will accept you, right? It's like a family. We spend more time here than with our own family, so it really ends up becoming a family, right?"

own ways to handle things. For Larissa, this is synonymous with being able to be authentic, yourself, "who you are" – something she obviously rates as a highly desirable and necessary value. Consequently, this is also the point where she locates her own affective bonds with the brand. Although her presence at *Visibly Hot* is work, it does not resemble work as such. For the company included, as she holds, literally everyone in its family, no matter if one was "strange" or "gay".

Being authentic in one's own subjective being or becoming seems then to describe the idea of freedom as shared by the salesclerks. Their approval (and admiration) of the branding project – "be different" – finds here its nodal point of 'suture' (Hall 1996). Authenticity and personal brand identification appear as counterparts of rational work ethic: they oppose conformity and disciplinary phasing as being the assuring factors for market productivity and efficiency. The suturing effect, as it seems to me, lies surprisingly in the phenomenon that work is being reinterpreted as an arena of individual self-expression and freedom. It would certainly be wrong to say that this is completely new. In Western societies, especially the work of artists – musicians, painters, writers, and so on – is commonly seen as the locus of self-realization, of creativity and opportunity to live out a supposedly unique identity[38]; an activity that advances and enriches people in their personality. Activities such as service work, however, are typically not regarded as such deliberating jobs. Rather, they rank among monotonous or repetitive tasks, empirically closer to the factory than to the artist's studio.[39]

Together with the salesclerk's suturing identifications, the proceedings of companies like *Visibly Hot* are very plastic examples of how, in the sense of Rose, freedom can be deployed as a form of (self)government (Rose 2004). Individuality at work is woven into the feeling of "gratify-

---

38 In comparative cultural sociology, the view of a coherent Western valorization of arts has also been challenged. As Michèle Lamont (1992) argued, creativity and morally valued self-realization varied by national context and social background. While French elite classes tended to mobilize the arts as a means of social distinction, American upper classes rather accessed individual success at the professional, corporate level in order to draw symbolic boundaries.

39 Regarding the Brazilian context of service employment, sociology of work has mainly pointed to the case of telemarketing (Braga 2012; Singer 2012).

ing". As is pervasive in the speech of Larissa and other salesclerks, this good feeling emerges because being personally authentic is the entrance ticket to the brand community they describe as a "family". Due to the diversity discourse that dominates *Visibly Hot*'s branding rhetoric, salesclerks tend to equate authenticity to the deliberate expression of a gay identity, a "strange" character, or a cool and deliberate lifestyle. In other words, one would neither have to hide her or his sexual orientation, nor to feel bad about being a weirdo or to adapt conformity of speech, dress nor body codes that are common to the world of work. In some cases, this forwards the sensation that doing service work is "cool" or "fun". Indeed, this remembers Arlie Hochschild's (2003) argument about the flight attendants; they need to show the customers that their work is fun, too. But different from the stewardesses' smiles, the nature of the *Visibly Hot* salesclerks' identifications is not something that is artificially trained. As they distinguish the necessity and unapologetic aspiration to be authentic, they ease any doubt that their work is not about playing a role, but to effectively "be" and inhabit that role.

3.3.1 The freedom of style

As we have seen with the group I named the artistic improvisers, having style often appears as a benchmark for one's authenticity. Consequently, the obligation to wearing a uniform[40] is repeatedly referred to as a kind of enemy image that other brands incorporate. *Visibly Hot*, the salesclerks assure, would be far more "awesome" than other enterprises, because the employees could partially wear their own clothes and always showcase their own styles. As Pedro had caught this idea, he went to the job interview without any special preparation.

---

40 Du Gay (1996) also encountered the working uniform as something quite relevant to how salesclerks in retail perceived their own identity performance. Salesclerks in his inquiry tended to compare their status with that of higher employees who were not affected by a dress code: "staff felt that the uniform attacked their sense of who they were and that they wanted to be seen to be." (du Gay 1996: 172)

"É porque a [*Visibly Hot*] não é uma empresa de engenharia. Ela é uma empresa descolada, entendeu? Então, eles querem escolher aquela pessoa que fala bem, pessoas que não têm vergonha. O estilo diz muita coisa, né, o estilo como você se veste diz muita coisa sobre a sua personalidade. Então, eu fui como eu sou mesmo. Eu não estava criando- passando impressão do que eu não sou."[41] (Pedro, 21, salesclerk at *Visibly Hot*)

According to this conviction, pretending to be something different than someone really is would be the biggest mistake a sales candidate (or worker) could commit. Style, in this view, is what expresses personality and is further attached to a way of self-confident acting. While Pedro sees style primarily as having to do with fashion, Juliano locates *Visibly Hot*'s coolness in the liberty to behave informally at work, like kidding around or speaking in colloquial language. This, too, refers to a person's authenticity.

"A gente- a marca prega muito estilo, né? Quando você chega lá, com o seu estilo, está tudo certo. Contanto que você não finja ter um estilo- ótimo! Chega aqui, sendo você mesmo, o seu estilo, falando do seu jeito, brincando como você quer. Beleza, fica tudo certo! Não tem nada para se preparar. [...] Aqui não é tão formal do modo de se vestir, do modo que você fala. A gente brinca também, a gente fala sério."[42] (Juliano, 21, salesclerk at *Visibly Hot*)

Juliano emphasizes a behavior, allowed at work, which refers to individual style as expressed by a specific language and jokes. Actually, I could bet-

---

41 "Because [*Visibly Hot*] is not an engineering company. This enterprise is cool, you know? So, they want the kind of person that knows how to speak, people that are not ashamed. The style says everything, right, the way you dress says very much about your personality. So, I went there the way I really am. I didn't create- give the impression of something I am not."

42 "We- the brand holds forth style very much, you know? When you get there, with your style, everything's fine. As long as you don't pretend to have a style- perfect! You get here, being yourself, your style, talking in your way, kidding as you want. Great, everything is fine! There is nothing you should prepare for. [...] It isn't that formal here, they way to dress, the way to talk. We both joke and talk seriously."

ter understand what he and his colleagues meant by this, thinking about my observation notes I had made during the inquiries at different shopping centers. The way of joking and behaving means exactly the usual interactions perceivable among the employees. Especially at the moments of waiting for next customers, the salesclerks often joke and bodily "hang around" the sales point in ways that remember the sociability of "hip" youth localities.[43] For example, they would use a lot of "gíria" (slang) specific to younger generations and youth cultures they eventually also integrated in their sales strategies. What is more, many of the salesclerks express their easy-going lifestyles by a styling of their bodies. This, too, was seen as a central proof to living one's own individuality and to the brand's libertarian benevolence.

"Eu gosto da liberdade que a empresa te dá. Para poder ser quem você é. Eu acho que foi um dos principais motivos para eu procurar a [*Visibly Hot*] foi isso. Eu sabia que ia ser uma empresa que ia me aceitar com os meus piercings, com as minhas tatuagens, com o meu jeito de me vestir, jeito de falar. Porque, eu acho que eles dão essa oportunidade para todo mundo, não interessa o seu padrão. Interessa o que você faz de bom. Muitas empresas olham para sua aparência. E daí, eles vão te aperfeiçoar para fazer daquele jeito, vender daquela forma. Aqui não. Aqui eu tenho liberdade de ser do jeito que eu sou. E mostrar que eu faço um bom trabalho sendo do meu jeito. Não preciso seguir um padrão para ser boa no que eu faço."[44] (Bruna, 19, branch manager at *Visibly Hot*)

---

43 Almeida and Tracy (2003) show in their study on "nomadic nights" in Rio de Janeiro how young people experience their nocturne meetings by affective categories like "zoar". The latter means having fun, being excited to hang out with friends, trashing people and eventually flirting, experiences that altogether supersede the importance of the places or localities where they happen (Almeida and Tracy 2003: 126). In this sense, hip localities could be defined by the young people's sensation of participating in a group, actively producing the semantic field of what counts as cool and valuable.

44 "I like the liberty the enterprise gives you. To be able to be how you are. I think this was one of the major reasons I was looking for [*Visibly Hot*]. I knew it was going to be an enterprise that would accept me with my piercings, with my tattoos, with my way of dressing, talking. Because I think they give this opportunity to everyone, your type doesn't matter. What matters are the things

Once again, the strategies of diversity seem to unfold in the affect that echoes in Bruna's stance. She says that other enterprises tend to physically and behaviorally mold – normalize or standardize – their vendors, because they believed in the success of a one-sized way of selling. Larissa opposes such regulations to the proceedings of *Visibly Hot*, affirming that "good working" and efficiency did not depend on uniform body standards, but precisely on the need of individual self-realization, like through tattoos or piercings. In other words, her notion of authenticity diametrically contrasts the traditional recipe of a worker's identity; it incorporates personal and professional success as an integrated value of freedom.

3.3.2 The necessity of style

At the beginning of my first interviews, Marina, cashier at a *Visibly Hot* kiosk, asked me perplexed: "But what is the profile of that person? Do you think that I fit in?" She was curious to know why I had chosen precisely her as an interlocutor of my research. Actually, as it turned out later, until the moment when she handed in her CV, Marina thought that she would not "have the style for *Visibly Hot*". And her doubts apparently caught up with her when she felt obligated to speak on behalf of her teammates. Marina's insecurity also stems from what we just discussed about the freedom of style. While several salesclerks say that they enjoy the brand's valorization of (their own) genuine identities, there are these other voices, experiences that challenge the notion of an all-including diversity politics. Marina's self assessment points to the fact that the company's branding strategies are keeping alive a set of guideline identities that demand a certain degree of commitment. Branch manager Andrea, for example, makes it clear that there is a style specific to the brand that someone who works with sales should identify with.

---

you're doing well. Many companies look at your appearance. And then, they will perfect you in order to make it that specific way, to sell in a specific way. Here it's not like that. Here, I have the liberty to being the way I am. And to show that I'm doing good work, which is done my own way. I don't need to follow any standard norms to be good at what I'm doing."

"Eu acho, assim, ter o estilo da marca. Tem que ter a cara da marca. Tem que se identificar um pouco, querendo ou não. O estilo da [*Visibly Hot*] é bem diferente do que, por exemplo, o estilo da Mr. Cat. Até o nosso atendimento é mais agressivo. Mas, ali é editado."[45] (Andrea, 22, branch manager at *Visibly Hot*)

Although Andrea insists that the candidates unconditionally need to identify "at least a little bit" with the brand, she specifies that this imperative is different to precast style as is common in other enterprises. *Visibly Hot*'s way of customer service and attendance would be more "aggressive", that is, emotionally more involving[46]. Consequently, during the job interviews she holds with sales candidates, she would always ask for commitment and personal motivation:

"Para mim, você tem que ter o perfil, tem que ter- é! [...] Eu pergunto também: porque você escolheu a nossa marca, porque você gosta? É muito importante, é muito importante essa pergunta. E a última também acho muito importante: porque você acha que eu devo te contratar?"[47] (Andrea, 22, branch manager at *Visibly Hot*)

Andrea comments that most candidates are getting nervous with the latter question. But to her, this inquiry would be necessary because she wanted to know exactly "what the person wants", be it regarding future plans in their lives or just about what they wanted to do with the money.

Salesclerk Carol also agrees that identification with the brand's ideals is preferable. Actually, she even holds that identification is a resource, a kind of requirement that salesclerks of her branch should be striving for.

---

45 "I think it's like having the brand's style. You have to have the brand's face. You have to identify a little bit, whether you like it or not. The style of [*Visibly Hot*] is quite different from, for example, the style of Mr. Cat. Even our attendance is more aggressive. But there, it is standardized."
46 I further discuss this aspect in chapter four.
47 "For me, you've got to have the profile, you've got to have it- yes! [...] I' m also asking: why did you choose our brand, why do you like it? It's very important, this question is very important. And the last one I think is important, too: why do you think I should engage you?"

"A [*Visibly Hot*], cara- você tem que entrar- gostando mesmo da marca. Se você não gostar, você não fica, assim, se você não gostar. Vou te falar por quê. Vender acessórios, óculos, relógios, não é a mesma coisa do que vender uma blusa, uma bermuda que a pessoa precisa. Então, você tem que convencer aquela pessoa que ela precisa. Por isso, você tem que gostar desse óculos!"[48] (Carol, 21, salesclerk at *Visibly Hot*)

Carol holds the view that a salesclerk in the sunglasses branch is only successful and will want to continue for a given enterprise if she or he is passionate about the brand. Since sunglasses are not objects of utility, it is the task of the vendor to actively create the customer's need for that product. The only way to do that, in Carol's opinion, is to "really like" the products, a feeling of enthusiasm that would affect the customers. Differently from other fashion items, Carol summarizes that "óculos – a gente faz gostar"[49].

3.3.3 The malleability of "ser diferente"

Although the salesclerks had given me various entry points for a better understanding of what they meant when they talked about their opportunity to be who they are, I was not yet completely satisfied. I still wanted to insist on the question of how *Visibly Hot*'s promise, "be different!"[50], was taking shape within this individual search for authenticity. For, other than my initial research agenda had presupposed, it was obviously not only a question of the body surface, or say, of appearance. As previous salesclerks' references suggest, they link very diverse aspects to their own performances of incorporating that being different: a way to act and speak; a

---

48 "[*Visibly Hot*] man, you've got to join- really liking the brand. If you don't like it, you won't stay, if you don't like it. I will tell you why. Selling accessories, sunglasses, and watches is not the same thing as selling a shirt, some shorts that somebody needs. So, you need to convince that person that she/he needs it. And that's why you need to like these sunglasses!"
49 "Sunglasses – we make you like it"
50 It must be mentioned that the term *diferente* in colloquial Brazilian Portuguese, especially in the given context, carries also the meaning of something special or outstanding, in a much more positive sense than the English term *different*.

way to ornament and style the body; a way to feel passionate about the brand and its products; and finally, a way to think about identity, as for example, inhabiting the categories of gay or "strange". Even though most methodological textbooks in social sciences advise against directing research questions to the informants[51], at some point I decided that it would be more than helpful to un-code the research interest and to immediately request the salesclerks to define what they understood by being different. Salesclerk Eloisa, for example, discusses not only her own perception of what could be classified as different, but also the role identity politics play in retail strategies.

"É mais uma questão do visual: ser quem você é. [...] Agora, eu tô mais normalzinha, assim- mas, eu já raspei a cabeça aqui. Eu acho que as outras pessoas vêm com um estilo mais diferente, com um rótulo de um tipo de pessoas, assim, que não querem nada, que fazem nada. Com certeza. E seguem um visual- a sua pele realmente mostra quem você é! Mas nem sempre. Às vezes, você tá com uma roupa, mas não quer dizer o que você faça realmente, o que aquela coisa quer dizer. E aqui na [*Visibly Hot*] não, a gente tem vários estilos diferentes, se você for reparar nos vendedores que passam por aqui ou nas outras lojas. Na SportMix ou nessa Lior, você não vai ver uma pessoa toda tatuada na Lior. Eles não vão colocar uma pessoa com uma tatuagem na cabeça. [...] É que nem você vai colocar uma pessoa magra para trabalhar numa loja que vende roupas para pessoas mais cheinhas. As pessoas vão se sentir...sabe!"[52] (Eloisa, 23, cashier at *Visibly Hot*)

---

51 Naturally, this depends on both theoretical and methodological commitment. Commonly, qualitative social research is more receptive for open and self-reflexive aspects of the research process.

52 "It's more a question of looks: to be who you are. [...] Now I am more like normal- but I already shaved my head here. I think that the others come here with a more different [= outstanding] style, with a label of a certain kind of people, like those who don't want anything, that don't do anything. Definitely. And they adhere to a look- your skin really shows who you are! But not always. Sometimes, you're in an outfit, but it doesn't mean what you are really doing or what it wants to say. But here at [*Visibly Hot*] no, we have various different styles, if you look at the salesclerks that are going around here and in other shops. At SportMix or Lior, you won't see anybody fully tattooed. They won't let anyone with a tattoo on the head. [...] It's like you cannot put a thin

Intuitively, Eloisa defines being different as a question of appearance, something she scales on her own body. Other salesclerks were more different, she says, opposing them to her currently rather "normal" style. In her opinion, *Visibly Hot* attracts a label of easygoing, somewhat nonchalant persons, who also performed this through their looks. They were consciously showing their tattoos and would not hide another person behind this facade. It is this coolness linked to tattoos that Eloisa highlights as *Visibly Hot*'s main attribute. Her argument that a slim person should not work in a shop for overweight fashion further supports du Gay's (1996) explorations on how contemporary retail used the salesclerks as primordial mediators – representatives – of their entrepreneurial marketing strategies. For the salesclerk's identifications are always aimed at evoking a possible identification that comes from the customer. In this sense, Eloisa's definition adds the aspect that being different can mean two processes at the same time: first, the self-perception of the salesclerk as representing what is different, and second, the customer's attribution of what is seen as different. She subsequently argues that *Visibly Hot*'s "being different is you being normal", suggesting that it is one's authenticity reverberated through the eyes of others that makes the difference.

The mutuality of these two processes can also be found in Leidiane's evaluation. She notes that once the salesclerks speak the same language or like the same music as a given customer, they can close a sale more easily. But this, according to Leidiane, would only be possible if the space around you was a free, that is, not standardized one.

"Acho que a [*Visibly Hot*] tem essa diferença das outras marcas, entendeu, você pode falar o mesmo diálogo com cliente, entendeu? Depende do cliente, né? Não tem esse padrão, você tem que ser assim, assim, assim. Aqui é livre, entendeu? Você fala a mesma língua do que o cliente, sabe. Aí resultando uma boa venda e tal. [...] Na loja, como a gente também pode escolher as nossas músicas, então, o pessoal fica super à vontade, sabe. Aí tem cliente que só entra pela música, né?"[53] (Leidiane, 24, cashier at *Visibly Hot*)

---

person to work in a shop that sells clothes for chubbier people. The customers would feel like…you know!"

53 "I think that [*Visibly Hot*] has this difference compared to other brands, you know, you can have the same dialogues as your customers, right? It depends on

The affective capacity of music is apparently not only something that makes customers enter the shop, but again associates the parable of diversity to freedom. For Bruna, for example, music taste is crucial to think about *Visibly Hot*'s characteristic variety of styles.

"O ser diferente, para mim, é a mistura de todo tipo de pessoas. A gente gosta de rock, de punk, de pagode. A gente gosta de cabelo curto, raspado, cabelo longo. É- sabe- é isso! A junção de diversas pessoas que gostam de diversas coisas e que elas conseguem se dar bem, se respeitar trabalhando juntos, mesmo sendo diferentes. Que conseguem conviver."[54] (Bruna, 19, salesclerk at *Visibly Hot*)

Unlike Eloisa's indication of how the attribution by others (customers) influenced the contours of what is seen as different, Bruna thinks of being different more in terms of an irreducibility of difference among humans. Although style (of music and hair), too, is her characteristic benchmark of what makes young people different from one another, it is a grouping of singularities, that is, the diversity as such that defines the being different. This is a remarkable point because most of the other salesclerks' statements related to difference in more individualistic terms. In Bruna's case, however, difference has to do with her understanding of diversity as treating other people well and respecting their being different.

---

the customer, doesn't it? There is not that standard, like you have to be like this, like this, like that. It is free here, you know? You speak the same language as the customer, you know. From there, you can close a good sale. [...] At the shop, as we can also choose our own music, the customers are getting crazy, you know. There are customers who only step in the shop because of the music, right?"

54 "The being different, to me, is the mixture of all kinds of people. We like rock, punk, and pagode. We like short hair, shaved [hair], and long hair. It's- you know- that's it! The coming together of diverse people who like diverse things and who do well together, and respect each other while working together, despite being different [from one another]. Who succeed in living together."

3.3.4 Style as a becoming

Even though many salesclerks report on style and being different in terms of attributes that someone already has or is when she/he gets to the company, it would be misleading to grasp *Visibly Hot*'s diversity strategies in a literal sense; that is, that several salesclerks who start working for the company neither would nor ultimately should stay the same as before. Indeed, there is much evidence that having style and being different are simultaneously gone through as a process: once affected by the brand's ideals, a salesclerk can (and better, should) *become* different, become part of the *Visibly Hot* family. Larissa confirms that she has gone through a real metamorphosis since she began working for the company. Her personal transformation was of such an extent that the salesclerk trainer chose her as the prime example of the week.

"Quando eu entrei- a gente passa uma semana em treinamento. [...] É o que a gente chama de treinamento baby. São os primeiros três dias, a gente passa lá no escritório em [Ipanema]. E lá, ela [a treinadora] fala: todo mundo que entra, entra de um jeito e sai de um outro jeito. Esses dias, no treinamento que eu fui- ela sempre escolheu alguém para homenagear, para falar, botar foto lá- e aconteceu comigo! Ela estava falando que eu cheguei lá, com vestidinho vermelhinho até aqui, com cabelinho até aqui, toda [imita voz de menininha]. E hoje está aí esse monstro. A gente se comunica mais, se abre mais, a gente aprende a falar. E muda, não adianta. Não é a mesma pesso- pode ser a mesma pessoa – não posso ter medo de piercing, de tatuagem – mas muda o jeito de se portar, o corte de cabelo. Ela falou que isso acontece muito. A pessoa muda o cabelo, raspa o cabelo. A gente acaba se influenciando pela moda e a gente vê, pô, como que faz e a gente faz. Eu, por exemplo, mudei bastante. Bastante. A gente vai tendo uma visão mais ampla da moda, a gente vê pessoas estilosas, pega algumas coisas para a gente, entendeu. Foi legal."[55] (Larissa, 21, salesclerk at *Visibly Hot*)

---

55 "When I started- we have one week of training. [...] It's what we call the baby training. It's about the first three days we stay at the office in [Ipanema]. And there, she [the trainer] says: everyone who enters in here, enters in one way and leaves in another. These days, in a training I went to- she would always choose someone to honor, to speak about, put a photo there- and it happened with me! She said that I got there, with a sweet little red dress up to here, with darling

Larissa is proud of her transformation process into a "monster". Interestingly, she relates this feeling of success not only to her personal progress regarding fashion taste and creativity, but also to the company's accomplishment of changing people's thoughts and actions. The brand's training section awarded her with the title of representing the way employees (positively) changed their behavior over time. Larissa feels overtly pleased to being "honored" in that role, also because this means recognition of her as belonging and actively contributing to what makes the brand so successfully different.

These ways how the expression of a personal becoming is lived and portrayed resembles contemporary mass media language. *Visibly Hot*'s digital review evaluations of its employees – by using different photos and narratives – follows a logic quite typical in reality television, namely in internationally circulating programs such as *Next Top Model, The Voice*, or *RuPaul's Drag Race*. Commonly, the ones awarded are the candidates that most proved their abilities of self-improvement and hard working within their style performances (Wei 2014: 206), pointing to the fact that incorporating the role of an outstanding and authentic star is the result of a hard and sometimes dramatic journey. In the entrepreneurial jargon of *Visibly Hot*, a (sales) candidate is especially interesting for the brand from the moment she or he expresses an inner will of dedicated "growing" (*crescer*) within the company. Branch manager Andrea confirms that she liked *Visibly Hot* so much because she felt always highly valued and given opportunities for personal "growth". Consequently, she also understands her job as consisting in transmitting and stimulating such capacities of (self) improvement.

[long] hair, all like [imitates a girlish voice]. And today, what we've got here is this monster. We communicate more, we are more open-minded, we learn to talk. And we change, there's no doubt. It's not the same perso- it could even be the same person – [like that] I won't be afraid of piercings, of tattoos – but what changes is the way you behave, your haircut. She said this happens very often. The person changes a hairstyle, shaves off the hair. We get influenced by fashion and we see it, man, how to do it and we do it. Me, for example, I changed completely. Completely. We are given a broader sense of fashion, we see stylish people, pick some things for ourselves, you know. It was great."

"O meu trabalho é desenvolver pessoas. Pessoas que fiquem até mais capacitadas do que eu. Porque eu quero sempre desenvolver pessoas que sejam melhores do que eu. E tem muitas pessoas aqui que querem crescer na empresa, entendeu. Então, assim, eu estou aqui para desenvolver pessoas. Pessoas que querem crescer."[56] (Andrea, 22, branch manager at *Visibly Hot*)

Similar to what Souza (2012) observed with staff in telemarketing, the present sales employees tend to naturalize entrepreneurial jargon to an extent that it affects moral values with respect to various aspects in their lives. The internalization of "growing", for example, takes shape as a compass function that thoroughly integrates personal with professional development. When I asked my informants about what they perceived as their difficulties encountered at work, some of them reported that they had gone through a transformation process of their behavior that had been quite exhausting. Besides the adaptations in physical appearance, Bruna emphasizes that she had to overcome her shyness and to develop an overt attitude in handling sales.

"E eu acho que a dificuldade, por incrível que pareça- eu era tímida quando eu entrei aqui. Foi uma dificuldade para eu vender, para conseguir entrar no salão de venda como eu entro hoje. Hoje em dia, eu acho super fácil. Mas não era, no início foi muito, muito difícil. Acho que é isso, foi a maior dificuldade que eu encontrei aqui. Perder a timidez, comunicar melhor."[57] (Bruna, 19, salesclerk at *Visibly Hot*)

Just as Larissa, Bruna evaluates this experience of a personal-professional metamorphosis in highly positive terms. Even if the process was hard for her, she feels grateful to the company for the fact that she has succeeded in

---

56 "My work consists in developing people. People who end up having even more capacity than I do. Because I always intend to develop people who will be better than me. And there are many people wanting to grow within the company, you know. So, I'm here for developing people. People who want to grow."

57 "I think the main difficulty, however incredible this might appear- I was very shy when I started here. It was difficult for me to sell, to enter the salesroom the way I do it today. Today, I find it very easy. But it was not like that, at the beginning, it was very, very difficult. I think it was the biggest challenge I encountered here. To leave behind that shyness, to communicate better."

leaving behind her shyness. Mariana, one of her direct colleagues at the sales point and whose working experience at *Visibly Hot* is but of a couple of weeks long, also agrees. The longer one is part of the group, she holds, the more she or he strives to adopt the style and behavior of the peers: „Eu estou começando a mudar meu estilo, meu pensamento- acaba que você vai mudando"[58]. As already suggested above, these individual becomings not only heighten instantaneous feelings of social recognition, but often effect more long lasting, affective liaisons to the brand; feelings that drive several former salesclerks to want to come back to the company. Jéssica, who initially would have preferred to work for FARM but ended up becoming a branch manager at *Visibly Hot*, respectively summarizes:

> "Até quem não entra muito a ver com a marca, acaba saindo muito a ver com a marca. A gente diz que a gente sai da [*Visibly Hot*], mas a [*Visibly Hot*] não sai da gente. Por isso, têm várias pessoas que querem voltar."[59] (Jéssica, 23, branch manager at *Visibly Hot*)

3.4 RECOGNIZING AND MODELING DIFFERENT SELVES

The manifold aspirations for authenticity just described are pointing to the ineluctable fact that "ser diferente" is not an arbitrary business: there are boundaries and recipes of how to successfully inhabit the fanciness of difference. At *Visibly Hot*, the employee is subjected to a range of selection criteria in order to be recognized as a part of the brand's "family". In general terms, there is a need to be or to become recognizable in the enterprise's terms and conditions, that is, one has to be seen as (minimally) similar to other employees or consumers. In other words, the *Visibly Hot* employee should not be different in unrequested ways, because this could prevent her or him from being perceived as an equal, as it were, as failed before the brand's decision if she or he pertained to the common bond.

---

58 "I'm starting to change my style, my thinking- you end up changing."
59 "Even someone who enters without having much in common with the brand will end up having much in common with the brand. We use to say that you may leave [*Visibly Hot*], but [*Visibly Hot*] won't leave you. That's why there are many people that would like to come back here."

Truly, this condition of (whatsoever) similarity or sameness genealogically pervades the modern Western idea of equality. As Maihofer (2009) argues with historical examples from the thinking of Montesquieu and Lessing to the emergence of the modern discourse on gender difference and of race theory, the heritage of Enlightenment is highly ambivalent. On one hand, its insistence on the universality of human rights allowed it to overcome the old inequality as dictated by feudal division. On the other hand, Enlightenment's simultaneously emerging principle of identity forged the idea of the peaceful coexistence of different religions, ethnic and cultural groups, but with reservation: as the references to this claim of universality go until the present, these different groups are conceded equal rights and the status of equality *despite* their difference to the Western and explicitly male self-conception (Maihofer 2009: 21). In this understanding, equality is embedded not only in a prerogative of interpretation by the dominant forces, but also in the legitimization of possible procedures to exclude certain people from equality. "The idea of equality in itself contains a dialectic structure, letting equality turn into inequality, recognition into social exclusion" (Maihofer 2009: 21).

Such denial of sameness and subsequent social marginalization are contemporarily best known with the case of Muslims in (many) Western countries. In this case, equality discourse often strives to prove their absolute, "qualitative" difference from national populations. Maihofer further illustrates this logic by her interpretation of a fairy tale, namely Umberto Eco's and Eugenio Carmi's *The Three Astronauts* from 1966. The story is about an American, a Russian and a Chinese astronaut who simultaneously arrive at the Mars for an expedition. But as they think that they are all very different, they do not like each other. This only changes when they discover that they have something in common, namely a feeling: they miss their mothers. It is their new and emerging friendship in this sameness that guides her sudden encounter with a Martian. This one has six arms and appears them so much different from their selves they cannot but decide to kill it. "If somebody's ugly, he must be evil" (Maihofer 2009: 33). When all of a sudden a Mars bird falls out of the nest, and the Martian, out of pity, warms it with his six arms, the astronauts however realize another truth: actually, they see that even the Martian is somewhat a similar. They all understand, as the book says, that all beings have their own customs and traditions; what counted was to understand each other. As a summary of her argument about the dialects of the idea of equality we inherited from Enlightenment, Maihofer critically asks why was it that only on the basis of similarity or sameness that a mutual appreciation between these beings could concede them recognition and equal rights? And why, moreover, was it that evident that the Martian was a threatening creature and hence worth killing – only because the astronauts primarily could not find any similarity (Maihofer 2009: 34)?

Returning to our present inquiry we note that the promise of difference within *Visibly Hot* is paradoxically such a search for similarity. What may be rather recent or specific in this case lies thereby in the processes of how the brand spirit animates to create selected new groups of similars that are subsequently recognized by the brand's common sameness, the "family". As we have seen earlier with the mostly negative response on whether *Visibly Hot* was a gay brand, the sameness is precisely not established by putting gay, lesbian or black identities at the center. Rather, it lies in each employee's identification with the brand and her or his abilities to develop a specific attitude at work. As described in detail with the urge for authenticity, the salesclerks at stake are producing sameness and similarity through their individual consent to the (market) ideal of striving for beauty, coolness and, first and foremost, the unconditional disposition of self-perfection.[60] It is only on this basis that they are summoned to give free reign to their singular identity, be it attached to tattoos, alternative style or more specifically to lesbian, gay and black identities. As we have heard in the words of Larissa, it did not matter if one was gay or strange – such a "different" person was conceded equal opportunities *albeit* or even *precisely because* of this difference.

As I will show in what follows, the distinction of these two levels within the present brand's logics, namely the consensus of self-perfection on one hand and the freedom to act on differentiated difference (like the one attached to black skin or homosexual desire) on the other hand, has – like the modern discourse of equality – ambivalent effects. The young people at *Visibly Hot* may surely experience the promise of difference as a positive, and temporarily even as an empowering asset within their biographies. At the same time, these employees are exposed to changing pro-

---

60 Conversely, those who deny or get tired of this ideal, need to expect sanctions and eventually exclusion (see the cases of Pedro and others in chapter five).

cesses of in- and exclusion: since the recognition of the differentiated difference remains conditioned by and dependent on the logic of brand perfection, there is not always official protection of minority rights. In many situations, employees need to individually defend their definitions and styles of incorporating the cool difference against the viewpoints of other employees or consumers. Masculinity, for example, reveals to be a field of high contestation when it comes to employees debating the value of one's feminine traits and homosexuality, while femininity seems to present a rather fixed and consensual trait within the brand's beauty ideals.

3.4.1 Posing in contested differences

For the subsequent look at how a group of employees interacts and negotiates, not without conflicts, attractiveness and cool difference, I propose to leave my data sources from traditional face-to-face interviews for a while. Actually, the operational openness of grounded theory (Thornberg and Charmaz 2013) also led me to use photographs and comments on social network platforms as instruments for both cross-checking information given to me in interviews and shedding light on forms of self-depiction less influenced by the researcher or the research situation. Facebook has proved to be an invaluably rich source of inquiry, especially because it contemporarily represents *the* space where identity management or the management of the self takes place: identities that are consciously being made and controlled with the aim of being accessible (and attestable) to a broader mass (Kneidinger 2010: 50). *Netnography* (Kozinets, Dolbec and Earley 2013) is one of the recent research approaches striving to grasp this type of data.

In social networks like Facebook, people use manifold texts and pictures for describing themselves, that is, for sharing how they would like to be or be seen by others. According to Kozinets, Dolbec and Earley (2013), these self-representations are classic examples of what the authors call archive data[61]. Since they were normally not products of the researcher's involvement, they could be seen as the "cultural baseline" (Kozinets, Dolbec

---

61 The authors differentiate archive data from elicited data and field note data, whose meanings are directly influenced or guided by the researcher (Kozinets, Dolbec and Earley 2013: 267).

and Earley 2013: 267) of a given social phenomenon[62], similar to how social historians use written testimonies as their sources of inquiry. Differently from common research praxis in social sciences, *netnography* also bears an operational advantage because the registration of such archive data is less intrusive than a face-to-face interview or than observation as usually practiced in traditional anthropology. On the other hand, one is confronted with the ethical dilemma that results by the covered, spy-like proceeding of the researcher. Even the fact that networks like Facebook "successfully" animate its users to completely abolish their anonymity (Kozinets, Dolbec et al. 2013: 273), making their self-representations fully public, researchers should be careful with this data. Generally, it is necessary to assess whether the involved informants could suffer any form of consequences if they were recognizable in their offline identities.

In the present case of the *Visibly Hot* salesclerks, I opted for turning their publically shared information (photographs and forum discussions) into a form that prevents them from being traced back to their original authors. While names are given aliases which are different from those I had created for them as interviewee informants above, I tried to tackle the problem of photographic "reality" with the paintbrush-tool-effect. The latter has the advantage that we don't loose the contours and poses of somatic self-depicting, which is important information for both my and the salesclerks' analysis of difference(s) they make in their posted discussion comments. Figure 12 and its corresponding comments illustrate this methodological vantage and equally take us back to the contested character of how difference is performed and (mis)recognized by others.

---

62 I agree with the authors that the only way to prevent the researcher from disorientation – due to the enormous data flow encountered in a *netnography* – is to be guided by a clearly defined research question (Kozinets, Dolbec and Earley 2013: 265).

Figure 12: "A equipe mais irada", The coolest team ever

Source: facebook

1 Alexandre
2 Hygor
3 David
4 Wagner
5 Camila

H = Homem, usuário desconhecido M = Mulher, usuária desconhecida A = **Usuários retratados na imagem**	H = Man, unknown user M = Woman, unknown user A = **User depicted on photograph**
H1 Cadê o alargador na outra orelha? H2 Alexandre, você é estiloso, mas são todos feios, a loira salva legal. **Alexandre** Não quis botar na outra hehehehehehe H1 H1 tá e quem é a loira? **Alexandre** Minha gerentchy... hehe **Alexandre** Hahahaha, os nego amam uma loira, heeeeinnn H2 H2 Loiras amam negões Alexandre. **Hygor** quando era eu [heart] **Alexandre** Já foi o seu tempo, hahahahahaha Hygor H3 Loira 10 memo M1 no estilo escadinha haha **Alexandre** e olha que nem foi proposital hahahahaha aloooookaaaaa M2 camilaaa! M3 linda amiga **Wagner** [LESTE SHOPPING] >>>> ALL **Alexandre** SO OS MANO TRETAAAA **Wagner** HAHAHAHAHA **Wagner** só nego doido **Camilla** Adoro!!!!!!! **Alexandre** Eu me amarro, chama a [Mari], faz quadradinho de 4... hahahahahah hahahahhahahaha H4 tons of alargador **Wagner** Engraçado como o David sempre sai com cara de viado nas fotos **Alexandre** David chupa rola hahahahahahaha **David** Wagner, o menino mais menina da [Visibly Hot] **Camilla** Kkkkk tadinho... **Alexandre** menina de rola... hahahahahahhaha	H1 Where's the stretcher [piercing] in the other ear? H2 Alexandre, you're stylish, but everyone's ugly, the blond's the nice exception. **Alexandre** I didn't want to pierce the other [ear] hehehehehehe H1 H1 OK and who's the blond? **Alexandre** My branch manager...hehe **Alexandre** Hahahaha, the black dudes love a blond one, heeeeinnn H2 H2 Blonds love black dudes, Alexandre **Hygor** when I was me [heart] **Alexandre** Your time has gone, hahahaha Hygor H3 Blond really top score M1 in ladder lace style haha **Alexandre** and it was not even intended as such hahahahaha the craazyyyy M2 camilaaa! M3 handsome friend **Wagner** [LESTE SHOPPING] >>>> ALL **Alexandre** ONLY THE BAD GUYS **Wagner** HAHAHAHA **Wagner** only the crazy gang **Camilla** I love it!!!!! **Alexandre** I adore it, get [Mari] here, do the quadradinho de 4... hahahahahah hahahhahahaha H4 tons of stretcher [piercing] **Wagner** Funny how David always has this faggish face on fotos **Alexandre** David cocksucker hahahahahahaha **David** Wagner, the most girlish boy at [Visibly Hot] **Camilla** Kkkkk poor boy... **Alexandre** ladyboy... Hahahahahahhaha

As the caption reveals, Alexandre intended the photo (Figure 12) to depict his work team that he wants us to know as the "coolest" ever. The picture thus displays himself with his four colleagues, who are all wearing glasses and making a hand signal common, amongst others, within heavy metal music crowds expressing enthusiasm and group identity[63]. Further, several participants hint at their body ornaments like tattoos and piercings, giving a proof, as it were, of their genuine coolness. Especially the ear stretching piercings (*alargador*) are then also the object of the initial comments. While Alexandre gets a compliment for his style by H2, the same commentator states that "however", all depicted men were ugly and the only beautiful person on the photo was the "blond". H1 also critically judges Alexandre because, unlike his colleagues Hygor and Wagner, the picture shows him with only one ear piercing.

Alexandre counters that he did this on purpose, but the first interlocutor H1 rapidly insists on changing the topic. Like the other male commentators H2 and H3, he again expresses his interest for the blond girl depicted in the middle of the group. Alexandre endorses these male commentators' desires, remembering that "os nego" liked blond girls, extended by H2's argument that it was in the blond girls' nature to like blacks. But it is not only by male and racialized desire that Camilla is the center of attention. Female commentators M2 and M3 also affirm her female beauty and her own comment "I adore it" shows that she feels quite comfortable with the ways she has been represented on the photo. Alexandre completes the topic around Camilla's beauty performance, sarcastically alluding to the "quadradinho de 4", a hyper sexualized pose performed by female dancers of Rio's *baile funk* music scene.

Aside from further approval of coolness and authenticity, the conversation between those people actually depicted on the photo also takes up the topic of homosexual desire. Since David is the only of the four boys who defines himself as heterosexual, his colleague Wagner mocks him for always having such a "faggish" face in photographs. Alexandre obviously likes Wagner's teasing, probably considering himself in a position of ma-

---

63 The so called "mano cornuta" (*mão chifrada*) or sign of the horns goes back to ancient Circum-Mediterranean belief of the evil eye and made part of protective manual gestures (Elliott 2011). Mainly through rock music, the same gesture has contemporarily spread in "selfie"-aesthetics as a sign for coolness.

jority. But David, in turn, counters by pointing to Wagner's distinct femininity, which is further confirmed by Camilla's expressed feeling of pity. Strikingly, David's intention to offend Wagner is not challenged, giving the impression that not only the idea of a man looking feminine is finally accepted to be something bad, but also that being gay is something rather undesirable: although Wagner's teasing could be read as a comical way to include the heterosexual other, David cannot help using heterosexist arguments in order to defend his own masculinity.

This brief insight on how the salesclerks intend to depict themselves and how they handle both recognition and critique of their (identity) aspirations sheds a more conflicting light on the brand's diversity rhetoric. While the employees had emphasized only the positive aspects of "being different" in the interview narratives, the Facebook conversation above reveals that the topic of difference is much more complex. Naturally, the difference created by using tattoos and piercings is a softer one, because it easily fits in an image of youth and youthfulness capable of winning a majority[64]. Now other differences, although also often defined in terms of style, appear to be stickier regarding their normative content: being black, being gay as well as the supposedly right way to show masculinity are at the crossroads between oppression and emancipation. As the digital commentary board above reveals, one's denial to pertain to beauty or to hegemonic masculinity is repeatedly faced by dislocating the attention to unchallenged ideals. As both men and women in the extract express, the closest consensus is in the (sexual) attraction of the young blond woman. It is once again the entanglement with retail marketability that make individual investments and defenses of identity aspirations rather spontaneously reenact rather than undo heteronormativity and whiteness.

3.4.2 Sexy white girl

The arrangement of the photo above (Figure 12) is already suggestive of the person who is at the center of desires. With her long blond hair and her white legs exposed, Camilla turns Alexandre's project of the team's au-

---

64 As it is the case for many Western societies, tattoos have lost their somewhat "underground" stance and turned into a fashion statement, embracing "young people at almost all levels of society" (Kornblum 2012: 186).

thentic self-staging simultaneously into an image that could easily be confounded with the intentions common to fashion ads. As shown by Beleli (2007) and as I argued in chapter two, contemporary Brazilian advertisement has a main objective: seduction. This erotic charging continues to be mobilized by depicting especially young women's bodies, as well as by addressing male desire. For women, the identification demanded by such advertisements easily slips into what Beleli calls an aesthetic dictatorship (Beleli 2007: 202): it presents feminine bodies most women hardly conform to. In turn, those who represent the "narcissist femininities" in fashion propaganda can count on broad recognition of a specific and promising cultural capital. As they can give proof of their beauty, they count as real women. In the semantics of globally circulating advertisement, Beleli concludes her argument, this demand was heightened to a degree that femininity commonly turned into a synonym of seduction (Beleli 2007: 203).

However, both the norms and the centrality of the feminine body in contemporary advertisement may not be as stable and unquestioned as Beleli wants us to believe. While I pointed to the tactics of the heterosexist gaze in *Visibly Hot*'s early advertisement (chapter 2.2), it became equally clear that more recent marketing is pluralizing the beauty offers and new groups are hailed into the aesthetic marketability of the self. The self-depiction of the enterprise's employees in Figure 12 echoes this trend. Even if H2's comment is in favor of the blond femininity, his depreciative judgment about the depicted men also reveals his implicit demand that males should care for their beauty, too[65]. Moreover, the representation of the sexy white girl I used in interview settings (Figure 8) proved to provoke different reactions. The salesclerks' opinions on whether the depicted woman was able to work for the company or not turned out contradictory. On the one hand, the explicitly erotic advertisement was generally assessed as representing the brand's spirit, that is, the brand's sexually connoted daring (*ousadia*). Although all salesclerks emphasized the coolness of the girl's sexiness, something that generally provoked a malicious grin by both young men and women, some of them were in doubt about her ability to work for the company. They thought that her wide neckline and

---

65 For an exploratory study on the growing beauty consumption amongst men and the mutual effects for masculinity in Brazil see Fontes, Borelli and Casotti (2012).

her heavy make-up were a bit too daring or "slutty". Others, in turn, saw exactly this moral provocation as marking the critical, positive difference between *Visibly Hot* and other brands.

Branch manager Andrea, for example, goes into rhapsodies about the femininity projected in Figure 8. She immediately links the model's beauty to her own person, a comparison that several of her sales team members also made. Her enthusiasm for representing the girl's sexiness coincides with her admiration of the brand, that is, of the conventions and the individual opportunities given to her as an employee. To the picture, she reacts thus with a decided self-identification.

"Olha, vou falar por mim, eu sou bem perua, eu sou bem assim mesmo. Então, trabalharia mesmo [sorriso]. Você duvida, com aquele salto, com este vestido, roupinha, short? Se você entrar no meu Facebook, você vai ver, eu sou assim. Eu me identifico até com essa mulher sexy. Não me acho feia, me acho bonitinha, ela é bonita, né? Trabalharia, sim, ela trabalha, né?"[66] (Andrea, 22, branch manager at *Visibly Hot*)

Andrea spontaneously invites me to visit her Facebook profile. There, she suggests, I would get the proof of her authentic femininity and sexiness. She really liked the photograph because she sees herself in it, and as she specifies, it is about the character of the flashy woman (*perua*). Consequently, she also concludes that the photo model could undoubtedly work as a saleswoman at *Visibly Hot*.

According to her own explications, Andrea's identification refers to her aspiration of being both a "beautiful woman" and a "sexy woman". If we look at that affirmation from a broader perspective, the model in figure 8 is apparently transmitting hegemonic beauty ideals of regional, national or even global significance. One of the inherent aspects, although hardly named, is that the contours of this body are thoroughly white. Suzana Ma-

---

66 "Look, I will speak for myself, I am quite the flashy girl, I am really like this. So, she could work here [smiling]. Do you doubt it, with these high heels, with that dress, outfit, shorts? If you enter my Facebook profile, you will see, I am like this. I identify with this sexy woman. I don't think I'm ugly, I think I'm cute, she is beautiful, isn't she? She could work here, yes, she works here, doesn't she?"

ia (2012) has inspiringly traced back this discursive formation of unnamed whiteness on an international level by analyzing the case of the global top model Gisele Bündchen. The latter's body, Maia argues, experienced an overlay of stereotypes about what it signifies to be a Brazilian woman, mobilized by both national and Western/US-American cultural industry. Bündchen is dark blond, has blue eyes, white skin and comes from Rio Grande do Sul. While American media tends to stage her as exotically different, as having the spicy something that legitimizes her ascent to the throne of global beauty, Brazilian media praises her as a new national model, as it were, representing the beauty of Brazilian women. A brief look at Maia's analysis might explain better why the author diagnoses a considerable transformation of racial discourse inherent in these stereotypes that are complementing one another.

In the Brazilian context, Bündchen's biographical background in Southern state Rio Grande do Sul is of importance. As also her family name suggests, the model is a descendant of German immigrants who had major cultural influence in that region. Maia (2012) is thus curious to understand how and why Bündchen – as a tall white woman –could turn into a national icon, in a context where a long lasting discourse of racial mixture (*miscigenação*) was hegemonic to official state and nationalist ideology[67]. To put it in other words, how could she replace the *mulata*[68] as one of Brazil's most important brands? For Maia, Bündchen's success is a proof of the fact that "whiteness, invariably associated to social, economic and political privilege, is still presented as a transparent norm" (Maia 2012: 314). Actually, the author interprets this phenomenon as being due to political transformations of the past decade. Only a reawakened "white consciousness", the conservative elite's response to the strengthening of black

---

67 As I commented earlier, this ideology has been adapted by the state in the 1930s and was, at times, of high political importance because it abandoned scientifically based theories of racial degradation and their projects of "whitening" the population (Costa 2007). Today, however, ongoing polemics around racial quota since the early 1990s show that the myth of "racial democracy" (*democracia racial*) serves rather to veil and depoliticize racism, newly naturalizing white privilege.

68 To the historical rise and contradictory figure of the *mulata* in Brazilian national narratives, see Corrêa (1996).

movements and affirmative actions in the recent past would have helped to put Bündchen into that position (Maia 2012: 319).

In US American media discourse, however, Gisele has a somewhat different fame. After the Rolling Stone magazine had discovered Bündchen's sex appeal in 1999, she gained a sort of bi-racial identity: on the one hand, she is subjected to erotic exotization (belonging to "the Amazons"), a racial attribution that makes her non-white because of her Latin American descent. On the other hand, US media tend to emphasize her natural health, tracing a contrast to common stereotypes about dirt and poorness within third world discourse. "Gisele is at the same time looked at as typical and as the exception" (Maia 2012: 320): at the same time as she serves as a global example of diversity discourse in which she is valued in her difference because of her Latin American sensuality, she equally passes in white looks because she seems so surprisingly white (even if the category white as such remains unnamed). Maia also finds this complexity of being white as a non-white or being non-white as a white within the commentary of a fashion marketer. The specialty of Brazilian female beauties, the latter holds, was due to their Nation's "melting pot", enabling them to have "globalized faces", but with "fewer traces of ethnic stereotypes" (Maia 2012: 319).

3.4.3 Black beauty and identity

The transnational discourse about Gisele Bündchen remembers not only the modern idea of equality, according to which recognition of others is conceded by sameness and similarity. Moreover, it shows that – within beauty market – race is being designed as a crucial cultural capital. While media and marketers may sometimes accentuate the exotic affectivity of non-white models, they equally reiterate white looks and norms: as the example above suggests, only those Brazilian models whose traces are of few "ethnic stereotypes" have the power to turn into real global stars. In other words, if their bodies are still decipherable as white or quasi-white – which is the opposite of having "traces of ethnic stereotypes" – their career will be saved from many obstacles[69]. Following the logics of cultural capi-

---

69 This finding is also consistent with the illuminating argument of Deliovsky (2008), who underlines that women's hair and other physical markers as accen-

tal, race can thus be pragmatically enacted. As Andrea's enthusiastic identification with the sexy white girl proved, her beauty performance helps to increase her professional success and equally to be desired and recognized by broader social circles. The question then remains: what happens to those salesclerks who are, to use Butler's words (Butler 1993: xi), not intelligible as white bodies? How do they relate to race within the logics of cultural capital? And, again, by which ways do they identify with *Visibly Hot*'s diversity discourse?

The diversification of beauty ideals, resonating in the brand's promise of "being different", does not necessarily mean that the newly valorized appearances are making available social places on strictly equal terms. Foremost, this diversification stands for the fact that more people are given the chance to prove their individual style. Considering the above outlined dominance of whiteness, it is almost self-evident that people have very unequal resources at their disposal: while for some, generally whites, the proof of their beauty is but a question of putting on some fancy clothes, for others, in turn, there is much more effort involved in getting themselves into a recognized position. Machado-Borges (2009) has addressed this power relation with an empirical study about lower social class beauty parlors in Minas Gerais. To her interlocutors, manly black women that highly frequent or work at these parlors, beauty praxis is a question of vanity. Their considerable investments of time and money, the anthropologist argues, reflect their tiring efforts to be seen, something that is often denied to them in the every day and that is culturally equated as "being someone" (Machado-Borges 2009: 208). Consequently, the consumption of beauty and personal hygiene products would take on the role of every day life struggles: bodywork, allowing both to "stress and/or erase social difference" (Machado-Borges 2009: 209).

---

tuated for the sake of globally circulating beauty capital "represent a powerful political aesthetic that belies the salience of race for gender normativity" (Deliovsky 2008: 50). Whiteness and white femininity, she holds, are reproduced through the very "compulsion to adopt styles and attitudes consistent with an imposed white feminine aesthetic"; white femininity was paradoxically normative because "it is not seen as white per se but rather as just femininity" (Deliovsky 2008: 54).

The women described by Machado-Borges may certainly be scratching on the surface of structural social and racial inequalities. However, their beauty performances should also not be reduced to mere embodiments of resistance against white supremacy. At the same time, those women express compliance with the meritocratic logics of the body as a social capital. In my inquiry about the role style had for the salesclerks, I encountered a similar, complex relation the latter maintained with race and the body. Leidiane, who equally mentioned the importance of vanity, underwent a process at *Visibly Hot*, which led her to recognize both her own black beauty and the application of style as a way to work on her professional attitude.

"Bom, eu pretendo muito mudar o meu [estilo]. Tipo- particularmente o meu, mais para chamar atenção mesmo, para aparecer. Porque cliente adora essas coisas. 'Gente, amei esse cabelo!'- e tal. Tipo, eu mesma não ligo para essas coisas, mas é bom também parecer maneira, sabe. Uma coisa mais vaidosa, higiênica. E aí, eu tô tentando adaptar isso para mim. Toda semana, estou aqui com uma fantasia diferente, chique. Tipo eu, por exemplo, sempre me julguei- tipo, dei uns toque no meu visu pelo fato de eu ser negra. Aí, eu não vou usar louro, tá maluco! Só que esses dias veio uma cliente, grande demais, loura, negra, mais preta que eu- é Angolana. Aí eu, duvido, eu não posso. Mas quinta-feira, eu tô loura, sabe, ah! É isso que eu quero para mim, sabe, atitude. Ah, chega de padrão!"[70] (Leidiane, 24, salesclerk at *Visibly Hot*)

---

70 "Well, I heavily intend to change my [style]. Like- particularly my own one, it's more about calling attention, to pose. Because, customers like these things. 'Man, I loved this hair!'- and so on. Like, myself I don't care for such things, but it's good to appear cool, you know. Something more vain, hygienic. So, I'm trying to adapt that for me. Every week, I'm here with a different, fancy disguise. Like me, for example, I always judged myself- like, I care for my appearance because of the fact that I'm black. So, I wouldn't wear blond, too crazy! But these days, there was this customer, way too tall, blond, black, blacker than me- she's Angolan. So I said, no way, I can't. But Thursday, I'm blond, you know, ah! That's what I want for me, you know, attitude. Ah, enough of that mainstream stuff!"

Leidiane observes a change of how she relates to style today. In the past, she says, she did not really care about "these things", but since the customers she serves at work would love a salesperson's stylish outfit, she also came to appreciate the importance of appearance. Particularly her hair turns out to be the medium Leidiane stresses as positively valued difference. On the day of our interview, she had "African braids" (*tranças afro*), a hairstyle she repeatedly got compliments for. In addition, several customers approached her saying that she was "stylish" and sometimes inviting her to date them.

Along with the brand's incentive for having a cool and fancy appearance, these individual experiences of being seen as a beautiful young woman provoked a shift in her former perception of black skin. As she insinuates a few times during our conversation, the feeling of seeing herself as someone with style and beauty is fairly new to her. In both social circles around her home and previous occasional jobs, being black seemed to her to be an obstacle to beauty, something she would have to style against. But, abstracting her own words above, she felt very restricted in terms of her styling options. As Leidiane makes clear with the example of the Angolan customer, the job for *Visibly Hot* made her rethink her properly imposed aesthetic norms. While using blond coloring was a sort of no-go criteria in the past ("too crazy!"), she came to like that kind of playful styling, to an extent that led her to perform a "different disguise" (*fantasia diferente*) from one week to another. Such "crazy" combinations, like a black woman wearing blond hair, are what defines Leidiane's notion of "being different" and equally denominates her aspiration for a specific professional attitude at work.

On one hand, this example shows that the promise of "being different" in racial terms can give rise to one's self-confidence. Leidiane effectively experiences the valuation of her black skin as something that grants her economic success in both the material and the affective aspects. On the other hand, the same example points to the fact that in order to get this kind of recognition, one needs to overemphasize, stylize, invest in attributes of racial difference – as it is primarily the case with "afro" hair. In other words, it would not be enough for Leidiane to merely have black skin. Differently from white salesclerks, she has to prove a much higher ability to change and perform her black race in hyper-stylish ways. Remembering Machado-Borge's theses on the beauty parlors, failing to do so could mean to be unseen by others. It is this fear that echoes in Leidiane's statement that she had to learn that a cool appearance had to do with hygiene and vanity. In summation, it is only a very specific – stylized – form of being black (or performing black skin) that matches the norm of *Visibly Hot*'s "being different".

While the stylization of blackness is a unisex requirement for black salesclerks, young men are confronted with other cultural and political stereotypes than women. It is less their invisibility that they need to struggle against. Rather, they are confronted with national mass media's discourse that associates them with crime and death in the urban peripheries. As Pinho and Rocha (2011) show, black rap musicians (MCs) in Bahia are directly challenging these stereotypes in that they question the national discourse of "alegria, mistura e cordialidade"[71] in their texts. Raposo (2013) further points to the empowering effects young men (although not only, but in majority of black skin) from the Maré district in Rio de Janeiro find in breakdance. In a society, the author writes, that strives to condemn them to a subaltern status due to structural violence they suffer by both police and drug trafficking, their "desire to be someone materializes in dance" (Raposo 2013: 53). In many cases, this opens them new scopes of action and self-esteem.

"A prática desta dança proporcionou a alguns deles um conjunto de capitais culturais e simbólicos baseados na solidariedade mútua, no respeito e na amizade geradoras de uma autodisciplina que os faz ter outra 'atitude' perante a vida. Os seus discursos realçam a necessidade de ser um B-boy (dançarino de break dance) não apenas quando dançam, mas também no trabalho, na escola ou na família."[72] (Raposo 2013: 36)

---

71 "happiness, mixture and cordiality"
72 "The practice of this dance bestows a set of cultural and symbolic capitals on some of them, which are based on mutual solidarity, respect and friendship. Again, this puts forward a self-discipline that confers another 'attitude' towards life. Their discourses highlight the need of being a B-boy (break dancer), not only when they dance, but also at work, at school or with their families."

The performances and identification as B-boys, as Raposo argues, lend the young men a positively loaded identity. Moreover, this identity transcends the sphere of dance for it unfolds cultural capital and access to new spaces.

Although not into breakdance, salesclerk Pedro aligns the brand's understanding of difference with his biographical search for black identity in a similar direction. As he enthusiastically tells me in our conversations, he was reading books by black Brazilian feminists who had travelled to the US and who compared the local racial regimes to those in Brazil. The positive valuation and accentuation of black identity is important to him because it bestows upon him higher degrees of self-esteem and identification with the self-optimizing logics of the brand. Pedro thus agrees with the feminist author's conclusion that black people in Brazil were not seeing their race and that they needed, respectively, to raise their consciousness. Style is what he puts at the center of this process, ranging from his interest in Afro-brazilian religion to black music on a global level. He reacts thus with ardor to the photograph on Figure 9: "Têm cara de gringas. Maneiro, Maneiraças! Bem Brooklyn, negona!"[73] Finally, Pedro sees desire as something attached to race. Referring to my European origin, he insistently points to his opinion that white Europeans (in his perspective different to Brazilians) loved black girls or boys.

3.4.4 The gay theme

Both stylized black identity and white "sexy" femininity are some of the cornerstones of what *Visibly Hot* is mobilizing as representing the brand's difference. This understanding of difference, however, only crystallizes through the individual investments of the salesclerks: their styles. Being at the same time the proof of one's individual authenticity, having style might even be said to be the central requirement for the worker's identity. Now there is this persistent common sense discourse in Western societies, saying that especially gay people would have a talent for fashion taste, style and arts, leading them to work in areas where related skills are valued. Frequently, gay men "are thought to be disproportionately represented among the arts (especially dance), fashion careers (hairdressing and design), and decorating (interior decorating and florists)" (Bailey and Ober-

---

73 "They look like *gringas*. Cool, fucking cool! Quite Brooklyn style, *negona*."

schneider 1997: 433). Apparently, these stereotypes are also activated through *Visibly Hot*. As I mentioned earlier, there is a high number of young salesclerks who do not define themselves as heterosexual, contributing to a strong visibility of gay and lesbian people publicly associated with the brand[74]. When I explicitly directed the questions to my informants, whether *Visibly Hot* had a specific link to sexuality and whether the company was eventually a gay brand, several of them started again – although in varying meanings – talking about style.

"Eu acho que- relação com sexualidade, talvez sim. Agora, em qual ponto eles querem chegar, eu não sei. Mas eu acho que tem, sim. Tem uns 80%, 70%, assim. Até porque, muitos pontos de venda, vejo muitos gays, muitas lésbicas, assim. E, tem- não fui em muitos pontos, mas têm, assim, pacatos. E tem, lá em Copacabana- que gente linda naquele lugar! E é pimenta, sabe, caraca- é pimenta. Muito demais, toda vez com um estilo diferente. Tipo, diferente do padrão, assim, sabe. E a forma como eles falam, sabe, ay, é outra coisa!"[75](Leidiane, 24, salesclerk at *Visibly Hot*)

Leidiane, who has worked only a couple of months at *Visibly Hot*, is still ravished by the brand's style. While during our interview she relates that working together with so many lesbian and gay people was very new and somewhat strange to her, she equally expresses a sort of admiration for

---

74 When Marco Feliciano, evangelical pastor and federal deputy, was elected president of the Commission for Human Rights and Minorities in March 2013, several social movements and civil rights organizations began to engage against his openly homophobic and racist speeches. As he even intended to incorporate psychological treatment for homo- and transsexuals, phrases like "Feliciano, who is gonna work at [*Visibly Hot*] after your treatments?" rapidly spread in social media.

75 "I think that- related to sexuality, maybe yes. Now, where they want to get to by this, I don't know. But I think there is [a link], yes. There are about 80%, 70%, like that. Because at many sales points, I see a lot of gays, a lot of lesbians, you know. And there are- I haven't been to all the sales points, you know, but there are also boring ones. And there are, in Copacabana- very beautiful people in that place! And it's spicy, you know, holy cow!- it's spicy. It's incredible, every time with a different style. Like, different from mainstream, you know. And the way they're talking, you know, ah, it's something very special."

them. Although consciously rejecting the stereotype of all queers being flashy ("there are also boring sales points"), Leidiane is moved by several lesbian and gay salesclerks' different style and amazing beauty. In her perspective, "they" incorporate the emblematic stance of transgressing mainstream culture ("diferente do padrão"), something also present in their ways of talking. However, Leidiane would not go as far as wanting to adopt this difference for herself. In describing one of her teammate's transformations of style at work, she outlines her personal limits of identification.

"Por exemplo, tem a menina ali [apontando para Larissa, a uma distância de 20m da nossa posição], que é vendedora. Conheci ela quando eu entrei na [*Visibly Hot*], sabe. Só que eu não conversei com ela, sabe. Aí, ela era uma pessoa super calma, boa vendedora, mas nunca- mas quando eu desci [para este ponto de venda], gente, ela- eu acho ela um travesti. É uma papagaiagem de maquiagem- e ela conhece um público grande de gays. E vira uma gestão aqui, sabe, fazendo aquela cena, ai, sabe. Tipo, vontade de ficar no meio desse pessoal gay. Eu fico super com vontade. Não tenho esse tipo de preconceito, não. Mas as conversas deles, o patamar de pessoas, é muuito diferente. Nunca conheci tantas pessoas tão diferentes em um só lugar, sabe. A [*Visibly Hot*] proporciona isso."[76] (Leidiane, 24, salesclerk at *Visibly Hot*)

According to Leidiane, there are diverse levels of how to deal with style and identity attached to sexual orientation and/or gender. While some cases are worth her admiration because of cool style, in others she just sees a desperate attempt of belonging. Specifically colleague Larissa serves as

---

76 "For example, there is this girl over there [pointing to Larissa, in a distance of 20m to our position], she's a salesclerk. I met her when I came to [*Visibly Hot*], you know. But I didn't talk with her, you know. Well, she was a very calm person, a good vendor, but never- but when I came [to this sales point] here, oh my god, she- I think she's a transvestite. It's an acute clown-like [*papagaiagem*] make-up- and she knows a lot of gay people. And it turns into a marketing here, you know, like making a scene, ah, you know. Like, she wants to be in the middle of these gay people. I'm very keen on this. I'm not prejudiced in this way, no. But their conversations, the sort of people, it's veeery different. I've never met so many people that different in one and the same place, you know. [*Visibly Hot*] renders this possible."

her example of someone who would exaggerate in styling (catchword *papagaiagem*) in order to take part in gay social circles. Leidiane's description depicts Larissa as performing bad taste travesty. Although she defends her own sympathy and anti-homophobic stance, Leidiane makes it clear that she feels a personal distance to this "kind" (*patamar*) of people and their sort of conversations.

The overlap of admiration and distancing reflects, as I argue, the ambiguity inherent in contemporary discourse about deviance from heteronormative behavior. Strikingly, many non-heterosexuals at *Visibly Hot* also tend to affectively attach themselves to the idea of being both hyper stylish and potentially threatening, deviant, or distastefully different. And they perceive the brand as a space where they could express or playfully arrange these attributes through style. Salesclerk Carol liked *Visibly Hot* from the first moment she met with people working for the company. Still an adolescent at times, she got excited, as she says, by that "alternative crowd", something she highly identified with and she perceived as the guarantee of her being accepted as a young lesbian. Carol systematically emphasized this aspiration, imprinting the brand's symbol on her forearm.

"Eu amo [*Visibly Hot*], é uma paixão mesmo. Tenho até isso aqui [mostra tatuagem no braço], [*Visibly Hot*] na veia! [...] Eu posso sair da empresa, mas não vou me arrepender disso. Eu amo a marca mesmo, é a minha cara [sorriso]."[77] (Carol, salesclerk at *Visibly Hot*)

Carol's overemphasis of her affectively loaded identification with the company is emblematic because she literally brands her related aspirations into her flesh. If, according to her declarative statement, she *is* just like the brand, she will consequently provoke – through her mere presence as a salesclerk – a co-engineering of what the brand so emphatically communicates to embrace the "being different": that the brand is to be seen also in her individual terms of both an alternative and a lesbian identity.

In spite of this empowering aspect, I don't focus to overestimate Carol's or other salesclerks' agency with regard to struggles against heter-

---

77 "I love [*Visibly Hot*], it's really a passion. I even have this here [showing her tattoo on her forearm], [*Visibly Hot*] in my veins. [...] Even if I leave the company, I won't regret this, because I love the brand, it is just like me."

onormativity. As will be discussed later in chapter five, time, precarious working conditions and the normative regulations of *Visibly Hot*'s diversity discourse are setting limits too strongly as to affirm a queer liberation movement. Rather, I want to draw attention here to how, in the present context of Brazilian cultural industry, the category "alternative" is enmeshed in processes of both challenging and normalizing meaning of lesbian and gay lifestyles. While Carol seems to use the label alternative as a vehicle or resource for articulating a lesbian identity, other queer salesclerks bemoan the same, local stereotype that equates alternative style with being gay or lesbian. For the latter position, such as the one held by Antônio, this stereotype supports heteronormative prejudice. In this way, Antônio is very careful about agreeing with the supposition that *Visibly Hot* could be seen as a "gay brand".

"Eu nem diria não nem sim. É que hoje tem gay em todo lugar. Então, os gays gostam de todas as marcas. Eu acho que não é uma marca só de gays. Eu acho que, antigamente, era uma marca mais alternativa. Então, associavam o alternativo ao gay, por ser diferente. Mas eu acho que [hoje] não, eu tenho amigos héteros que adoram a marca, que se identificam bastante, que usam roupas mais extravagantes que as minhas e são héteros. Nunca tive essa restrição alternativo-gay. Por mais de ser de São Paulo, lá não tem essa associação. O pessoal é mais livre já. Eu acho. Aqui no Rio, tem muita gente reprimida."[78] (Antônio, 22, salesclerk at *Visibly Hot*)

For Antônio, associating alternative style to gay identity is something of the past. According to his explanation, *Visibly Hot* is commonly thought of as a gay brand because it was formerly "more alternative". But today, since there were gays "everywhere", this stereotype was no longer mean-

---

78 "I wouldn't say either no or yes. Because today, gays are everywhere. So, gays like all brands. I don't' think that it's only a brand for gays. I think that, in the past, it was a more alternative brand. Consequently, they associated the alternative to gay, because it's different. But I think that [today], no, I have heterosexual friends who adore the brand, who highly identify with it, who wear fancier clothes than me and they are heterosexuals. I never had this alternative-gay restriction. Even more because I am from São Paulo, where this association doesn't exist. People are already freer there. I think so. Here in Rio, there are many repressed people."

ingful. *Visibly Hot*, in this sense, had already turned into mainstream. Antônio makes this assertion also to deconstruct the idea that there was a natural link between being gay and having style. His heterosexual friends, he stresses, would have more style than him. Finally, he thinks that this is a current liberating process, which happened already in São Paulo, but was still to come in Rio.

Unlike Carol, Antônio defends that being alternative as well as being gay has already become (or at least should be part of the) normal. Overemphasizing difference in terms of sexual orientation is thus not everyone's aspiration. However, both positions seem to go together with the all-embracing diversity discourse. The latter, I argue, constantly mobilizes "being different" as a messy category: especially when it comes to stereotypes attached to sexual orientation, both progressive and reactive attributions are salient. Some salesclerks also heavily argued against the provocation of *Visibly Hot* representing a "gay brand". "Homossexuais não fazem esporte"[79], Eloisa explained by pointing to the company's product assortment, which included glasses with sporty style. Mariana, in turn, even understood the provocation as a form of prejudice against the brand:

"Ah, tem muito esse preconceito. Se for por esse lado, todo mundo tem. Só que eles jogam para nosso lado. Gays, lésbicas, pessoas que usam drogas- só que na prática, não é nada disso. É totalmente diferente."[80] (Mariana, 23, salesclerk at *Visibly Hot*)

While such highly caricatured stereotypes are rather rare in the salesclerk's views, everyone defends the principles of *Visibly Hot*'s benevolent inclusionary politics. In other fashion stores in shopping centers, they say, gays and blacks were not welcomed. But at *Visibly Hot*, everyone who had enough "competence" and "interest" would be given a chance.

"Por exemplo, se vier uma pessoa mega afeminada aqui, com cabelo como homem mas perfil completamente feminino, se ele se mostrar competente, se mostrar

---

79 "Homosexuals don't play sports"
80 "Ah, this is a common prejudice. If it were like that, everyone would have it. But they say it's us. Gays, lesbians, people who take drugs- but in reality, it's completely wrong. It's totally different."

interessado, ele vai ter uma oportunidade aqui. Coisa que outras lojas não dariam."[81] (Diogo, 23, salesclerk at *Visibly Hot*)

"Being different" seems to be a rather messy category when it comes to sexual orientation. It entails, as we have seen, associations that range, on one hand, from benevolent admiration to old-fashioned stereotypes and meritocratic strategies regarding gays and lesbians. On the other hand, lesbians' and gays' self-perception vary from enthusiastic identification with to distancing from alternative style as representing queer lifestyles.

In spite of these antagonistic projections, there is a consensus that *Visibly Hot* makes a difference: both hetero- and non-heterosexual salesclerks agree that the brand would have a somewhat transformative power. This power is associated with combating exclusion of gays and lesbians in the service sector, with enhancing the value of queer identities to icons of style or with normalizing, heteronormative[82] effects for non-heterosexuals. What is more, this power is intrinsically attached to the idea of individual performance. As Diogo makes clear, even "extremely feminine" men could get a chance at *Visibly Hot*, as long as they proved professional competence and interest in the brand. Actually, the salesclerk's perception of identity based on sexual orientation follows the logics of diversity management and market inclusion. Through self-perfection, it goes, everyone can improve her/his queer bias, can finally become cool and take part in the family of "being different".

---

81 "For example, if someone extremely feminine comes here, with hair like a man, but with a completely feminine profile, if he's showing his competence, if he's showing his interest, he will have an opportunity here. Something other brands wouldn't do."

82 This tendency can be drawn from Antônio's example above. In his aspiration, gays should no longer be stereotyped as alternative, because this would contribute to repressing gay people. This idea is also quite common in contemporary cultural industry. As different studies about the representation of lesbians and gays in Brazilian telenovelas argue (Colling 2007; Beleli 2009), the intensified visibility of queer characters is often subjected to heteronormative plots such as monogamous relationships, "an image more easy to digest for the general public" (Beleli 2009: 117).

4. Affective labor

The present chapter aims at bringing together the insights of chapters two and three, though with a change in perspective. I will understand salesclerks' individual and joint efforts towards "being different" as a crucial part of their daily labor. Most professionals at *Visibly Hot* are convinced that a salesclerk has to establish an intimate bond with the brand and its products if she/he wants to be successful. This is also why the sales force is made to participate in monthly training sessions, where they are instructed on how to develop their individual commercial skills. On one hand, these skills playfully include the processes of identification as discussed in the precedent chapter: fancy style and sex appeal are what make salesclerks attractive and hence enhance sales opportunities. On the other hand, workers are learning about a broad range of sales tricks that could help them come to terms with the rapid interactions with customers at the sales points. My general argument contends that these two aspects of sales skills pertain to affective labor. Processes such as learning to love the brand, to treat the customers as if they were friends, or to sexually affect the potential clients not only displace the private and the public, but also deeply somatize entrepreneurial messages through feeling and hence alter the workers' ways of feeling, thinking and acting in a range of social situations.

I start my argumentation with a review on Hochschild's incisive notion of emotional work (Hochschild 2003). While emphasizing the conciseness of this notion with respect to describing the ways employees are being trained to align their feelings with the goals of a given enterprise, I critically question the author's analytical distinction of true and artificial feelings as being synonymous to the leisure-work divide. By analyzing the case of

Visibly Hot salesclerks' aspirations for authenticity through the lens of queer, feminist and affect theorists, I argue that feeling at work is (coercively) producing and re-arranging real, not artificial, social places and identities. A dialogue with both the notion of sexual labor (Lorenz and Kuster 2007) and the (post)Marxist notion of affective labor (Hardt 1999) will thus address the general shortcomings in studies about commercial service work. As McDowell noted about the state of art:

"If sociologists of sexuality and the body forgot, or at best under-emphasized, the social relations of employment, then theorists of work and employment tended to forget the laboring body and its sexual desires and fantasies." (McDowell 2009: 12)

In commercial service work, the desiring body is aligned to business goals to an extent that it turns both into a resource of work and – rather unanticipated – into a means to disturb a strictly profit-oriented work ethic. Publicly famous for their "aggressive" attendance, *Visibly Hot* salesclerks mobilize spontaneous flirts or lead customers into feelings of intimacy. Not infrequently, these affectively charged bonds result in private meetings or relationships of customers with salesclerks in leisure time. At the same time, affective labor bears misadventurous dangers, for the provocative attendance repeatedly triggers bad sentiment between already allied couples, and is thus counterproductive to sales. It is as if capitalist engineering of consumer behavior does not only activate good feeling, but also gets imminently involved in the uneasy, sometimes bad feeling mechanisms of gendered hierarchies and narcissism.

The final section of the chapter discusses another ambiguity of the affective labor in question: its cultural traits of friendship and affectivity. As already central in the work of classics like Sérgio Buarque de Holanda (2014), Brazilian's "cordiality", oriented towards friendships and emotionally proximate behavior, is often associated as being natural to Brazilians or to Brazilian culture. "Provincializing" (Chakrabarty 2002) this knowledge by recent studies on both sex and domestic work (Piscitelli 2007; Vidal 2007), it turns out that affective labor is culturally enmeshed with power and domination. Strikingly, these relations at *Visibly Hot* are mediated through the workers' allusion to the ideal of the sales team as representing a family. As the employees seek social recognition in this collectivity, their sales-driven rivalries are being naturalized as an allegedly "healthy" and harmonious part of their affective labor.

4.1 EMOTIONAL WORK, AUTHENTICITY, AND AFFECTS

Arlie Hochschild's approach of emotional work (Hochschild 2003) has made history within the social sciences. Elaborated in 1983 as pioneering in the field of the sociology of work, the notion has proved to be highly topical. Up to the present day, no less than 10,000 publications run under the title of emotional work. As Hochschild recently concedes (2013), this success may stem less from emotional work's theoretical conciseness and probably more from the social change within the last three decades, namely the massive extension of the service industry and its respective workforce. In the USA alone, 25% of the gross domestic product is due to this sector. In Brazil, the service industry has gone through an even higher expansion, so that it represents more than 60% of the present-day GDP (Ministério do Desenvolvimento 2014). While Hochschild's precursory study focused the emotional work of flight attendants and tax collectors, sociological studies are now covering a broad range of occupations. Most worth mentioning may be the debates on care work (Arango and Molinier 2011; Hirata and Guimarães 2012), domestic work (Brites 2007; Gutiérrez Rodríguez 2010), commercial services like telemarketing (Braga 2012; Sproll 2013) or supermarket cashiers (Soares 2000), but also the studies on hairdressers and beauty salon workers (Arango 2013) or on public officials such as post office clerks (Sauer and Penz 2014).

Above all, the notion of emotional work enjoys great popularity not only in sociology, but also in other areas of knowledge. Foremost psychology, organizational studies and management see in it a new concept in order to tackle workers' emotional troubles. According to Hochschild's classic argument, the professional valorization of human feeling would bring about a process of alienation to the workers. These could no longer access their true feelings, which in turn caused them psychological problems. As one of Hochschild's interviewed flight attendants put it: "Sometimes I come off a long trip in a state of utter exhaustion, but I find I can't relax. I giggle a lot, I chatter, I call friends. It's as if I can't release myself from an artificially created elation that kept me 'up' on the trip" (Hochschild 2003: 4). The sociologist based her notion, amongst others, on the Russian theater theoretic Stanislavski and his problematic distinction of surface acting versus deep acting. According to Hochschild, emotional work is only a problem (of exploration, alienation and hence psychic burden), when artificially induced feeling threatens to blur the borders of the self. To be more precise: when the flight attendant's smiles become too much of a reality, to such an extent that – as in a theater play – one can no longer draw a line between the performing and the performed.

But where do "real" emotions begin and where do they end? Who may define what feelings are genuine and what feelings are artificial? Hochschild gives clear responses to these questions throughout her book. She sees the "true" feelings as pertaining to the private realm, that is, the flight attendants' emotional life in leisure time. According to the training sessions of Delta Airlines, these emotions need to be suppressed when boarding the airplane and serving customers. The all-encompassing rule states: keep smiling and perform a slightly sexy and serviceable young woman. And in fact, there is evidence that such kinds of emotional training of workers, as a form of (self)disciplining power, have spread in several institutional and entrepreneurial sectors. As Penz and Sauer (2014) show with the example of the Austrian post, the neoliberalization of state institutions would not stop at the formerly most bureaucratically and rationally defined jobs: even post office clerks had to participate in new emotional management courses and were thus actively engaged in re-engineering hierarchical arrangements of masculinity and femininity.

It is precisely because of this global expansion of emotional and sexually coded self-management, which is requested of so many service workers, that I see the necessity to critically reconsider Hochschild's somewhat normative assertion of what would happen to both the supposedly true feelings and the workers' identities. As outlined in chapters two and three, most of these employments are framed by an economic conduct that has moved on to align people's emotions with brands and business targets. Bruno Latour (2014) has recently alleged that capitalism created the feeling of helplessness. By this, he means a historically specific constellation of the present, which makes us feel about capitalism as an always surviving and unavoidable power. He writes:

"I will take capitalism to mean not a thing in the world, but a certain way of being affected when trying to think through this strange mixture of miseries and luxuries we encounter when trying to come to terms with the dizzying interplays of 'goods' and "bads". Capitalism is a concept invented to help absorb this odd mixture of enthusiasm for the cornucopia of riches that has lifted billions of people out of abject poverty and the indignation, rage and fury in response to the miseries visited on billions of other people. Especially troubling to me is the feeling of helplessness that is associated with any discussion of economics and that I have so much trouble reconciling with what I consider science's and politics' main effects, these being the opening of new possibilities and the provision of margins to maneuver. Why is it that when we are asked or summoned to combat capitalism, we feel, I feel so helpless?" (Latour 2014: 3)

According to Latour, capitalism is generative of power lines, which are able to provide global markets' planetary induced, perverted relation of poverty and wealth with the feeling that one had to sustain this misery due to the lack of any alternative. This feeling, by which we were all in some way affected, proves to be difficult (if not impossible) to relate to being either real or artificial. Rather, the example of helplessness makes it clear that economic and political power relations are compromising even the supposedly real feelings.

Inspired by Spinoza, current studies on affects underline human feelings' immanence of both constraining and liberating powers. Clough (2007) goes as far as to understand capitalism's intervention in the emotional world as representing a power that works pre-individually and hence modulates both the emergence and creativity of affects. With this, she lines up with Arvidsson (2006), who sees the modulating tool of capitalist control as exemplified in brands and their respective procedures to interweave social groups and aspirations. Common to both authors is their effort to reformulate the critical questioning on the truths of feeling. Differently from Hochschild, Clough and Arvidsson are challenging the view that real emotions could be separated from displayed, performed, or artificial ones. It lies in their core argumentation that there was a distinguishable neoliberal governmentality, which systematically obliterates such domains of truth. In the words of Clough, it is a government of productivity that embraces the very tension of control and "indeterminate emergence" (Clough 2007: 63).

The affective mobilizations that circulate within and around the brand of *Visibly Hot* (the Brazilian case study as discussed throughout the last two chapters) are emblematic for such complex processes of subjectivation in the sector of service work. As I have tried to show by the salesclerks' enthusiastic identification with the enterprise, their will for both individual authenticity and "being different" turns out to be an important factor of juvenile self-government. On one hand, the workers succeed in associating positive feeling to the employer. On the other hand, the same affective alignment causes renewed states of dependence and commitment. Hence the sensation of being just yourself and – by this authentic identification – of representing a particularly stylish and outstanding figure is for most of the salesclerks both a proof of their very personal success and a measure of their contribution to the enterprise's profits. Sales employee Carol notes that the worker's mode of being-affected by the brand actually encompassed the volume of resources one had for selling products to customers. Salesclerks had to really like and love the brand, or as her direct superior Andrea puts it, in the best case they have the brand's face, its style and creative but corresponding behavior.

Feeling that arises through this labor is not alien to the emotions of the workers. Actually, the opposite is the case. The individual claim to be authentic in a sexually, racially or youthfully fashioned social role is being spatially and temporally aligned with interactional tactics of appearance in front of the customers. Differently from Hochschild's flight attendants, these sales workers are not trained to pass on a feeling of being in good institutional-like hands to their clients (which is important under the circumstance of eventual turbulences), but they are instructed to bring in some of their real emotions and ideals they advocate for in their life beyond the sales point. The strive for individual authenticity, as I will show later, even permeates the micro interaction techniques of the sales employees. Circulating feeling is affectively effective, now engaging surface and depth at once. As a consequence, commercial labor is meant to be the ambiance where salesclerks, at least in parts, autonomously work on their identities; where they become different for the sake of the employment and its mission of profit optimization.

A body of work and studies, which uncritically adapt Hochschild's notion, currently examine and naturalize psychic burdens as suffered by emotional workers (Bonfim and Gondim 2010). However, without the intention of ignoring or disregarding this concern, it seems to be urgent to reflect on those current transformations in commercial service work, which will perhaps prove to be more unsettling. The fact that there was not a single sales worker in my case study who would have mentioned mental suffering as being caused by her/his job might neither be a coincidence nor correspond to an isolated case. In contrast, the salesclerks' continuous enthusiasm charts the functioning of new forms of (self)control at work. Since it has become evident in entrepreneurial contexts that salaries alone do not guarantee a worker's motivation to work well, identity politics in the commercial sector have become an ever more crucial part of corporate management (du Gay 1996). In somewhat more dramatic terms, this indicates a conversion of large parts of human life into labor. As Sauer and Penz rightly note, sociology has widely concealed this topic: particularly the corporal and emotional aspects of subject formations, that is, "the literal somatization of the government of the self and of others" (Sauer and Penz 2013: 126) has been ignored.

Consequently, the guiding questions I strive to tackle in this section refer to the modes of subject constitution specific to contemporary capitalist market logics. But rather than analytically presupposing alienating effects, that is, what the labor in question undoes in subjects, I am interested in the manifold emergence at work: what are generally speaking the products of affective labor in commercial service jobs? And what are the emotional and somatic demands for workers in order to mobilize these products?

4.1.1 Double productivity: sexual labor

Taking into account the notion of sexual labor [*sexuell arbeiten*][1], as elaborated by queer art theorists Renate Lorenz, Pauline Boudry and Brigitta Kuster (Lorenz and Kuster 2007; Lorenz 2007a, 2007b and 2009), I argue that the role of the desiring body is crucial to the affective labor in commercial service employments; to those jobs, in which the immediate inter-

---

1 The original term *sexuell arbeiten*, in German, could be more precisely translated as "working sexually", a term that would possibly prevent common misunderstandings given the closeness of "sexual labor" to sex work. However, I adapted "sexual labor", because it is the term the authors use in their English texts.

action with the public is continuous and in which the sale of a given product defines the main outcome of the worker's tasks. Sexual labor is the conceptual result of a group of German authors who started, throughout the 1990s, their project *queering work*. The latter aims at bringing together two topical strands of critical social theory, which are often separated today, if not declared as conflictive: work and sexuality.[2] While the former continues to be the core of (post)Marxist thought, the latter has gone through a long journey within psychoanalysis and clinical sciences until its more recent consolidation as a field of critical social inquiry. Amongst other interventions and books, the group of authors around Renate Lorenz started the experiment to integrate sexuality in the field of work through the exposition *Normal Love* (Lorenz 2007b):

"For sexuality, and this is the thesis, is an important factor in how power functions within the field of labor: 'normal love' traces these connections between the 'love of work' and the 'norms of sexuality'." (Lorenz 2007b: 8)

The connections the authors envisage between social constraints on sexuality and the articulation of work motivation represent a theoretical effort, which is salient in the form of everyday experiences of salesclerks in my present case study. As discussed in chapter three, sales workers at *Visibly Hot* literally say that they "love the job". And at the same time, their identification with the brand's promise to "be different" is involved in the reworking of heterosexual normality: being gay, as goes the brand's diversity discourse, can be a cool thing, and the workers themselves should show how much this is true.

It is central to the notion of sexual labor that capitalist labor demands a double productivity. Labor produces not only products in the sense of commodity value[3], but also social subjects. Once subjectivation is consid-

---

2   The exception of this common divide are contemporary studies on sex work (Piscitelli 2007 and 2009; Hofmann 2010), in a wider sense also feminist interventions about reproduction and domestic work (Dalla Costa 2004) as well as Preciado's (2008) provocations on workers under the conditions of pornographic and pharmaceutical industries.

3   Marx (1957) defined commodity value as socially necessary labor time. The latter results of a complex interplay of both use value and exchange value,

ered as an equally crucial process of labor, then the critical analysis of the control over workers will further include the examination of rules and social norms of masculinity, femininity as well as of sexual orientation. Lorenz (2007b) illustrates this very clearly with the photographs and diaries of Hannah Cullwick, a domestic worker in Victorian England (see also McClintock 1995). In addition to the hard and sweaty tasks of cleaning her master's house, Cullwick was demanded to comply with a range of sexually connoted rules of conduct: as a woman, she must not walk on the streets at night (there were the dangers of seduction by strange men, and therefore the moral request of sexual abstinence had to be pronounced as encompassing both work and leisure time), she had to obey her masters and to avoid talking freely. Following Althusser's refelctions on *savoir-faire* (1976), Lorenz theorizes on Cullwick's case:

"By learning such practices, according to Althusser, individuals are 'interpellated' as subjects. They become capitalists or workers, men or women. Individuals learn the practices that are necessary to production, and by learning them they simultaneously become subjects that subordinate themselves to social rules." (Lorenz 2007a: 110)

By pointing to the work of Butler (1993), Lorenz further adjusts that the subjects' subordination under the cultural imperatives on sexuality were never to be understood as totally enforceable. Subjects had a certain room for maneuver. Sexuality as a power, she insists, was simultaneously a possibility and an obligation to improvise (Lorenz 2007a: 109). Sexual laborers, in turn, always encountered this tension.

Accordingly, Lorenz et al. define sexual labor as an (individual and collective) effort, which is attached to a continuous need for improvisation, and which is ensnared in the intersection of submission and potential revision (Lorenz and Kuster 2007: 15). On one hand, it elicits something like a seduction into promising social identities, whose recognition is at-

---

which have no real essence but rather phantasmagoric powers that reflect historically specific modes of production and social relations of domination. Marx made it clear that the workers' investments of time and physical energy would make them dependent on the capitalist system, since they sold their labor power for money.

tached to professional and emancipatory success. On the other hand, this identity work is part of a (written or orally pronounced) labor contract the worker agrees to as if it were out of her/his own free will. The irony of sexual labor's socially necessary efforts lies in the challenge that the social identities on offer are not necessarily already there. Social places like "the lesbian" or "the black woman" need to be (re)constructed in order to be able to participate in a roundly profitable articulation. Indeed, the regime of sexual labor stipulates from its workers a playful and desirous will to invent or rework social identities. However, the point here is that the starting positions are not the same to everyone: some workers need to expend more effort than others in order to fall in with the ruling identity politics.

Lorenz outlines these differing subjective efforts with a photograph by Laura Aguilar, from the 1987 series entitled *Latina Lesbian* (Lorenz 2007b: 66). The image depicts a middle-aged, non-white woman wearing jeans, a black leather jacket and short hair; a figure who, in the US context, can ostensibly be deciphered as a Latina butch dyke. Accompanying the photograph, the caption says: "My mother encouraged me to be a court reporter...I became a lawyer." By this example, Lorenz comes to highlight the manifold social expectations and interpellations addressing the depicted woman. The portrait comments on the stereotypes attached to the person's status as a woman and equally as both a Latina migrant and a lesbian. This human is exposed to far greater efforts than if she were white, heterosexual or a man. She has to make crossings of various social places, which under the common cultural belief in norms are often irreconcilable. Consequently, the obligation and unequal distribution to make crossings is what describes precarity: "places that cannot and should not be fully taken" (Lorenz and Kuster 2007: 22). Crossings are related to high individual efforts: mobilized through aspirations, one has to confront not only cultural norms at work, but also to arrange, readdress or solve social contradictions (Lorenz 2007b: 10).

Commenting on the same photo series, queer theorist Muñoz ascertains:

"The Latina lawyer's image is most certainly disidentification inasmuch as it is neither merely a stereotypical depiction of the model minority nor is it the simplistic outcast." (Muñoz 2007: 130)

By "disidentification", Muñoz denominates labor that takes place in everyday practice and that is a "simultaneous work on, with and against dominant ideological structures" (Muñoz 2007: 127). In this sense, sexual labor refers to the production and performance of posing, which point towards the possibility of another, queered future. Regarding the dominant sexual order, Muñoz continues, the portrait of the *Latina Lesbian* is claiming forms of democracy and freedom that are "not-yet-here" (Muñoz 2007: 129), but that become think- and desirable through the same image. Sexual labor involves identity work and therefore distorts the rigid distinction of the private and the public. Although this may disclose a site of broader emancipation, even disidentified identities are placed in danger to reproduce the same logics that previously suppressed them. Referring to Foucault, Muñoz concludes on sexual labor: "It is an expenditure that puts us in the position of constantly having to be concerned with ourselves and with the questions of 'what we are'" (Muñoz 2007: 130).

The latter aspect of sexual labor reminds us of Foucault's insights on how, throughout Western history of the 19th century, sexuality came to denominate the truth of the subject's inner self (Foucault 1987). Applied to the field of contemporary service work, it seems as though this logic has expanded to the beliefs in sales. As I have tried to show up to here through the example of a Brazilian fashion enterprise, sexual attractiveness and youthful coolness are being mobilized for the sake of both individual self-realization and commercial profits. Sexual labor, in this area, is moving a range of enthusiastic emotions, thus affecting present and future customers. In turn, these would experience their purchase not only as a pleasant enrichment, but also as linked to emotional proximity or sexual attraction. In summation, the instigation of subjectivity —focused on the customers as well as on the salesclerks themselves – is crucial to service work. And particularly because this labor charges the vitality of bodies (it excites, affects them with emotional proximity or ardor, and identifies them through particular feelings), the opposing contours of inside and outside, of private and public as well as of leisure and work are being thoroughly displaced.

4.1.2 Exuberant sexuality, or, back to affect

We can understand sexual labor as a provocative means to reflection, allowing us to broaden our perspectives on work in general and thus to overcome canonized forms of labor studies within the sociology of work. In this respect, the notion is nothing less than a continuation of feminist critiques on unpaid domestic labor (Federici 2012). For several decades, this questioning directed the mutual conditionality of female reproductive work and male wage labor, thereby challenging capitalist society's systematic alliance to masculine domination through labor relations. Women were not only exploited as unpaid labor forces, but also subjectively configured, as one could say, according to the dominant norms of bourgeois modernity. Lorenz and Kuster (2007) further this theoretical basement, dilating the focus on female reproductive work by including literally all vital and aspiratory powers, which are participating in the subjectivating effects of gender, sexuality and wage labor. Their *queering* of work consists strategically in highlighting how heterosexist norms are part of performative processes at work and how these processes are both subjecting and enabling subjects to face social rules (Lorenz and Kuster 2007: 19).

However, it is necessary to adapt and reformulate one of the core aspects of sexual labor, namely the restriction of its performative outcomes to a subject's stringent sexual and gender identity. As Lorenz later concedes, the concept of sexual labor reached its limits, as the products and subjects of work "turn out quite differently" (Lorenz 2009: 15). As I illustrated in the precedent chapter, labor and self-subjectivating processes within the fashion service sector are attached not only to the reiteration/challenge of heteronormativity, but also to that of whiteness, black race and of social norms related to youthfulness. The efforts salesclerks spend are capitalizing the desiring body through labor, but this body includes even more aspects than being binary sexed and hetero- versus homosexually coded. Fashion salesclerks' efforts are setting the worker's body in particular states of feeling that affect other bodies (of both customers and sales colleagues). This affection is often – like flirts – of sexual content, but it equally assembles friendships or admiration for another's style. In summation, it represents a switching system of power that transcends a uniquely sexual mode. Affective labor fosters cunning powers; it leads workers to being "able to be deceitful, persistent, opportunistic, a trickster" (Tsianos and Papadopoulos 2006).

Considering the conceptual narrowness of the notion of sexual labor in its focus on sexual norms, I advocate – based on the case study on *Visibly Hot* in the present book – for the term affective labor. As a theoretical proposal, it is meant as a critical appraisal of and as an intrinsic attachment to both Hochschild's perspective on emotional work (2003) and Lorenz and Kuster's notion of sexual labor (2007). By affective labor, I thus refer to two interconnected, though analytically separable arenas of subjectivation: on one hand, it embraces processes of identification, directed towards abstract aspirations, particular social places or utterly towards the employer; in other words, it is identity work. On the other hand, affective labor designates the whole range of social interactions that come along with commercial service work. Flirts, emotional proximity, friendships – all are partially induced by skills affective laborers are taught through training sessions and that are subsequently adjusted spontaneously and in an individual authentic manner. The two arenas – identity work and sales interaction – have in common the fact that they bring processes of subjectivation forward and that they keep these processes in motion. While the phenomenon of hyper identification with a product brand pertains to the realm of technologies of the self (in the example of *Visibly Hot*, the idea of "being different" unfolds through the worker's identifications), affective sales strategies on the micro interactional level are concerned with stimulating feeling as attached to a situation, to a person or to a space. Affective laborers mobilize and attach both themselves and others with feeling.

The insight of seeing both affects and emotions as circulating powers with subjectivating effects is not least inspired by recent debates on affect in cultural theory (Clough 2007). These debates relate to a long lasting distinction between affects and emotions, which commonly defined the concepts of feeling in the humanities. Affects were commonly conceived as pertaining to immediate and mostly unconscious reactions. Emotions, in contrast, were seen as longer processes, which are deeply anchored in the individual and its modes of feeling. In other words, it was emotions that said something about one's personality, while affects meant hasty, uncontrolled impulses that were rather alien to cultural scripts of human feeling. This separation also resonates in Hochschild's notion of emotional work (2003). She analyzes the feelings of flight attendants always with respect to the question of the ways their true individual emotions – as localized in the inside of the individual and further pertaining to the realm of the private – were being compromised, if not manipulated, by artificial emotion. While this leads to an overemphasis of true emotion as representing one's allegedly private personality, it paradoxically does not go far enough in considering the role of pre-individual feeling in molding or hailing a worker into a given identity.

Lorenz and Kuster (2007) fundamentally question whether the truth of any individual identity is tenable as an analytical presupposition. In their view, it is the circulating (sexual) desires within the realm of labor regimes that summon workers to actively produce (and sometimes shift) the very spheres of the individual or the private. Both one's identification and disidentification with, for example, the role of the housemaid are contributing to establish the culturally legitimate spheres of labor *and* sexual affect/emotion. Here, I see a connecting point to Ahmed's (2004a) work on feeling. According to this author, neither affects nor emotions are naturally pertaining to the private or the individual. At the same time, they are also not simply representing, as it were, social structure.[4] In the terms of Ahmed, emotions and affects are movements, in which humans are inserted in a state, so to speak, of swimming (Maihofer 2014). It is thus only in our reactions and impressions by others, she holds, that we find our orientation within these moving powers. This orientation is generative of our experience of what pertains to the inside and the outside, the individual and the social, the private and the public. What makes feeling historically and culturally specific lies thus finally not in affects and emotions as such, but in our ways of directing them towards objects (Ahmed 2004b; Schmitz and Ahmed 2014)

Commercial service labor, as we know it today in industrialized countries, demands considerable efforts in directing feeling. Since its historical provenience in the 19th century, it became ever more usual that workers like salesclerks, particularly in the fashion area, would need to represent the aesthetic zeitgeist; that compliance with cultural expectations of both their physical appearance and emotional behavior towards customers would crucially increase the profitability of a given enterprise. In conformity with Bröckling's suggestive analysis of contemporary knowledge that circulates within personal management (Bröckling 2013), today's successful sales workers appear as those who self-reliantly manage their feelings

---

4 At this point, Ahmed distinguishes her approach from that of Durkheim or Mauss (and therefore form the so-called anthropology of emotions), according to which emotions are necessarily bearing a cohesive and socially integrative character.

as well as their personal identities in a profitable manner. Playful sex appeal, charm, emotional talk and socially desirable life styles are some of the now strategically canalized exercises affective laborers are asked to perform. Affective workers in the consumer service sector need to give proof of their high emotional adaptability to a range of daily situations (with customers, sales colleagues, moments of tension, changing fashion trends) and they must never cease to cultivate affective flows of attraction.

Remembering Clough's (2007) thesis on neoliberal governmentality, it is of importance to note that feeling as a resource of work is never fully subjected to entrepreneurial control. As affects participate in inducing emergence, they simultaneously help to unfold a sort of surplus socialities at work: intimate bonds like close friendships or relations of love, to cite only the more plastic examples. In these terms, affective labor produces, enhances desire (Hardt 1999). Be it intentionally or not, feelings between people can turn into a coping strategy for workers to put up with or partially escape the demanded labor routine. However, the cultivation of these emotions at work always runs the risk of subscribing again to profit maximization, of being "colonized" by management's efforts to canalize them towards service orientation, as Carls (2007) put it. In fact, workers' affective skills are thoroughly multifunctional. They can be directed to different aims and objects. Finally, as René Pollesch reminds us through his provocative theater pieces about subjectivity under the postmodern technological age: once the whole person unfolds in work, she/he includes both her good and her bad qualities. And the latter "want to work", too (Mennel and Salzmann 2008).

The idea that a subject's (unintentional or intentional) compliance with and resistance against the ruling order are work-immanent is what actually connects the notion of sexual labor with post-marxist thought on immaterial/affective labor. The latter also "supports the analysis of a double productivity" (Lorenz 2009: 15). As Hardt argues, affective labor creates value and simultaneously produces subjectivity en masse (Hardt 1999). By re-reading Marx' *Maschinenfragment*, post-marxists presuppose that contemporary, capitalist value creation is foremost supported through immaterial, cognitive and affective labor (Lazzarato 1996; Lazzarato and Negri 2001). As a renewed motor of capitalism, both immaterial energies and bodily capacities would create the biopolitical scenario of a global empire (Hardt and Negri 2000). Unfortunately, most post-marxists do not sufficiently take into account queer and feminist approaches on the processes of subjectivation. In defiance of their insistence on the political notion of multitude, they often leave the reader with the impression that subjectivity and exploitation were primarily carved in one's position of social class, and that masculine domination or sexual regimes were but of second, subordinate importance (see the critique in Preciado 2008). Accordingly, the collectivities and "spontaneous revolts" – in Negri and Hardt's view welcomed byproducts of affective labor – remain considerably indebted to the idea of proletarian class consciousness rising, a modus operandi which has for a long time predominated in the sociology of work.

However, and as Lorey (2012) puts forward with the example of several subject-decentered social movements, the potentiality post-marxists see in the activities of affective labor can be broadened as a potentiality (specific) of the precarious. Affective laborers are (re)working the social, that is, the very relation of individual and collectivity. Thereto, they make tough efforts in traversing given social places (Lorenz and Kuster 2007), stereotyped norms attached to gender, sexual orientation, race, age and social class. These transitions are part of work control, although they proceed with the chance to start something new. Compulsory flexible subjectivity, like the emotional adaptation to sales customers, on one hand incorporates social promises made to affective workers, which might never be realized. On the other hand, the same affective precarity induces ongoing movement, and hence potential powers that effect – intended or not – displacement of existing social places. To work affectively means to subject one(self) to two types of imperatives: to produce products and to become a desirable subject. Yet the effects of this work are never as predictable as it would please the management.

4.2 THE SEDUCTIONS OF RETAIL SERVICE WORK

Skills as gained through retail jobs have apparently entered into the neoliberal guidebook aimed at forming one's business competencies. As a UK-based agency for internships, graduate jobs and career planning promotes:

"Working in retail, you've seen first-hand how a fast-paced business operates and how commercial decisions are made. What made the business you worked for profitable, and what role did you play in its success?" (Targetjobs 2015)

This passage is part of a broader catalog, pushing ten major skills to be the landmarks for students who are interested in getting a well-paid job in their future. It gives advice on how retail work experience could be used for someone to show that "you have got the attitude and abilities the employer wants". These skills embrace the know-how (*savoir-faire*) of working under pressure and with a busy team, taking on individual responsibility, and showing initiative for suggesting improvements. "Good self-management" is a key term, involving "being punctual, flexible, getting work done on time, and being willing to improve your own performance" (Targetjobs 2015).

These self-improving aspects of contemporary employment have been vividly discussed in sociological debates on neoliberal agency (Boltanski and Chiapello 2005; Bröckling 2013). But the role of the body and its affective capacities have still been neglected by or separated from these studies[5]. This is rather surprising, since the individual, emotional realiza-

---

5 As Wolkowitz (2006) points out regarding the sociology of employment, the role of the body has for a long time been restricted to studies of nursing, care or sex work. Her notion of body work aims at widening such contractions, highlighting the contradictions of social relations, human values and labor as inherent in a broad variety of jobs (beauticians, fitness instructors, dentists, nannies, tattooists, and so on). Unfortunately, Wolkowitz herself restricts body work in retail to jobs that include "measuring or touching customers as a matter of course" (Wolkowitz 2006: 147), shifting the empirical and theoretical focus on the worker's sensory practices and thus losing sight of broader power relations as mediated through the composition of labor.

tion of a worker's contribution to the enterprise's success (as also salient in the citation above) is very often based on a thoroughly somatic experience. Particularly service work in retail, as the job agency itself reminds us, demands a training of one's interaction skills and a know-how on handling the customer's feelings and desires: "Good customer service is friendly and polite", it is about "dealing tactfully" (Targetjobs 2015). Service work hence constantly calls for mobilizing the bodily capacity to be empathetically affected (by customer needs) and to affect other bodies (those of the customers). This even holds for employments where an encounter with customers is merely virtual or distant, as it is the case of operators or online-chat-agents. Retail jobs that rely on full exposure of the worker's somatic presence or agency, such as are the situations of shop workers or cashiers, may however be more immediately affected by the self-improving imperative, since they urge on the production of an embodied performance which is locally verifiable and controllable. As McDowell (2009) puts it, interactive service employment is highly confronted with a demand for the commodification of the worker's bodily self, because "sexuality, pleasure, desire and fantasy play an increasingly significant part in the employment relation" (McDowell 2009: 50).

Pringle's classic text about the work of female secretaries (Pringle) also made an important point here. Following a Foucauldian perspective, the author understands sexuality not primarily as a synonym of sexual activity but as a historical, regulatory force of identity (Foucault 1987). Consequently, her studies about daily interactions between male bosses and female secretaries of Australian enterprises show how flirting or "having fun", as scripts of these interactions, are reinforcing organizational hierarchies as well as wider social attitudes regarding gender/sexuality that go beyond the workplace. Female secretaries, Pringle tellingly observes, are often involved in "personal rapport" and intimacy with the male boss, "capable of generating intense feelings of loyalty, dependency and personal commitment" (Pringle 2013: 66). This arrangement of power led secretaries to willingly do tasks very distant from bureaucratic or rationalized logics. Making coffee or preparing food for guests, for example, were assignments oriented towards creating the sphere of a cozy home, (re)producing voluntary submission under the bourgeois order and its device of masculine domination.

4.2.1 "Trabalhar com acessórios é ser apaixonado pela marca"[6]

Concerning affective relationships, contemporary retail jobs often go further than the services of secretaries. Salesclerks are not necessarily sexually committed to superiors, but they are intrinsically immersed in a relationship with the brand, its products and consumers. As I showed earlier with the case of *Visibly Hot*, retail workers commonly stress their passionate bond with the brand's spirit, entailing a specific sex appeal that draws from the promise to "be different". Strikingly, this passion for the brand is often seen as the basic requirement for someone to both work and keep working as a salesclerk.

"A [*Visibly Hot*], cara, você tem que entrar, gostando mesmo da marca. Se você não gostar, você não fica, assim, se você não gostar. Vou te falar por quê. Vender acessórios, óculos, relógios, não é a mesma coisa do que vender uma blusa ou uma bermuda que a pessoa precise. Então, você tem que convencer aquela pessoa que ela precisa. Por isso, você tem que gostar desse óculos."[7] (Carol, 21, salesclerk at *Visibly Hot*)

First and foremost, Carol's account suggests that a salesclerk needs a very high level of identification with the brand, if she/he wants to do a good job. The affective conviction of the brand's products can then be passed on to the customers: this would help to persuade them to buy a pair of sunglasses or accessories, products that no one really needs. Secondly, Carol also distinguishes that being passionate about the brand constitutes something like a survival strategy at work. Identification keeps someone from disliking and quitting the job. This view is also shared by other salesclerks

---

6 "Working with accessories is being in love with the brand", Carol, 21, salesclerk at *Visibly Hot*.

7 "[*Visibly Hot*], man, you have to get into it, to really like the brand. If you don't like it, you won't stay, you know, if you don't like it. I'll tell you why. Selling accessories, glasses, watches, it isn't the same thing than selling a blouse or some shorts, something someone needs. So, you have to convince that person that she needs [that product]. That's why you need to like these glasses."

who emphasize, for example, that they were working at *Visibly Hot* without any constraints: "Eu faço por que eu gosto. Não é por obrigação"[8], Pedro's somewhat defiant statement goes. This and other evaluations with the same content are reflecting modes of perception, whose effects unfold in revealing work in a light of both arising from an individual will and pertaining to sensations of "fun" and enjoyment.

Analogous to the theoretical considerations about the role of feelings at work above, it is this kind of retail service work I have in mind when I discuss affective labor. Such work takes place in a diverse and globally dispersed range of capitalist economies, mostly those attached to consumption, shopping centers and the marketing of those goods that exceed the needs of human survival. It is labor, which fosters individual identifications, desires and emotional bonds to brands, and often turns the same into an economic measure of a worker's capacity. What is more, such labor is based on the idea that the "souls" of retail workers are central to assemble the anticipated "emotional proximity" to customers (du Gay 1996: 98). The worker's authentic enthusiasm is engineered to be infectious: customers should finally become convinced of a product's outstanding benefits, in other words, they have to be moved by a bundle of ideas and feelings if they are to buy these products. Consequently, the question arises: what does a retail worker do in order to suborn such feelings? Larissa shares an introductory account of a salesclerk's required strategies when in ordinary interaction with a customer.

"E, assim, é uma tática. Porque- as pessoas- todo mundo é meio carente. Então, você chega assim, pô, cabelo bonito- elogiar o cabelo já muda a pessoa. Ali, já alegra o dia dela, pô. Daí- o meu dia com esse elogio! Traz isso para o seu lado. A pessoa começa a confiar- em você, entendeu? Ah, um óculos mais bonito, ah, é uma só-tal-coisa. Aí a pessoa: ah, é mesmo! Entendeu? É que nem você vai numa balada e você vai tentar conquistar alguém. É a mesma coisa. Só que em vez de vender um beijo, você vai vender um óculos. É tipo isso."[9] (Larissa, 21, salesclerk at *Visibly Hot*)

---

8 "I do it because I like it, there's no obligation"
9 "It's like- tactics, you know. Because- people- everybody is somewhat needy for love. So, you're like, man, what beautiful hair- complimenting the hair will already change the person. Like, it already cheers up her day, man. Hence- my

Affective labor in fashion retail is primarily a matter of developing the right tactics: strategies, which are based on the assumption that customers are looking for affection, for compliments and self-esteem. The affective worker has to exploit these needs and, in the best case, establish a relation of trust. If the salesclerk manages to induce a good feeling in the customer, like "I am so handsome" or "I am so good", then much is gained. It is no coincidence when Larissa compares this process with seducing someone at a party. Selling glasses, in her view, is entangled in the same affective tension; it has to do with an economic game of exchanging and selling affects. It is an activity that consciously channels feeling and where the truth of one's intentions can hardly be tested.

4.2.2 Training, individuality, and attitude

In the history of capitalist service work along the 20th century, the exploitation of human feeling has initiated a trend in entrepreneurial government, aiming at directly accessing the workers' emotional (self-)management. Thereafter, transnational firms such as Delta Airlines began to design internal training courses for their employees. Through these, as an instructor observed by Hoschschild said, workers would learn individual techniques related to "thought processes, actions, and feelings" (Hochschild 2003: 24). Today, such training sessions are common in a variety of employments (see Hughes 2010 for a discussion on "emotional intelligence") and they all share the purpose of, first, heightening the worker's identification with the brand or enterprise and, second, of advancing the worker's skills in selling a product. In the view of Althusser (1976), the acquisition of know-how (*savoir-faire*) was crucial to the reproduction of capitalist labor power. Since the workers' salary alone is not sufficient to ensure the ruling order, he argued, capitalist society would take state apparatuses in his service: the school system as well as other institutional facilities and instances. There, individuals would be taught to express

---

> day with this compliment! Turn this in your favor. The person begins to trust you, got it? Ah, nicer glasses, ah, it's such a singular thing. So, the person [returns]: Ah, really! You know? It's like going to a party and trying to seduce someone. It's the same thing. Except instead of selling a kiss, you'll sell glasses. That's it."

themselves through the right language or how to command, including scientific and literary culture that helped them to function in their respective positions within the production process. These forms of know-how, Althusser concluded, are not only assuring subjection (*assujettissement*) under the dominant ideology, but also the "mastery of its practice" (Althusser 1976: 76).

Albeit not focusing on the role of the state and its institutions, Althusser's reflections are still enriching for one to think about the function of contemporary training entities as conventional in both public and private economy. Knowing how to act and behave according to the expectations of the employer likewise implies bringing into service individual or private abilities, which in a certain way reproduces capitalist labor force. Larissa's image of selling kisses at a party as an analogy to her individual selling tactics might be emblematic. Her narrative is colored by business jargon and widely embedded in mindsets supported by her monthly training in sales. João, working at *Visibly Hot* for but a couple of weeks, explains why these training sessions were so central to the sales job.

"Tudo começa com o nosso treinamento. A gente tem treinamento, assim, realizado todo mês. É para a gente saber o que apresentar aos clientes. Os clientes que vêm em nossas lojas- para que eles gostem de um modelo, a gente fala a história do modelo. Porque a [*Visibly Hot*] trabalha com toda a coleção, um modelo com maior história. É diferente. Então, a gente acaba contando essa história para o cliente, porque- a gente não vende só óculos escuros- são peças, são jóias raras. Por isso, a [*Visibly Hot*] lança toda semana uma coleção diferente. Para realmente dar uma diversidade maior para os clientes. E com esse treinamento, a gente vai pro salão, o que é o ponto de venda, e acaba passando o que a gente aprende para os clientes, mas da nossa forma. Você acaba conquistando os clientes."[10] (João, 18, salesclerk at *Visibly Hot*)

---

10 "Everything begins with our training. We have training sessions, you know, taking place every month. Because we have to know what to show and demonstrate to the customers. The customers who come to our shops- to get them to like a [certain] model, we tell the story of that product. Because [*Visibly Hot*] promotes a whole collection, a model with great history. It's different. So, we end up telling this history to the customer, because- we are not only selling sunglasses- these are (single) pieces, rare jewels. That's why [*Visibly Hot*]

Getting the customers to like the products is the salesclerk's ultimate goal of labor. Consequently, the monthly training sessions at *Visibly Hot* do focus on teaching sales arguments, and especially the particular "histories" of each accessory model to its employees. João, whose account is clearly branded by having memorized the key instructions of his latest training, points to the significance of emphasizing each sunglasses' precious singularity to the customers. Individuality and diversity, the brand's discourse wants to make one believe, is what comes out of these products. Strikingly, this specific market ideology also instructs the nature of the salesclerk's know-how in selling. João notes that the lessons learnt at the training has to be passed on to the customers in individually engineered manner ("our own way"). Affective labor is then meant to be the opposite of mass processing; in its logic, only the singular and personal touch, as elaborated by the salesclerk, will secure the "conquest" of a customer. João further refines this idea during our conversation, simultaneously indicating the social condition of communicative strategies.

"A gente recebe uma estratégia padrão. Mas depois, a gente vai manejando ela da nossa própria forma. Ah, a gente aborda o jeito padrão da empresa, mas a gente muda algumas coisas, para poder dar uma diversidade maior. [...] A gente vai precisar de algumas coisas- que a gente sabe que vai funcionar com uma pessoa, mas com outra pessoa não vai. Aí, cada um usa o padrão, mas na sua personalidade. Essa é uma coisa legal."[11] (João, 18, salesclerk at *Visibly Hot*)

Most of trainers and trainees alike identify and evaluate this task of gaining customers through individually adapted strategies by the category of attitude. As I showed earlier, *Visibly Hot*'s managerial discourse sees in it

---

launches a different collection every week. In order to really provide major diversity to the customers. And with this training, we go to the salesroom, that's the selling point, and we pass to the client what we are learning, but in our way. You end up conquering the customers."

11 "We get a standard strategy. But afterwards, we will handle it in our own way. Ah, we address the standard style of the enterprise, but we change a few things, in order to give it a major diversity. [...] We will need some things- that we know that will work with one person, but with another person it won't. Therefore, everybody uses a standard, but in his/her personality. That's a cool thing."

a measure of an employee's behavioral commitment as expressed, for instance, by physical styling of blackness (see section 2.4.1). Salesclerk Leidiane echoes this giving proof of one's singular authenticity as representing her very personal desire (3.4.2). Personality and styling of the self appear as crucial resources for the kind of affective labor that salesclerks at *Visibly Hot* have to administer. The category attitude refers though not only to the styling of the surface body (like hair, tattoos, and additional fashion accessories), but also to an overall conduct of the self that further includes a management of both emotions and desires. "You have to look good and be nice", Marina, one of my first interview partners commented on the central trick of a *Visibly Hot* salesclerk. Though branch manager Andrea shares a more detailed definition of what "having attitude" means in terms of one's interaction skills. According to her, attitude refers to

"saber falar bem para o cliente, atitude para mostrar um produto, não ter vergonha e falar muito bem. Acho que atitude é isso, você ser dinâmica, você falar bem para o cliente, interagir bem com ele."[12] (Andrea, 22, branch manager at *Visibly Hot*)

Attitude can thus be understood as the hallmark of *Visibly Hot*, in other words, it comprises the case specificity within the field of affective labor in Brazilian retail. Its demands for professional self-improvement regard an overcoming of shame, as well as being provocative, fast and highly eloquent. Andrea proudly adds that *Visibly Hot* is famous for its "aggressive" service workers, something also attested by João and his colleagues. Especially at night, the latter enthuses about this quality, "a gente dá uma arriscada- de uma atendimento mais despojado. Pô, nãoseiquê, você ta bonyta, oi que tal?"[13]

---

12 "knowing how to speak well with the customer, having the attitude to show a product, not being ashamed and speaking very well. I think attitude, that's it, being dynamic, speaking well to the customer and interact with him."

13 "we dare- do a more exposed service. Shit, I dunno, you're so beautiful, hey how are you?"

4.2.3 Desires and sticky social bonds

Highly trained skills in interaction and conquest of customers not infrequently imply affective commitments. Selling sunglasses as if they were kisses, to paraphrase Larissa's recipe, creates an ambience in which desires are spinning. Larissa thinks that the flirty atmosphere at *Visibly Hot* is peculiarly intense, first, because the salesclerks are all so young and second, because this kind of sales labor was "not a formal job".

"A gente está aqui, a gente se veste cada um do seu estilo, mesmo tendo uniforme. E, pega, né? Acontece. Às vezes, a gente vê até- deixa o telefone- a gente provou o nome, joga o nome no facebook, procura para ver, às vezes adiciona. Acontece muito."[14] (Larissa, 21, salesclerk at *Visibly Hot*)

As in many cases the employees told me about, Larissa, giggling, recounts the practice of mutual affective interests between salesclerks and customers. "Stalking" or checking out a client's profile on facebook is quite common amongst her colleagues. But such expectations do not only stem from the sales crew. Salesclerk Leidiane says that mostly customers are looking for fondness [*carinho*].

"Ontem eu estava conversando com moço, tipo, ele tinha esse perfil completamente sério. Começou, oi, bota noite- eu sendo defensiva, assim. Aí ele veio, começou falar, que tinha problema de visão e tal, que ele gostava muito da armação da [*Visibly Hot*]. Aí, eu fui conversando com ele, falei para ele que eu nunca usei óculos, que nenhum óculos combinava comigo. Aí ele: mas você é tão estilosa! Como assim? Nada combinava com você, menina?! Sabe, eu fiquei- gente, ele falou que eu sou estilosa. Sim, é mais os clientes que têm essa relação."[15] (Leidiane, 24, cashier at *Visibly Hot*)

---

14 "We are here, everybody dresses in her/his own style, even while wearing a uniform. And it's alluring, right? It happens. Sometimes, we even look for- we leave the phone number- we try the name, put it on facebook, check it out, and sometimes add [them]. It happens a lot."

15 "Yesterday I talked with that guy, you know, he had like this completely serious profile. It started, hi, good evening- me taking a reserved position, right. Then he came [closer], started talking, saying that he had problems with his

Leidiane stresses that even customers she would not expect to be provocative are frequently hitting on salesclerks. In her example, a male client started chatting and sweet-talking to her. Although she expresses astonishment in her narrative, fishing male compliments, precisely the one about her having style, seemingly pleased her. It confirmed her in her efforts taken to belong to the brand's ideals. When I asked further questions about her opinion on the aspect of self-authenticity many salesclerks loved regarding *Visibly Hot*, Leidiane approved:

"Na loja, como a gente também pode escolher as nossas músicas, então, o pessoal fica super à vontade, sabe. Aí tem cliente que só entra pela música, né? [...] tem cliente que eu- coisa atendeu e depois ele veio no caixa, ai fui conversando com ele várias vezes, sobre rap, reggae, e tal. A gente se- a gente se esbarra na Lapa e vai tomar uma cerveja, sabe. Então, sim, a gente pode ser quem a gente é, sim."[16] (Leidiane, 24, cashier at *Visibly Hot*)

The mutual interests between customers and salesclerks seem to fluidly transition into leisure activities, such as sharing the same taste in music or in hot spots for going out at night. It is common that salesclerks describe these relations in terms of having or making "regular customers" [*cliente fixo*]. Jéssica, who was promoted to a branch manager within a couple of months after she had started at the firm, even sees in it her very individual formula for success.

---

eyesight and so on, that he liked a lot the spectacle frames from [*Visibly Hot*]. So I started a conversation with him, told him that I never wore glasses, that there was no model that fit me. But he [returned]: But you're so stylish! How come? Nothing fits you, girl?! You know, I was struck, my god, he said that I am stylish. Yeah, it's more the customers who open up that kind of relations."

16 "At the shop, since we can also choose our own music, staff is super comfortable, you know. And then, there are customers, who only enter the shop because of the music, right? [...] there are customers I- so-and-so answered and then he came to the cash register, so I started talking to him several times, about rap, reggae, and so on. We meet in Lapa [on of Rio's bohemian downtown areas] and have a beer, you know. So, yeah, we can be who we are, yes."

"Eu fui a melhor vendedora do Rio em 2014. [...] O que eu faço de diferente, é me envolver com a pessoa mesmo. Eu me envolvi com os clientes, eu tinha muitos clientes fixos. Não só vendia o produto, eu procurava saber um pouco da história da pessoa. [...] Trabalhar pós-venda- às vezes, se você vender, dá uma ligada depois para a pessoa- ah, você gostou da peça, nãoseoiquê; não? Vem aqui, a gente troca. Então, eu trabalhava muito cliente. Eu criava vínculo, criava um elo, né?"[17] (Jéssica, 23, branch manager at *Visibly Hot*)

Jéssica's secret recipe apparently lies in diminishing the frontiers between one's role as a customer in the shopping center and the same person's condition as a broader social subject. Getting involved, in some way, with the customer, is this salesclerk's procedure: she would show interest for the person's life and repeatedly call her/him even after the sales process. Such feeling of a social bond, Jéssica further explains, is promising because it prompts customers to naturally get back to the shop and its products.

As a matter of fact, Jéssica's technique is not an isolated case. "Treat your client as if he was a friend" is one of the most expressed recommendations by salesclerks. But as in life in general, how does someone proceed in order to engage friendship? Carol prefers the so-called technique of *rapport*. To my surprise about her self-enterprising account, she invited me to read about it on the Internet. As I would investigate afterwards, this procedure refers to the French term *rapport* and literally means to establish a relationship with the customer. According to a Brazilian public education platform, *rapport* is based on three key commands:

1) Intention: get to know the other person;
2) Attitude: meet the other person through his world model and validate its "maps" such as values, beliefs, and individual reality;

---

17 "I was the best salesclerk in Rio in 2014. [...] What I do differently is that I really get involved with the person. I got involved with the customers; I had a lot of regular customers. I didn't only sell products, but I tried to get to know more about the person's history. [...] Post-sale work, sometimes- when you sell, just give the person a call afterwards, ah, you liked the piece, I dunno; no? Come here, we'll change it. So, I really worked [on] customers. I created bonds, a tie, right?"

3) Frame: move to the perceptual position of the other person. (Portal Educação 2013)

In further details, the manual recommends both non-verbal (body posture, gestures and breathing) and verbal elements (voice quality, adapting the language to the customer, as for example, by repetition) that would help to reach the target. Actually, this is about techniques of acting that put the salesclerk in the role of a dramaturgic performer. Her/his empathy, persuasiveness, as well as her/his skills of improvisation will decide on whether the customer feels pleased and buys a product.

Team leader Letícia also assumes that she has a bit of an advantage in selling products, since she was involved in theatre and film projects for many years. Sales acting, in her mind, is attached to a creative management of both time and concentration.

"O primordial é, também, não ficar quieto. Por que vender um óculos é uma coisa muito passional, muito momentânea. Não é uma necessidade, é a última coisa que alguém vai querer comprar. Mas é uma coisa muito impulsiva. Sabe, de você comprar, de você vender. Você não pode deixar a pessoa pensar muito. Às vezes, um suspiro, alguém chegou e te cortou- você perdeu a atenção do cliente. E você não vende. [...] Como você pode dar uma arte, de duas horas, da pessoa pensar, e no final, você vende. Vendas, não é uma regra, é muito suscetível a tudo."[18] (Letícia, 26, responsible salesclerk at *Visibly Hot*)

According to Letícia's account, the salesclerk has to maintain an impulsive climate: one should neither give too much time for reflection to the customer nor let the affective attention decrease. Passions for both consumption and sales, she holds, arise the same way as fugacious moments. The

---

18 "The most important thing, too, is to not keep quiet. Because selling glasses is something very passionate, very momentary. It's not a necessity, it's the last thing someone would actually want to buy. But it's a very impulsive thing, you know, for someone to buy, for someone to sell. You cannot let the customer think [too] much. Sometimes, a sigh, someone arrived and interrupted you- you lost the customer's attention. And you won't sell. [...] Like you can give your artistic masterpiece, during two hours, the person keeps thinking, and finally, you'll sell. Sales, it's not a rule, it's susceptible to everything."

salesclerk's efforts hence lie in constant talking and acting out all available artistic skills, which sometimes draws on bridging highly elastic temporal flows or fixing unexpected interruptions. Salesclerk Diogo likewise highlights the importance of a quick, eloquent and psychologically smart sales service:

"Você tem que falar muito mais. Por que- colocou, tirou! Se fosse bermuda, botou duas bermudas para experimentar, vai demorar bastante. Aqui- quando a pessoa vai experimentando, eu tenho um trabalho de raciocinar e falar uma coisa, depois dela trabalhar em cima. É tudo psicológico. Tem muito a ver. Você está falando, a pessoa ta colocando um óculos, vai se ver no espelho. O que eu vou falar ela vai absorvendo, e vai casando com o óculos, já está no rosto dela, e tá bonito: aconteceu e vendeu!"[19] (Diogo, 23, salesclerk at *Visibly Hot*)

Time pressure, according to Diogo, is more intense with products like sunglasses than with shorts. The salesclerk's acting thus needs to include not only a scan of the customer's psychic condition, but also the use of further devices: the mirror, amongst others, is crucial to that goal. As Diogo explains, he would use the simultaneity of his eloquent commentaries and someone's mirror image. Customers would "absorb" this moment, getting convinced of their beauty by "matching" their faces with the sunglasses at sales.

4.2.4 Compliments and sexual fantasies

As Letícia shared an elaborately reflected account about the sales job in our interview, I also tried to draw the attention to the gendered aspects of

---

19 "You have to talk much more. Because- put on, put down! If it was about shorts, [if] the customer put on two pairs of shorts to try on, it will take some time. Here- if a person tries on [sunglasses], my work is to reason and say something, and afterwards to work around it. This is very psychological. This has a lot to do with it. You are talking, the person is putting on a pair of glasses, will look at herself in the mirror. What I will say she will absorb, and [she] will marry with the glasses, they are already on her face, and it's beautiful: it happened and it's sold!"

what she had just told me about acting as well as about the management of affects. But the dedicated young saleswoman dismissed it with a smile:

"Eu não sou dessa teoria. Eu acho que- realmente, tem muita gente que acha que homem vende melhor do que mulher. Eu acho que isso depende muito da pessoa."[20] (Letícia, 26, responsible salesclerk at *Visibly Hot*)

Individual pursuit of sales goals as well as product knowledge, she insists, and not the salesclerk's sex would be vital for one's success. Such a dedication led her to bringing fashion advice to perfection, "agregando valores"[21], as she calls it. Although this downsizing of gender issues in favor of neoliberal logics of individual responsibility pervades both the enterprise's training ideology and several employees' accounts, a couple of other salesclerks dissent. They see a difference in whether they are selling to a male or a female customer, a factor which also affects their interaction performances. Cashier Marina, for example, closely observed one of her sales colleagues and distinguishes his singular skill in combining sympathetic manners with giving advice on fashionable appearance.

"Eu achava que ele fazia bem as vendas, porque ele era simpático e ainda dava dica, ainda, de beleza, de modelo. Tipo, ah, mas isso combina super com a sua sobrancelha, com a sua roupa. [...] Eu acho que ele ganhava muito com isso. Ainda mais com mulher, cara, ela se importa muito, né? Ah, mas a minha sobrancelha fica toda torta!"[22] (Marina, 19, cashier at *Visibly Hot*)

According to Marina, women were very concerned about looking beautiful. Therefore, she says, her salesclerk colleague, who is a specialist in giving fashion advice on eyebrows, had much more success with female

---

20 "I am not a fan of this theory. I think that- really, many people think that men are selling better than women. I think that this highly depends on the person."
21 "accumulating values"
22 "I think that he was doing well in sales, because he was sympathetic and above that, he gave advice, in beauty, of models. Like, ah, this goes very well with your eyebrows, with your clothes. [...] I think he gained a lot from it. Especially with women, my god, she cares a lot, right? Ah, but my eyebrows are all crooked."

than with male customers. The feeling of being attractive is what constitutes the sales interaction; it is what affects the very bond between the seducer and the seduced. But emotions and affects, to use again Ahmed's words, are always directed to an object (Ahmed 2004b). It is not the feeling of being beautiful as such that is circulating between the bodies, but rather the object of its directedness. Femininity and masculinity are such cultural objects. They are circulating as affective horizons between people and other objects, designing, as it were, a pretended feeling-in-common.

Many salesclerks are directing compliments and flattery towards customers in order to suborn such a gendered, and often heterosexually coded feeling. Pedro, one of Marina's teammates, has advanced his selling techniques in this manner. In fact, he mobilizes a series of fantasies that he believes to match with the customer's desires.

"O que eu falo muito para homem, quando o óculos está bonito, naquele com cara de patrão; patrão é aquele quem manda, né? Você tem cara de galã! Galã é um cara que seduz. Eles gostam, eles morrem de rir, eles gostam, acabam levando porque eu falei essa palavra mágica. [...] Olha só, as pessoas são carentes. Eles gostam de se sentir bem. Eu uso muito isso. Para mulher, eu uso muito a moda. Mas, às vezes eu falo que estão chiques, têm cara de riqueza, cara de rica, perua, elas morrem de rir."[23] (Pedro, 21, salesclerk at *Visibly Hot*)

Pedro identifies that the customers he serves do lust after (self-)complacency. Consequently, he meets this need with a procedure that incites for manifold imaginations. Firstly, he invokes the character of the stylish womanizer as to be identified by the male customers; equally, he intends to accommodate the female clients with flattery, animating them to experience their own feminine beauty. In both cases, Pedro gets to play with the urge for being sexually attractive to other humans by activating commonly known, binary gender performances. Most strikingly, these allusions (es-

---

23 "What I say a lot to the guys when the glasses are beautiful- that kind of guy that acts like a boss, you know- boss is the one who gives orders, right? You look like a heartthrob! They love it, they die laughing; they like it just because I said this magic word. [...]Look, people are needy for love. They want to feel good. I use this a lot. For women, sometimes I tell them they are fancy, that they are looking rich, like a celeb chick; they die laughing."

pecially those to female beauty) are tied to richness and fame: the all-encompassing aspiration for a better, brighter life. The customer's affirmative reactions ("they die laughing") do finally underline that this promise of material wealth is interlocked with sexual fantasies. According to Pedro, they can be "used", in other words, turned into sales.

Drawing on feminist film theorist Silverman (1992) and her critical enhancement of Althusser's theory of ideology, which privileged the role of state institutions as well as of identities as based on social class, (sexual) fantasies and desires equally contribute to establish social constraint. Subjectivity, the author holds, unfolds not only embedded in historically specific modes of production, but also due to a culturally charged symbolic order. Together, these two entities would establish a "dominant fiction", consisting of "the images and stories through which a society figures consensus" (Silverman 1992: 30). Now, the most impacting binary opposition of Western dominant fiction relied on "male" and "female". As Silverman puts it elsewhere (1997), since fantasies and desires are both collective and individual, they urge on subjects to "posing" in suchlike sexed bodies. Or, to state the case somewhat differently, fantasies are taking shape in people's aspirations for social belonging. Individuals such as the sales customers above are invited to willingly arrange a picture of their own within the cultural repertoire of gender screens. The individuals' investments in male or female bodies finally also reflect their need for being perceived, that is, for taking part in a specific scene of collectivity (Silverman 1997: 49).

Affective labor and its substantial sales strategies as reported by Pedro are constantly provoking customer "posing". Strictly separated in experiences of either women or men, the customers' fantasies are being enlivened by flattery and compliments that promise self-affirmation. Consequently, their feeling comfortable in the offered roles and positions make them fall in with both the brand's and broader society's regime of the gaze. To once more use Silverman's (1997) words, these regimes are setting the coordinates through which individuals are imagining and positioning themselves in space, costume and light. Representing the heartthrob [galã] on one hand, and the celeb chick [perua] on the other, seem to refer to historically specific ways how quite a lot of Carioca shoppers would like to be seen and desired by others. Pedro's knowledge about how to handle and "use" these customer aspirations finally constitutes the deeply gendered fashion of affective labor. Salesclerks not only have to identify with socially promising identities (chapter three), but also to summon customers to posing within the cultural repertoire of femininity or masculinity. Affective labor concentrates this repertoire; it endlessly associates singular aspirations to it, thus reassembling both the conditions to reproduce capitalist labor power and the symbolic contours of masculine domination.

4.2.5 Misadventurous affects

From what has been said about fantasies and desires in retail techniques, it follows that affective labor is both woven in and weaving in heteronormative arrangements. It is labor, which fosters what Preciado (2008) has tried to grasp with the ambiguous tensions characteristic of the "pharmaconographic era". According to her hypothesis, both the pharmaceutical and the porn industries have put sexual desires to their service. Desires would be celebrated and multiplied, but simultaneously distributed and particularized as "tangible realities" (Preciado 2008: 32). As Preciado provokes with her examples of Viagra, Playboy and Testogel, the present multiplication has indeed not necessarily a deliberating effect. In many cases, the sexual desires as stimulated by the pharmacopornographic industries are rather reproducing male supremacy and heterosexual affectivity. They are, for example, not interested in a female Viagra, neither are they critical to new constraints that come along with bringing people's testosterone balance to perfection. Preciado concludes that we were contemporarily captured in tensions of excitation and frustration (Preciado 2008: 37); that we were lustfully moved and reigned by modes of heteronormative desiring that would easily result in misadventurous reluctance.

Affective labor at *Visibly Hot* is about unleashing desires. As mentioned above, it can open up intimate liaisons. Several salesclerks report that they have been invited to dates, that they have hooked up or even married through their job at the sales point. However, the same are well aware that engineering feeling by encouraging desires is a risky and sometimes frustrating business. Customers' accidental irritations can easily backfire on sales. Salesclerk Juliano reported on repeated scenes of failure when heterosexual couples entered the store.

"Vem casal junto, a Camilla atende. Ela é uma menina bonita. A mulher fica com ciúme e faz o cara ir embora. É surreal isso. [...] Casal é bem complicado para atender."[24] (Juliano, 21, salesclerk at *Visibly Hot*)

Juliano's direct supervisor was frequently causing scandals when she started flirting with the male part of the couple. Her affective-sexual selling strategy would lead to high tension and a feeling of jealousy in the female customer of the couple. Jealousy and the abrupt abortion of sales form a sequence many salesclerks observe at work. Strikingly, the conflict is often ascribed to stem from female competition.

"Teve um lance aqui [sorriso]. Era o meu primeiro namorado. Veio aqui com sua nova namorada. Eu estava aqui no caixa. E eu o cumprimentei. O menino de vendas falou- pô, eu perdi a venda por sua causa! Por que a menina deu uma olhada assim, sabia, entendeu? E foi embora. Acontece bastante."[25] (Eloisa, 23, cashier at *Visibly Hot*)

Eloisa apparently once ruined a sale of her colleague because she said hello to her ex-boyfriend, who, at that very moment, was accompanied by a new girlfriend. The latter must have imagined an affective threat emanating from Eloisa. As that girl would defend her love property, stemming any possible sexual pretensions of others, she urged her boyfriend to leave the shop. Salesclerk João asserts that such situations always arise when serving mixed couples. However, not only women, but also men would be driven by jealousy and hence violently act on male suspects.

"Eu já tive momentos aqui que tipo- atendendo a mulher do cara, mas eu tava sendo simpático com ela. O cara era um brutamonte. O cara achou que eu estava em

---

24 "There comes a couple, Camila serves them. She is a beautiful girl. The woman [of the couple] gets jealous and makes the man go away. It's totally crazy. [...] Couples are very difficult to serve."

25 "We had an awkward situation here [laughter]. It was my first boyfriend. He came here with his new girlfriend. I was here at the cashier station. And I greeted him. The sales boy said- fuck, I just lost the sale because of you! Because the girl glanced at you like this, she knew it, you know? And went away. This happens very often."

cima da mulher dele. Chamou minha atenção. Eu falei para ele- até que falei assim, não, olha só, eu tô sendo simpático e tal, eu sou gay, e tal, até para não arrumar um conflito. Por que eu vi que o cara estava levando na maldade. Mas querendo ou não, os funcionários da [*Visibly Hot*] têm essa energia. A gente gosta de receber e transmitir energia. Então, assim, a gente vai ser simpático, a gente vai querer trocar ideia, vai conversar, ou vai- vamos marcar para sair um dia e tal!"[26] (João, 19, salesclerk at *Visibly Hot*)

In this situation, João has been menaced by the male part of a couple. As he tellingly describes, the sales job at *Visibly Hot* is risky because its salesclerks have a special energy, a sexiness, in other words, that would open up sympathy, conversations and spontaneous invitations to dates or going out. But this energy sometimes causes trouble. In the case of mixed sex couple customers, the salesclerk had to manage macho violence. To this respect, João personally starts with explaining to the man that he is just behaving "sympathetically". If that does not work, he will go on and say that he is gay (what he actually "is not", as he stressed in our interview). In some situations, however, this strategy would not work out, since in a momentary man's absence, he could be "really" affected by provocative signals purposely transmitted by the woman.

"Já teve a situação que veio um outro casal. Aí, a mulher ficou, o cara saiu. Aí, a mulher começou a ficar em cima de mim. Depois o cara voltou. Ela se pôs no lugar dele. Já teve muita essa situação assim. Caraca, essa mulher está tentando me ferrar!"[27] (João, 19, salesclerk at *Visibly Hot*)

---

26 "I already had moments here, they were like- serving the guy's wife, but I was only nice to her. It was this brute guy. The guy thought that I was into his wife. He caught my attention. I told him- I even said it like this, look, I am being nice you know, I am gay, and so on, right because I didn't want to enter into conflict. Because I saw that the guy was taking this badly. But, whether you like it or not, the employees of [*Visibly Hot*] have this energy. We like to receive and transmit energy. So, you know, we will be nice, we will chat around, talk, or- we will meet to go out some day and things like that!"

27 "There was already a situation with another couple. In that one, the woman stayed here, the man left. Soon, the woman started to hit on me. Then the guy

This time, João sees himself as beaten at his own game. In the latter scene, it was the female customer who initiated a provocative flirt with him. But when the same girl's boyfriend came back to the shop, she would skillfully take on the role of the innocent fiancée, charging solely João with the flirty tension in the air. Such situations confronted through affective labor relegate again to the ambiguous tensions of excitation and frustration. Although both customers and salesclerks are enthusiastically striving for exploring new limits of affective intensity, their relations maintained with the object of desire get stuck in heteronormative trouble about both the possibility of polygamous affect and loss of property. In Preciado's (2008) sense, there are the two sides emblematic of the "pharmapornographic era": first, a concentration of narcissist energy, thrilling and promising for new sexual excitations; and secondly, frustration fighting back through untamed jealousy and newly essentializing gender difference.

4.3 AMBIGUOUS FRIENDSHIPS

One could object now that *Visibly Hot* salesclerks' unabashed flattery and amicable customer attendance is culturally entrenched; that is, that there would be a certain "Brazilianness", fostering a sexually liberal ease of handling. For it is true that the enterprise's sales strategy in other countries such as Kuwait, Abu Dhabi or United States – where I could not conduct fieldwork – might be slightly less aggressive to this respect. Since *Visibly Hot*'s branding government is imminently playing on cultural traits and authenticity, the question arises to what extent this is true for affectivity attached to nationality. In what follows, I strive to respond to this relevant objection in tracing a short genealogy of how a specific affectivity continues to be ascribed to Brazilians and their emotional character. Most interestingly, this is not a recent question. Many intellectuals in and above Brazil have dealt with this topic along the 20th century because emotional behavior was often seen as hindering the project of European-style modernity. Emotionality, informality of the social encounter and especially the role

---

returned. She stepped back to him. There were a lot of situations like this one. Oh my god, this woman is trying to fuck me up!"

of friendships in the economic sphere have been at the center of their analytical interest. As Buarque de Holanda writes:

"O desconhecimento de qualquer forma de convívio que não seja ditada por uma ética de fundo emotivo representa um aspecto da vida brasileira que raros estrangeiros chegam a penetrar com facilidade. E é tão característica, entre nós, essa maneira de ser, que não desaparece sequer nos tipos de atividade que devem alimentar-se normalmente da concorrência. Um negociante de Filadélfia manifestou certa vez a André Siegfried seu espanto ao verificar que, no Brasil como na Argentina, para conquistar um freguês tinha necessidade de fazer dele um amigo."[28] (Holanda 2014: 178-179)

This citation stems from Buarque de Holanda's famous book *Raízes do Brasil* (2014; English translation 2012), originally written in 1936 and until today one of the most influential historical essays which both analyzed and gave rise to the experience of an allegedly specific emotional character of Brazilians: the "cordial man", an ethic of living together, as he says, which is solely dictated by a thoroughly emotive basement. In his understanding, Brazilians were outstandingly affectionate, but this was neither due to a ritualized friendliness (as it was the case, according to the author, of Japanese), nor to an innocent behavior. As an amalgamation of a socio-psychological ideal type and a pattern of sociability, Holanda's "cordial man" refers to constant, both individual and collective attempts to personalize whatever social interaction. As Costa rightly notes, the "cordial man" prefers feeling to the "anonymity of legalized order" (Costa 2014: 834); friendship and personal loyalty are more important to him than the institutionalized law.

In a broader sense, the "cordial man" describes a strategic, somewhat playful behavior, which aims at preserving personal interests. This applied to the political, the economic and overall social spheres. According to

---

28 "The rejection of any form of relationship not based on an ethos of emotion is an aspect of Brazilian life that few foreigners understand with ease. And this trait is so characteristic among us that it does not even disappear in activities normally based on competition. A Philadelphia businessman observed to André Siegfried that he was astonished to discover that in Brazil and Argentina, you have to be-friend the customer to win him over." [my translation]

Monteiro's foreword to the English edition of Holanda's essay, the "cordial man" could furthermore be read as a sort of an anti-US-American character.

"In contrast to the North American, the cordial man is the person who refuses all restraints, as well as all protective mechanisms, with regard to society and to the Other. In the Brazilian case, the public sphere would instead be the place for possible celebration of the proximity of bodies and souls. Intuitively, who can fail to recognize, in this kind of celebration, the *alegria* [joy] repeatedly attributed to Brazilians, backed up by an endless string of stereotypes?" (Monteiro in Holanda 2012: xi)

According to Holanda's concerns he shared with his intellectual compatriots in the 1930s, the "cordial man" could lead to problematic consequences. Since the latter was opposed to Max Weber's protestant work ethic and instead praised the emotional bonds of the patriarchal family, the evolution towards a European-styled modern civilization was in danger. However, maybe the most interesting aspect of Holanda's unease about the Brazilians' emotionality is that he was noticeably torn between its corruptive and its fortunate nature.

Holanda begins the analytical section on the "cordial man" with a glance at economic history and the correlated social change in the United States. Industrialization in the 19th century, he writes, brought about new hierarchies between workers, authorities and intermediaries; relations which substituted the old "bonds of affection and blood" (Holanda 2014: 171). While he clearly sees the problems that arose from this rationalization, namely the disappearance of human relationships and the consequent feeling of irresponsibility of employers towards the lives of workers, Holanda insists on its liberating effects. The detachment of strong familiar ties, especially that of patriarchal imprint, was in his view essential not only to triumph over individualist abuse of power, but also to adapt to practical life in modern times. This view was close to Holanda's heart, because he would disagree with Ribeiro Couto, a cosmopolitan intellectual contemporary and poet, who had actually first used the term "cordial man". For Couto was convinced that the "cordial man" had a civilizing effect:

"Essa atitude de disponibilidade sentimental é toda nossa, ibero-americana... Observável nos nadas, nas pequeninas insignificâncias da vida de todos os dias, ela toma vulto aos olhos do crítico, pois são índices dessa Civilização Cordial que eu considero a contribuição da América Latina ao mundo."[29] (Couto in a letter to Alfonso Reyes 1931, cited apud Bezerra 2005: 126)

Although Holanda highly appreciated the poet's oeuvre, he resolutely objects that the "cordial man" corresponded to a civilized character. Bad and corruptive traits, he argues, were equally implicit in cordiality: "a inimizade bem pode ser tão cordial como a amizade, visto que uma e outra nascem do coração, procedem da esfera do íntimo, do familiar, do privado"[30] (Holanda 2014: 241). Holanda may have widely agreed with Couto that Brazilian sociability contained a specific, exacerbated affectivity. But he disagreed in magnifying these traits in terms of good or even prosperous manners.

The emotive virtues of nice and wholehearted company, hospitality and generosity were "antes de tudo expressões legítimas de um fundo emotivo extremamente rico e transbordante"[31] (Holanda 2014: 240). To Holanda, the cultural politics of cordiality, which prevail in Brazil, have an inextricably ambiguous face. On the one hand, the excessive desires to establish intimacy with other people could easily result in a compulsive order. They might infiltrate the public sphere, causing a degeneration of politics into particular, individualistic interest, all at the expense of modern democracy. But even if Holanda sees this coercive danger unfolding through "overflowing" emotionality as predominant, he does not abandon, on the other hand, the idea of cordiality's potential. In Brazil, politeness was used as a powerful strategy. Once it was experienced and practiced as

---

29 "This attitude of sentimental disposition is all ours, Ibero-American... Observable in the inanities, in the small insignificancies of daily life, it takes shape in the eyes of the critic, because they are signs of this Cordial Civilization I do consider Latin America's contribution to the world." [my translation]
30 "hostility can easily be as cordial as friendship, since both do arise from the heart, and operate as emanating from the intimate, the familiar, the private." [my translation]
31 "above all legitimate expressions of an emotional depth, which is highly rich and overflowing." [my translation]

sort of formalized masquerade, it could keep "true" sensibility as well as emotions intact. As such, the cordial mentality also served individuals as a means of resistance against the constraints of society (Holanda 2014: 177).

4.3.1 Cordiality, a cultural politics of friendship

Due to Holanda's methodology of thinking contraries as embedded in a constant dialectic play (see Antonio Candido's preface to the 1967 edition, Holanda 2014: 13), his dynamic reconstruction of affectively legitimated hierarchies within Brazilian society has lost nothing of its topicality. Although it may be true, as Bezerra argues, that the romanticizing perspective on the "cordial man" of Ribeiro Couto now prevails in both internal and external attributions of Brazilianness as something imminently attached to candor and affection (Bezerra 2005). Anthropologist Rezende (2009) gives evidence of related identities Brazilian postgraduate students articulated during their long-term sojourns in European countries. Since most of them expressed difficulties in establishing stable friendships with locals, the former came to the conclusion that the problem laid in the cultural difference of affectivity. They would have more facility to become friends with other Brazilians living abroad, since their fellow countrymen would like parties and were much more "affective persons". Actually, these students' predominant discourse on friendship holds that Brazilians were warmer and more accessible than Europeans, thus pointing to the reason why they easily made friends. Quite often, being Brazilian gave them even a subjective feeling of superiority, a sort of "privilege they had compared to others" (Rezende 2009: 103).

The self-image of warm, cordial and sensual traits of Brazilians is both a collectively and individually experienced pattern. As such, it is also present within contemporary economic work relations. As Piscitelli (2007; 2009) has vividly shown, Brazilian sex workers in Europe eventually concentrate such identifications in order to accommodate their clients: joyful temper, warmth and sensuality form part of their accessories that serve to express their Brazilianness (Piscitelli 2007: 28). As a specific corporeal and affective style, the latter would have turned into a qualification, a competence that supported a sexualization as well as a racialization of nationality. Therefore, Nigerian sex workers, for example, were usually rejected because they were Nigerian, and not because they were black. At the same time, Brazilian women could make use of the exotic imagery about the *mulata carinhosa* – the affectionate mulatto girl (Piscitelli 2007: 26). Affective competency fills social markers with hierarchy. Those women who had fewer advantages than the Brazilians needed much higher individual investments as well as competitive efforts in order to become desirable to European clients.

Besides sex work, domestic work is another, virtually classic métier, which is thoroughly nerved by affective components. As a consequence of the bourgeois modernity on either side of the Atlantic, domestic work has not only been re-naturalized as the work of women, but also disregarded as pertaining to productive labor (Federici 2012: 92). To this day, this structural devaluation demands from female domestic workers a great deal of emotional demonstrations – like sympathy, manners and good intentions – towards their employers. While in European countries, such emotional subjection affects mostly migrant women (Gutiérrez Rodríguez 2010), in the Latin American and especially Brazilian scenario it is women from poor and mostly non-white strata. And in this context, the self-image of Brazilian cordiality goes even beyond the question of a worker's competence. According to Brites, emotional ambiguities within the hierarchic relation of employee and employer were a fundamental part of the "didactics of social distance" (Brites 2007). In other words, cordiality is what governs the relations between those who serve and those who are served (Vidal 2007: 183). For, similar to Holanda's "cordial man" in public commitment, emotionality in domestic work is pervaded by ambivalent powers. It can enable corporate bonds, heighten the feeling of familiar belonging, but once it gets too much formalized and imposed, it equally obscures the ways it exercises patriarchal dominion.

Sociologist Vidal (2007) demonstrated with an impressive sensitiveness how friendship and love were the affective references in the relation between female domestic workers and their mistresses from Rio de Janeiro's middle classes. Without romanticizing nor morally judging neither of the two parties, the author stresses all actor's daily insistence on the idea that Brazilians would share an emotionality which positively distinguished them from other people and which transcended the differences of social class that were actually separating them (Vidal 2007: 183). On the ideal of friendship he writes:

"Présent chez les unes et les autres, l'idéal de l'amitié entre les bonnes et les patronnes renvoie à une demande partagée de considération et d'affection, mais possède un sens différent selon la position occupée dans la relation: pour les premières, cela suppose de pouvoir recevoir une aide matérielle ou psychologique dans les moments difficiles; pour les secondes, c'est la loyauté, la confiance et la discrétion qui est attendue. Bonnes et patronnes savent d'ailleurs combien diffèrent ces attentes qui fondent leur amitié et combien l'affinité sur laquelle repose celle-ci permet que s'établissent des relations entre des personnes inégales dans un rapport hiérarchique."[32] (Vidal 2007: 192)

While both employer and employee share the same ethic ideal regarding friendship at work, the respective meaning turns out to be attached to their very different social positions. But as Vidal distinguishes, the women on either side are well aware that these positions are bearing disparate expectations. It is exactly therefore that they think that efforts from both sides towards establishing mutual affective bonds could enable a relation which bridges the gap of social class. The mistress, the women agree, "has to treat her domestic like a friend" (Vidal 2007: 191).

Since the employment contract between the serving and the served is lived in such terms of friendship, women experience its eventual breach as a withdrawal of amicable commitment. Both sides utter frustrations. Domestics complain, for example, that in spite of their affection to the mistress' children, they were suddenly betrayed in their friendship; that they didn't get the psychic or material support they were expecting from their employer. Mistresses again report on unanticipated disappearance of their employee. They say that they had never imagined, in the face of so much

---

32 "Familiar to one and the other, the ideal of friendship between the domestic and the mistress refers to a shared request for consideration and affect, but has a different meaning according to the position occupied within the relation: to the former, this means to receive material or psychological help in difficult times; to the latter, it is loyalty, trust and discretion that is expected. Domestics and mistresses incidentally know how these expectations which base their friendship actually differ and to what extent the affinity, on which that friendship is based, permits the establishment of relationships between unequal people in a hierarchical manner."

affection they shared, that their domestic would abandon them without any premonition (Vidal 2007: 194).

Conversely, the experiences of both personal disappointment and mutual loyalty do not suggest a primacy of a utilitarian attitude towards friendship. Vidal argues that women in both positions could actually never be sure about the feelings of the other person. In this light, the rhetoric of affectivity is rather referring to moral judgments on society's structural inequality. Gesture and hindrance of gratitude, Vidal provokes, actively regulate the feeling of social recognition. Mistresses commonly expected domestics to be grateful for occasional gifts or material support. By and large, domestics correspondingly express this feeling. However, they don't do this necessarily because they want to please their employers, but also because it would help them to put up with bad or paternalistic working conditions. Once again, this does not make domestics blind to gestures of domination. When secretly making fun of cheap perfumes they got by their mistress, and even more so when omitting a sign of the expected debt of gratitude, domestic workers actively challenge the social order they are immersed in. As we have seen above, "being affectate" is not just about effecting, but also about resisting social constraint. In the case of domestics, reserving the feeling of gratitude is an appeal for recognition as equals in a society which is formally democratic, but which in many respects continues to disadvantage or exclude them (Vidal 2007: 198).

4.3.2 Deprovincializing cordiality

If we follow the historical reconstruction of social philosopher and sociologist Honneth (2011), the institution of friendship, as we know it today, had historically emerged at the end of the modern age. Only with evolving capitalism, he writes, the idea spreads that men involved with profit-oriented markets would need a sort of counter-world, a sphere of retreat in which social relations were but of sympathetic and sentimental purpose (Honneth 2011: 241). Although this argument is inspiring at first glance, the author's noticeable pretense of universality seems to be caught in geographical and historical reduction. The emergence of modern friendship, Honneth claims, meant a gradual (and today definitive) release of its intrinsic attachment it formerly maintained to both economic calculation and policy of alliances, since members of all social strata implicitly attached to it the drive towards social freedom (Honneth 2011: 234). As I reconstructed until this point, the Brazilian case gives proof of another perspective. Both historical critique (Holanda 2014) and common sense in daily social reality (Brites 2007; Piscitelli 2007; Vidal 2007; Rezende 2009) are evidencing a deeply emotional entanglement of exactly those spheres Honneth suggests to have split up as a consequence of capitalism.

Meanwhile, efforts in transnational history have also taken up this issue. As a current German research project about emotions accurately provokes:

"Emotions are not the same for all people at all times. They have a history. In the Research Group for the History of Emotions at the Max Planck Institute for Human Development, researchers come together to investigate the history of Europe and India – not only to compare regions, but also to study what is called the provincialisation of Europe: overcoming the perception of Europe as universal, as the norm from which all other regions represent, to a greater or lesser extent, deviations." (Pernau 2015)

While Pernau emphasizes that a turning away of normative and Eurocentric views on emotion demanded the consideration of other world regions, she equally considers the heterogeneous, never absolute but always transnationally interwoven culturality of emotions. By this argument, Pernau aligns the research's inquiry on the project of "provincializing Europe", as famously put forward by Chakrabarty (2002).

According to historian Chakrabarty, the master narratives of European history, such as of the "public" and the "private" sphere, the nation state or citizenship, need to be transnationally unraveled (Chakrabarty 2002: 305). The methodological procedure must not be a cultural relativist one. In other words, it would be insufficient to switch allegiance from the "center" to the "periphery", thus running the risk of reproducing the logics of the "deviation". Rather, Chakrabarty writes, it is inevitable that dismantling Europe also includes the problematization of India (Chakrabarty 2002: 306). I assume that Holanda's reflections on the "cordial man" (2014) – even if written in a completely different context than Chakrabarty's postcolonial critique – has qualities, which inspiringly contribute to the latter's project. First, Holanda's analysis does not treat European modernity as culture specific. Holanda, we should not forget, was very committed to a European perspective, for which reason he repeatedly refers to European travelers and their view on Brazilian emotionality. But at the same time, his measure at the European norm of emotional management and modern progress also reveals his pragmatic intention to overcome colonial heritage in his native country.

To a certain extent, Holanda has actually written a transnational history of emotions and emotionality attached to social relations, namely friendships. On one hand, he problematized the traces colonialism and slavery had left behind in Brazil at the beginning of the twentieth century: a weak economy, a despotic elite, and a fundamentally authoritarian society (Costa 2014: 824). According to Costa, *Raízes do Brasil* has then also to be read as a kind of libertarian manifesto, aimed, at that time, at showing that "Brazil should not only find a place in the shady part of modernity, the country should also participate in the conquests of modernity" (Costa 2014: 824). So, on the other hand, Holanda indirectly offers the reader a critique of European modernity as exclusive, although he thoroughly preferred the same due to his still colonially flavored aspiration for social progress.

My point of deprovincializing cordiality goes in the direction of this tension Holanda might have felt in the 1930s and which Chakrabarty has put in a nutshell. How should the historian talk about a social phenomenon in his "colony" without falling into the trap of contributing to the logics of modernity's failed deviation? To Holanda, the former world system completely disregarded the potential advantages of the "cordial man". For sure, he had his own doubts about its real institutionalization, since colonial heritage had driven the Brazilian version to somewhat excessive, individualist outgrowth. But since he saw Brazil as a part of the West (and not of the "rest", as most intellectual contemporaries did), whatever emotionality expressed in the (post)colony was an aspect of modernity's manifold but entangled courses to him, be they histories of success or of failure.

Such conflicting feeling is still accompanying both discourse and practice of the "Brazilian emotionality". As shown by Rezende (2009), it emerges within transnational encounters in the form of individual identity constructs. What is more, Brazilian cordiality also embraces the cultural code of conduct most people share, especially when they stand in a hierarchical relation to each other or when the question of social equality surrounds the issue (Vidal 2007). Especially in this cultural politics of friendship, people's experiences vividly deconstruct the idea that there were necessarily "public" or "private" spheres to be traversed. The naturalness with which they handle personal commitments within relations of work may then bear witness of incomplete, if not imperially shaped, analytical tools regarding Western notions of friendship. As a similar occurrence to the "cordial man", the contemporary "Brazilian affect" is facing the difficulty of being articulated globally, if it does not want to comply with the suspicion of pertaining to either dishonesty or individualistic opportunity.

4.3.3 Recognition at work

If we bear this deprovincializing argument in mind, then Honneth's (2011) study on both possibilities and realities of democratic life can still be of interest. As Vidal so tellingly describes in his ethnographic encounter with the relation between Brazilian mistresses and their domestics, the cordial enunciation of friendship is embedded in a broader volition for social recognition (Vidal 2007). Hence, inspired by some of Honneth's key ideas, his study brings out that friendship is neither necessarily utilitarian nor opportunistic, but that the social bonds in question are often motivated by the need for self-affirmation. Honneth writes:

"It is modern society's will that personal relationships, in the midst of anonymization and isolation, come to represent those social relations in which the inner nature of humans finds its freedom by mutual confirmation" (Honneth 2011: 235) [my translation]

Rather unusual within contemporary social critics, Honneth challenges the commonly held perspective that growing, economically driven individualism was compromising friendship. This thesis, he holds, was hardly verifiable by empirical methods. Additionally, there would be evidence that the stability of friendship as an institution was far from being at risk (Honneth 2011: 252). While the history of Western modernity had undergone a series of erroneous trends in politics and economy, friendship could be seen as a space of contingent social progress. In Honneth's perspective, friendship as well as love are those kinds of social relations, which proved to have strongest "inertial power" [*Beharrungskraft*] as opposed to accelerated processes of individualization and increased flexibility at risk (Honneth 2011: 252).

At this point, Honneth might seem a bit too optimistic when he attaches his hope for a political counterstrike against neoliberalism to the achievements of same-sex marriage or, as he says, of friendships that transcend barriers of ethnicity, social class and space at risk (Honneth 2011: 252); in short, he truly misses out on neoliberalism's mobile technologies (Ong 2007), which are equally responsible for forging ambiguous regimes of femininity (McRobbie 2009), homonormativity (Mesquita 2011), xenophobia against migrants (Tsianos and Karakayali 2010) and, not to be forgotten, the global trends of increasing social inequality (Castillo and Maldonado 2015). Nevertheless, Honneth's claim that social bonds of friendship or love, even as articulated under present economic regimes and forces, are setting free a sort of communality through the need for recognition, highly matters in order to overcome the shortcomings of other critical views that perceive the economic sphere of markets and industries as monolithically alien to any democratic emotion. And this actually brings us back to the argument of Hardt (1999), saying that affects can never be fully engrossed by capital. Social bonds and ideas unfold also in the somewhat grey and dusty life of everyday work. At least the potentiality for it, we can assume, is already somewhere there.

Although – or maybe rather because – I could not find any institutionalized labor union within the affective laborers at *Visibly Hot* I studied, this question of friendship and social bonds' potentiality gained a certain importance for the present inquiry. Salesclerks mentioned foremost friendship, but also love as representing their patterns of emotion at work. They attached almost entirely good feeling to it; whether this was due to their aspiration to pertain to a peer group of gay or socially "different" people, to appreciation they found in flirty or amicable bonds with clients, or to the perception of friendship as a strategy to get along or come to terms with work. In any case, the experienced bonds were mediated by the brand, the spirit the salesclerks so often uttered to represent themselves. Notwithstanding the fact that this space of articulation seems to be a thoroughly commercial and economic one, these young people are not only embedded in the cultural context of cordiality and a supposed "Brazilian affectivity", but they are – as a mode of affective labor – also constantly immersed in a negotiation of their social position, which is both directed towards and modulated by an individual will for recognition.

Salesclerks at *Visibly Hot* stressed repeatedly the importance of a common language at work. Through shared slang or bad language, joking and sometimes coolness, they felt proximity to their sales colleagues as well as a sort of self-affirmation with respect to their own imaginations of being young. Salesclerks share and practice these commons when they meet each other at the brand's conventions, when they come together for the monthly training and actually experience it as a part of their daily routine at the sales point. Furthermore, the friendships experienced are not restricted to the sphere of the workplace. In most cases, they form a crucial part of social lives in leisure time. Regardless of whether sales employees were still new or already more experienced at the enterprise, everyone asserted that at *Visibly Hot*, "todo mundo é muito amigo"[33]. Branch manager Bruna, who is about to leave the company within the following month at the moment of our interview, says that these friendships were maybe the nicest part of the job.

"Quando eu sair da empresa, eu vou sentir muito falta disso. Porque é uma coisa que vai além do ponto de venda. [...] Todo mundo se conhece, está marcando uma coisa para sair, sempre- eles são basicamente a minha família. Todo dia a gente está se vendo. Sai daqui, liga um pro outro, na folga você encontra. Na folga, às vezes, a gente vem aqui. É absurdo como o pessoal da empresa tem um apego. Sabe, os gerentes, os vendedores, os caixas, os supervisores, sempre se comunicando."[34] (Bruna, 19, branch manager at *Visibly Hot*)

To Bruna, the social bonds she maintains at work correspond to the sensation of being part of a family. As a form of collectivity, family is generally

---

33 "we are all friends."
34 "When I quit the enterprise, I will miss this so much. Because it's something that goes beyond the sales point. [...] Everybody knows each other, will arrange something to go out at night, always- they are basically my family. We see each other all day. One leaves, calls another, and on day off you'll meet. On day off, sometimes we come here. It's crazy how people of the enterprise are so attracted to each other. You know, the branch managers, the salesclerks, the cashiers, the supervisors, they are always keeping in touch."

associated with a high degree of commitment while simultaneously representing a space where one can behave without having to pretend to be someone else. *Visibly Hot* seems to take advantage of this feeling in an astonishingly broad sense. The surprising affection of the sales crew, Bruna says, would even go as far as employees on their day off visiting or meeting their friends from work right at the sales point in the shopping center. Like the case of cashier Marina. She told me that the first months at the shop had helped her to finally separate from her ex-boyfriend, a process she now saw as decisive for her personal development and that she could not have coped with without the help of her new friends from work.

"Eu entrei em um época, assim- eu namorava. Tipo desde 12 anos. Quando entrei, era a época que eu brigava com ele. Brigando direto. E o [Vitor] me ajudava muito. Eu nunca consegui enxergar quem ele [o namorado] realmente era. Mentia, mentia- e, cara, foi o pessoal do trabalho, o [Vitor], o [Cleiton], a [Joísa], conversando comigo que- caraca! Eu acordei para a vida real. Assim, muito legal. E eu amei trabalhar, cara, eu prefiro muitas vezes trabalhar do que estudar até. [...] Nossa, fiquei muito mal. O que me dava fôlego para aguentar era aqui. Até dia de folga eu ia para cá."[35] (Marina, 19, cashier at *Visibly Hot*)

Friendships at work gave Marina the feeling of being mentally and affectively supported. Since her colleagues from her first employment encouraged her to break up with her boyfriend, she came to experience a new and liberating emotion through the group, as she says, the "real life". What is more, the atmosphere of friendship at the sales point also contributed to the positive, affectionate relation she maintains with the job. It is this pattern that generally appeared in the salesclerks' perception. The case of Diogo even shows that it is not uncommon that salesclerks recommend peo-

---

35 "I got here at a time, like- I was in a relationship. Like since I was 12. When I got here, it was at the time I was fighting with him. Really fighting. And [Vitor] helped me a lot. I never realized who he [the boyfriend] really was. Lies after lies, and man- it was people from work, [Vitor], [Cleiton], and [Joísa], talking with me, oh my god! I woke up in real life. Like, really cool. And I loved working, you know, I even prefer working to studying, actually. [...] God, I felt really bad. What gave me breath to endure was this place. Even on a day off I used to come here."

ple for new recruiting with whom they had already established closer friendships years before and outside of *Visibly Hot*.

"Eu trabalho com dois amigos meus, pessoas que eu conheci fora daqui. Acabei colocando os dois para trabalhar junto comigo. Então, eu me sinto super em casa. Eu venho trabalhar super empolgado. Mesmo quando ficar cansado, o que for. É um ambiente de trabalho que eu me sinto completamente à vontade por estar com as pessoas que estão comigo."[36] (Diogo, 23, salesclerk at Visibly Hot)

Friendship, in this case, becomes intelligible as a resource or strategy for someone to feel better when doing a given service job. It contains aspects of social freedom, which according to Diogo unfold in the midst of work and working relations. As a consequence of manifold emotional crossings of what one could still rudimentary attribute to either the private or the professional sphere, the feeling of "being at home" can easily spread at the workplace. To phrase it differently, the experience of friendship seems to have the power to align work and home, assemble the joy of leisure with labor.

Most strikingly, these crossings also hold for friendships with customers. Salesclerks proudly report on the common language that would "naturally" evolve when they treated the clients as if they were friends. Their personal and collective experiences of friendship easily turn into sales arguments: salesclerks literally affect customers with their own feelings. Cashier Eloisa, who mainly observes her sales colleagues, evaluates that the common points of being young and being a resident of the same large city helped a lot to engineer these emotions, because there was a shared language.

"Então, eu acho que quando você atende pessoas jovens assim da cidade, se torna mais fácil até pela língua já. A gente acaba criando situações que seriam situações para a gente, que a pessoa utilizaria esse óculos, tipo sair, tipo festa. Então, nosso

---

36 "I am working with two of my friends, people I have known elsewhere. I succeeded in putting them to work here together with me. So, I feel like really at home. I come to work extremely enthusiastic. Even when getting tired, or whatever. It is a working ambiance where I feel thoroughly at ease with sharing time with the people that are with me."

mundo é mais fácil a gente criar o mundo da pessoa com aquele óculos, criar uma situação que ela usaria este óculos, para convencer ela para levar. Eu vejo muito os meninos fazendo isso aqui."[37] (Eloisa, 23, cashier at *Visibly Hot*)

As already mentioned above, the creation of "situations that would be our own", as Eloisa puts it, repeatedly merge into more stable friendships or bonds of mutual attraction. The "outcome", as we could say, consists of what the salesclerks call the "cliente fixo", their regular customers.

"E o que tem também é cliente fixo. Sabe, que já é cliente dela muito tempo. A gente tipo- ah, ela quer um relógio, mas não tem aqui. Ontem, por exemplo, ela veio, e aí, não tinha aqui. A gente teve que ir lá para Copacabana para buscar, sabe- é aquele cliente certo. Eu fui lá para buscar o relógio. Ela ficou feliz; ela até deixou um brindinho, um chocolate, um carinho, né?"[38] (Leidiane, 24, salesclerk at *Visibly Hot*)

In the eyes of Leidiane, theses regular customers can be somewhat stressful. Since they already enjoy the special status of long-term clients, salesclerks must fulfill any special requests. But on the other hand, Leidane also makes clear that these are the "right" customers, not least because they usually return their gratitude with small and affectate gifts. In this way, the salesclerk may be happy because she/he gets recognition for her/his efforts, which are both personal favor and professional engagement.

---

37 "So, I think when you serve young people like that from the city, it's already way easier because of the language. We manage to create situations that could be our own situations, that the person would wear these sunglasses, like for going out, like for a party. So, it's easier for us to create our world as the world for that person to use those sunglasses, creating a situation, in which she would wear it, in order to convince her to buy it. I see the guys acting like that very often."

38 "And there are also the regular customers. You know, those who are already her customers for a while. We like- ah, she wants this watch, but we don't have it here. Yesterday, for example, she came here, and that's what happened. We had to go all the way to Copacabana to get it, you know- it's that kind of the right customer. I went there to get the watch. She was happy about it; she even left a little present, some chocolate, some affect, right?"

Branch manager Bruna also shares an opinion of the phenomenon "cliente fixo". In her view though, this is the outcome of a clearly professional competence, which is specific to *Visibly Hot*. Long-term friendships, Bruna holds, were part of the enterprise's procedure to both work on people so that they like their job and make customers come back.

"Eu tenho amizade pessoal com vários clientes que, ao longo do tempo, se tornaram os meus clientes. Eles compram só comigo, e fora da empresa, são os meus amigos. Eu saio com essas pessoas, tenho uma relação de amizade. Acontece, sabe. A gente trabalha muito com isso de, sabe, fazer as pessoas voltarem. Gostar de estar aqui, a gente trabalha muito isso, é uma característica da empresa mesmo."[39] (Bruna, 19, branch manager at *Visibly Hot*)

4.3.4 Competitive affects and collectivity

Although Bruna reminds us that friendships with customers were the consequence of a business strategy, her analysis is not to be seen as a critique. In her view, emotional proximity to both customers and colleagues are neither jeopardized by nor opposite to economic interest. Rather, these aspects seem to her to be closely connected. However, other salesclerks relate the social relations at work to the problem of individual profit seeking. Depending on the respective sales team, they say, competition could spoil team spirit and friendships.

"Existem equipes que são muito amigos. A gente aqui é- tem uma competição maior. A gente não é inimigo, a gente brinca, a gente conversa; há uma divergência às vezes, entendeu? No [outro shopping] era muito unida, eu adorava. Mas é isso, é tudo com respeito. Porque a gente passa a maior parte aqui do que em casa. Então,

---

39 "I have personal friendships with many customers who, over time, became my customers. They only buy with me, and outside the company, they are my friends. I go out with these people, I have a relation of friendship. It happens, you know. We work on this a lot, you know, to make people come back. To like spending time here, we work on this a lot, it is actually a characteristic of the company."

tem que respeitar o outro. Se não se gosta, pelo menos se respeita, aí vai dar tudo certo."[40] (Carol, 21, salesclerk at *Visibly Hot*)

Carol clearly rejects the excessive competition because she thinks that this made people lose their respect towards other teammates. Her own practices show though that she is not immune against the social tensions, which constantly unfold through affective labor. When Carol proudly posted a photo on Facebook that showed her with a "cliente fixo", a branch manager from another sales point, Bianca, felt visibly offended. The latter immediately reacted on the photo that Carol had so enthusiastically entitled: "Além de ser cliente VIP na [*Visibly Hot* da Barra], ele faz um bombom caseiro mais delicioso do universo. [heart symbol]"[41].

U = usuário desconhecido	U = unknown user
Bianca Deixa de ser puxa saco, Carol! [heart symbol][annoyed symbol] U1 Caroooooool [heart symbol] **Bianca** Sdd também, mas ele é MEU cliente VIP hein! Rum! Cuida bem dele! U2 Traz aqui para mimmmm **Carol** HAHAHA, Bianca tu é gerente ??? Rss ciumeeenta!! Ele é NOSSOO! [heart symbol] **Bianca** Ah meu amor Carol, sou gerente SIM! Quem é rainha nunca perde a majestade! Kkkk [heart symbol]	**Bianca** Stop being a bootlicker, Carol! [heart symbol][annoyed symbol] U1 Caroooooool [heart symbol] **Bianca** I miss you too, but he is MY VIP client ok! Hum! Take care of him! U2 Get some for meeee **Carol** HAHAHA, Bianca you are a branch manager??? Haha jealouus!!! He is OUURSS! [heart symbol] **Bianca** Ah my dear Carol, I am a branch manager--YES! Once a queen, always a queen! Haha [heart symbol]

---

40 "There are teams in which they are all friends. Here we are- there is more competition. We are not enemies, we are joking, we are chatting; there is some dissent sometimes, you know? In the [other shopping center], [the team] was very united, I loved it. But that's it, everything with respect. Because we spend more time here than at home. So you have to respect each other. If you don't like someone, at least respect each other, and everything will be fine."

41 "In addition to being a VIP client of [*Visibly Hot* in Barra], he makes the most delicious homemade sweets all over the universe. [heart symbol]"

Bianca's accusation of Carol as a bootlicker aims at setting boundaries of admissible cordial behavior at work. In her view, Carol has stolen a regular customer from her, an interpretation she made on the basis of the photo, which expresses an intimate bond (homemade sweets that Carol apparently tasted) to the regular customer. What is more, Carol's reaction, which exposes Bianca as a jealous person, even intensifies the competition between the two girls. Bianca considers it necessary to underline her hierarchical position as a branch manager and finishes by accentuating her queenly powers.

Actually, most of the conflicts reported by salesclerks have a gender, that is, they denominate conflicts between women. In some cases, these conflicts are described as conflicts that were additionally attached to conflicting sexual orientation. Salesclerk João comments about his boss, branch manager Letícia, and identifies her aversion to heterosexual women. As a consequence, the latter would prefer to choose either men or lesbian women to work in her team.

"Tem gerente que só gosta de trabalhar com mulher, tem gerente que só gosta trabalhar com homem. Tem gerente que gosta de trabalhar só com gay; tem gerente que gosta de trabalhar só com hétero. Tem gerente que gosta de trabalhar com os dois. Assim, a nossa gerente nunca consegue trabalhar com mulher vendedora. Todas as mulheres vendedoras que ela teve- mulheres hétero- ela teve dor de cabeça. Agora, mulheres gays, ela teve- tem uma compatibilidade até maior, tem um desenvolvimento maneiro da equipe, agora mulher hétero, sempre teve dor de cabeça. Por isso, se você reparar aqui, só tem hétero homem. Por causa disso. Por causa ela se adapta melhor. E também por causa do ponto de venda. Isso tem uma abordagem."[42] (João, 18, salesclerk at *Visibly Hot*)

---

42 "There are branch managers who only like to work with women, there are branch managers who only like to work with men. There are branch managers who like to work with gays; there are branch managers who like to work only with straights. There are branch managers who like to work with both of them. Like, our branch manager never succeeds in working with female salesclerks. All women she had here- straight women- gave her a headache. Now, gay women, she had- has even a higher compatibility, there is a cool development for the team; but straight women, always gave her headaches. That's why, if you want to have a look here, there are only straight men. That's why. Because

In João's view, there are very clear and separable categories of salesclerks: there are women, men, straights and gays. Due to branch managers' different tastes, sales teams were sometimes organized around but one or two of these categories, as it is the case of his boss. For Letícia, straight women were interfering too much in her vision of the team spirit. As she actually mentioned in our personal interview about one year before the conversation with João, she thought that women let their personal feelings compromise the sales. When they split up or were lovesick, they acted "de cabeça para baixo"[43]. Such feeling would not only jeopardize team coherence, she said, but also hindered the persuasive power that was needed for selling products to customers.

Notwithstanding their function and position, branch managers were commonly not looked at in terms of conventional bosses. As mostly same-aged colleagues, they are equally seen through the category of friends; friends, who sometimes share some personal advice or do personal favors for their salesclerks. Representing a crucial part of *Visibly Hot*'s feel good politics, all professional titles and positions are being symbolically diminished with respect to their hierarchical content. Salesclerks enthuse about their experiences at the conventions and training sessions, especially because they feel so emotionally close to their superiors; there are, as it were, no hierarchical borders that separate them. During trips, they report, everyone would share the same rooms and there was no distinction of whether someone holds a superior position within the overall company or not. Since these experiences endured and influenced the daily routines at the sales point, rivalry between salesclerks could be kept under control. As Diogo comments on the problem of competition:

"Mas, é nada que não consiga tirar de letra. A gente consegue, sim. A gente tem a Eloisa que, pô, ela ajuda, chega, fala. Todos vendedores podem contar com a ajuda do outro, não tem esse espírito de rivalidade. Até tem, mas é positivo. Todo mundo

---

she adapts better to it. And also because of the sales point. That's the approach."

43 "unhappy"

quer ficar primeiro, mas sem prejudicar o outro. Então, isso é muito bom, pelo outro lado."[44] (Diogo, 23, salesclerk at *Visibly Hot*)

Diogo shares an optimistic view on how social bonds and solidarity with colleagues at work can curtail bad or egoistic intentions of individuals. Since the atmosphere of friendship brings people to help each other, even competition could be something positive, as long as it would not harm or exclude members of the team. Diogo further concludes this consideration with an ethical stance on collective behavior at work: "Eu acho que todo mundo junto é mais forte do que um só. Acho mais bacana assim."[45]

However, the realization of a harmonic collectivity is often a difficult task, since the context of sales labor is in- or explicitly framed by competition. As we have seen above, it is not rare that salesclerks battle for so-called VIP-customers, for the primacy in beauty ideals or in reaching the monthly sales targets. Particularly in this regard, the high extent to which the salesclerks are praising the ideal of the family – right in the sense of "as all for one and one for all" – is striking. Their urge for individual recognition and social commitment cannot be reduced to a sole effect of corporate branding. The family and its values may also unfold within the cultural contours as traced by the "cordial man", including its ambivalent discourse of harmonic get-together that disguises unequal powers and its need for competition.

---

44 "But it's nothing you could not cope with easily. We succeed, yes. We have Eloisa who, man, she helps us, assists, talks. All salesclerks can count on the help from another, there is no such spirit of rivalry. Maybe there is, but it's positive. Everyone wants to be at the top [of sales], but without harming the other. So, that's really good, on the other hand."

45 "I think that all together are stronger than one alone. I think it's cooler like that."

5. (Un)fulfilled promises and different conflicts

The potentiality of friendships and collectivity is but one aspect when asking further questions about the limits of entrepreneurial promises. Actually, the complex interplay of branding government, self-conduct through processes of identification and new regimes of affective labor control urges us to further investigate the precarious effects on young people's lives. What happens to salesclerks after a period of employment at *Visibly Hot*? For how long do they stick to the brand's promises and where do they see the limitations of the propagated individual liberation at work? What are their decisions and possible futures in- or outside *Visibly Hot*? And finally, to what extent do these young people succeed (or not) in challenging the dominant logics of economic growth and affective self-perfection?

One of the main arguments of this chapter goes that the salesclerks in question – eventually representative of quite a large group of young employees of similar social background – inhabit precarious positions. Now, the precarious refers to quite differing, equally economic and cultural-coercive aspects. First, precarity refers to the structural conditions of retail service work in Brazil and hence to the factors of poor payment and heavy workloads. Second, *Visibly Hot* sales workers are engaging in logics of self-entrepreneurship and individual growth that today transcend very heterogeneous social classes. As I will argue, this lies not least in the cultural hegemony of beauty as attached to "cultural citizenship" (Edmonds 2010), which is generative of precarious subjectivities. On one hand, claiming individual aesthetic articulation can form a site of power and critique, as long as one succeeds in wrenching appreciation from other service workers and consumers. On the other hand, the same claims remain heavily exposed to economic turnovers and therefore to unsheltered, that is, insecure recognition. For some sales employees, this may produce the fatiguing sensation of ongoing and obligatory self-inventions. In other cases though, the rapid turnovers of identity claims may enable political articulations that were unforeseen by capital. As I will outline, particularly young people from the peripheries do not necessarily follow the social rules of product identifications they are previously hailed into.

The insights of the present chapter are mainly oriented towards and around the experience of three salesclerks I have met, about two years after the first encounter, for a second interview during my fieldwork. Directing the interests above mentioned, their stories illustrate different, singular ways of how they inhabit their precarious positions through work. Though general fatigue is the common feeling to all three sales workers after a while of their employment, they opted for very distinct strategies to tackle the situation, ranging from renewed enthusiasm for the brand to harsh critique and quitting. I end the discussion on inhabiting the precarious with opening it to the example of the *rolezinhos*, youth gatherings in urban shopping centers, which deeply unsettle dominant logics of consumer diversity and hence the pillars of how recognition and liberation through consumption are commonly thought of.

5.1 CONDITIONS, SUBMISSIONS AND MICRO REVOLTS IN SERVICE WORK

As we have already seen in the precedent chapters, *Visibly Hot*'s sales staff is being literally trained in both coping and agreeing with the rhythms of their employment – the entrepreneurial incentives range from a fine network of friendships and community events to promises for young-minded style and authenticity. In more practical terms, salesclerks also immediately experience the brand's virtues via particular teaching units. Every employee has to participate in monthly training sessions [*treinamentos*], which considerably resemble the training centers Hochschild (2003) described in her study about the instruction of flight attendants at Delta Airlines. Besides the specific trainings of cashiers and team leaders, most employees attend the sales trainings that embrace a classroom of about 20 persons. In the playful way of a theatre-like workshop and team competitions, the instructor – in the case of Rio de Janeiro, this is a former *Visibly Hot* salesclerk, who has about ten years of experience at the enterprise – conveys the latest sales strategies and codes of conduct to the employees. It is a crucial moment, in which the sales goals of the overall enterprise and of the respective sales points are communicated. Equally, initiating salesclerks are introduced to the demands for their individual performance that would decide on their monthly payment and premiums. As several salesclerks reported, it is common in these trainings that the singular stories of those persons who are already considered the "old hands" within the sales teams are honored (for their style or exemplary development of an authentic personal attitude) and presented to the "newcomers".

According to the survey of the international job website Indeed (2014), a sum of 80 current and former salesclerks evaluated *Visibly Hot* in widely positive terms. They stressed the nice and "dynamic" atmosphere of their employer as well as the "good friendships" they had found there. Furthermore, premiums for high sales performance were characterized as an advantage of the employment. On the other hand, several employees complained about the excessive and inconvenient working hours and about the lack of social security like health insurance coverage as well as of meal vouchers. As a different salesclerk elucidated in my interviews, *Visibly Hot* officially defines the employee's work schedule as a full-time job that includes a six-day week. While the day-off varies, salesclerks commit themselves to work shifts of six hours daily, including Saturdays and Sundays, alternating within the shopping hours that usually start at 10am and finish at 10pm. As is common within the entire consumer service sector in Brazil, the payment of commission makes a good part of the sales person's reward (see Sussekind 2005). In the case of *Visibly Hot*, the guaranteed salary is little more than one minimum wage [salário mínimo], which according to the Brazilian state is of R$ 788,00 in 2015 (Trabalhista 2015). Everything beyond this amount results from the employee's commission with respect to individual sales achievement, which on average doubles the fixed part.

Due to these commission-targeted conditions of consumer service jobs, overtime work is a crucial and thoroughly habitualized practice among *Visibly Hot* employees. As I could observe in many situations during my fieldwork, salesclerks are used to willingly stay for more hours if the shopping center is busy. It may then result from the factual full-time employment per day that several employees complain about the missing meal ticket. Although Brazilian workers' legislation does not obligate employers to furnishing this service, it is widely common in private and public employments (Redação/ON 2013). As different salesclerks explained, the situation was further complicated at *Visibly Hot* because they were not allowed to bring along their own food from home. Branch managers would generally forbid lunch bags because of the undesirable smell at the sales point. Consequently, employees need to eat at the facilities of the shopping center, which are normally not a very cheap option and hence often mentioned as an annoying aspect of the sales job. Furthermore, as *Visibly Hot* defines the daily schedule by six working hours, it succeeds in evading the employer's obligation to concede an official minimum lunch or meal break. According to Brazilian labor legislation, this duty comes to force only when the worker's schedule exceeds six hours daily. Hence, this is one more reason for why salesclerks hardly leave the shopping center at lunch break – there is literally no time for that.

5.1.1 Capital-competencies and personal growth, a phenomenon across classes?

In the tradition of the sociology of work, the questions of hierarchies and workers' participation within enterprises continue to represent important fields of investigation (Ramalho 2013: 100). Hence especially Marxist informed inquiries presuppose that the position of workers is illustrative for broader relations of domination and class struggle within a given industrialized society. The global expansion of service employments has now brought about new challenges for tracing such analogies. Braga's (2006) empirical research on Brazilian call center workers points to the disintegration of the working class formerly organized around Fordist relations of production and collective action based on labor unions. The rhythms to which these call center agents are subjected actually resemble in several ways those of salesclerks studied in my research on *Visibly Hot*. While team spirit and a great deal of collective feelings are being directly absorbed by the corporate brand, the enterprise's promises are fostering foremost the will for individual self-realization. Braga hereto contrasts the lack of collective mobilization with the call agent's individual interests for being recognized in their "personal dignity" (Braga 2006: 146). Their demands for the extension of breaks, for the improvement of catering as well as for being protected against aggressive behavior of their supervisors would be seen as the task of each individual and less in terms of a group interest. This phenomenon, the author continues, was further intensified by the fact that employments in the service sector were marked by high labor turnover (Braga 2006: 148). In other words, workers today were suffering highly flexible and timely limited contracts, urging them to perform periodic job seeking and simultaneously diminishing their nodal points for mobilizing collective action.

It is not only the theses of du Gay (1996) about the transformation of service employment and the rise of identity as a form of neoliberal government (see also my discussion in chapters three and four) within private enterprises that support Braga's diagnosed tendency that service employees primarily defended their personal integrity. Signs of fragmented group alliances are equally registered in broader terms. Within the vivid debates about the emergence of a supposed "new middle class" (Neri 2008), sociologists like Souza (2012) objected that it was more adequate to term these emerging groups as pertaining to a new working class, as he denotes, the "Brazilian strugglers" [*batalhadores brasileiros*]. Compared to the past, these groups were given more opportunities such as for higher education, but at the same time, there were not sufficient vacancies for these new kinds of curricula. Souza argues that people experienced the prospect of leaving behind dirty, hard and manual work, as it were, the socially stigmatized employments. However, structural conditions of the Brazilian labor market would restrain them within the service sector. According to the author, call center agents were the emblematic figures of an "exército de reserva minimamente escolarizado para o trabalho precário" (Souza 2012: 78)[1]. Telemarketing – and here lies also the proximity to service and sales jobs in shopping centers like at *Visibly Hot*[2] – pretended to pertain to "clean" and office work, lending a certain feeling of status to workers.

---

1 "a minimally educated reserve army for the precarious work"
2 As I argued in chapter two with the emergence of the early department stores, sales jobs may be even more tied to the idea of social status, since they directly mobilize a link to glamour and beauty.

Such aspirations for status are also the focus of Souza's study, when he discusses many service workers' incorporation of market driven ideals. His case study of Luciana, a former call agent that advanced to a team leader within her enterprise, points to the extensive impact of slogans stemming from career management and capitalist entrepreneurship on her personal plans for the future. Commenting on her actual private situation, she would make use of entrepreneurial jargon, like the "gestão da vida"[3] and the overall need for having a "visão de crescimento profissional"[4] (Souza 2012: 77). The sociologist concludes:

"Assim, ela transforma as exigências empresariais do trabalho precário em sua própria forma de olhar o mundo, em seu padrão de boa vida, mecanismo extremamente eficaz que faz com que ela converta em sua visão de mundo os novos critérios aos quais ela se adéqua, transformando-os em seus próprios. Dessa maneira, ela percebe a sua dominação não como algo imposto de fora, por um mundo cruel, mas como algo querido por ela, agora internalizado como seu padrão de boa vida. Se, por um lado, sua trajetória social ascendente lhe aparenta ser um mundo cheio de possibilidades, por outro, ela também não escapa de se tornar o suporte social por excelência da exploração do trabalho formal precário."[5] (Souza 2012: 78)

Despite Souza's problematic insinuation that Luciana could not perceive the forms of domination she subjects herself to[6], the observation of a nar-

---

3 "management of life"
4 "vision of professional growth"
5 "In so doing, she transforms the entrepreneurial requirements of precarious work into her own way of looking at the world, into her standard of a good life, which is an extremely effective mechanism that leads her to convert her own worldview into the new criteria to which she adapts herself, turning them into their own. That way, she does not perceive her domination like something imposed from the outside, by a cruel world, but as something dear to her, now internalized as a her standard of a good life. If, on one hand, her upward social trajectory appears to her as a world full of possibilities, she also cannot escape, on the other hand, from turning into the exemplary social support of the exploitation emanating from precarious formal work."
6 The author tends to an idiosyncratic reading of Bourdieu's concept of *habitus* (Bourdieu 1979) which prompts him to presuppose that subjects incorporate

row (and even linguistic) integration of personal life with market values seems to aptly record a transnationally operating zeitgeist of precarization (Lorey 2008). Also in the example of *Visibly Hot*, both branch managers and salesclerks explicitly (and linguistically) referred to the unquestionable need for self-optimization. *Crescer pessoalmente* – growing personally – was consensually seen as the key for success in both business and life. Today, the watchword of growth seems to embrace a broad range of occupations. Thus at least in Brazil, it also captures the experience of what are socially very heterogeneous groups.

While the vast majority of young service workers highlighted here pertains to lower social classes, a look at the coeval progeny of middle and elite classes illuminates that the grammar of personal/economic growth is not strictly class-specific. As Foucault had predicted, the imperative discourse of being an "entrepreneur of the self" (Foucault 2008: 301) now permeates, as it were, even the capillaries of society. In a research project on the construction of the self and the related professional prospects among young adults from socially privileged strata in Rio de Janeiro, Almeida and Eugenio (Almeida 2009; Almeida and Eugenio 2011) detected several individual strategies that unfold within proportionally insecure or flexible contracting. Young executives, stylists, artists and entrepreneurs would defend and convey values such as improvisation, attitude, calculation or spontaneity, without tracing any strict boundaries between life and work (Almeida 2009: 5). Beyond the aspirational need for personal "growth", as also diagnosed among small employees (Souza 2012: 77), the privileged young adults explain their tactics in terms of an artist-like act: "virar", that is, trying to cope with a difficult situation. As the authors of the study comment:

"Se a lógica do virar é caminho para arranjos idiossincráticos que permitem atingir circunstancialmente autossuficiência e 'dar conta do recado', é também um

---

structural values both literally unconsciously as well as in linear and uncritical ways. Although I do not share that misleading reading of Bourdieu, we may refer here to Boltanski's (Boltanski and Thévenot 1999) commendable efforts to theoretically insist on critical capacities that unfold as an integral part of an individual's need to formulate justifications for her/his actions in a given situation.

fenômeno diversas vezes atrelado, mais amplamente, a um novo desenho mais situacional e presentificado da vida profissional, no qual a carreira pensada como *totalidade* cede lugar a uma autonomia do fragmento: a cada projeto, é possível mudar de posição e de atividade e 'aprender fazendo', incorporando novas habilidades. 'Ninguém é mais uma coisa só', decreta o descolado colunista Tom Leão, em matéria sobre a *slash generation* publicada pelo jornal *O Globo* em 09 de setembro de 2010."[7] (Almeida and Eugenio 2011: 14)

According to Almeida and Eugenio, the project bound proceedings of young people meant an alternative to former career-focused trajectories. In other words, these people learned by doing, improvising and re-arranging rational job requirements, thereby echoing the hegemonic media discourse from *O Globo*, which formally declares that one had more than but one face, identity, and job.

Although Almeida and Eugenio are theoretically trying to see "aprender fazendo" and "virar" in terms of liberating and inventive practices (Almeida and Eugenio 2011: 14), it remains unclear from what these young people actually disengage themselves. From what the authors call "rhizomatic capitalism" they obviously do not. Similar to the employees in my case study on *Visibly Hot*, the young self-entrepreneurs' practices and explications rather seem to approve of the mechanisms of flexible and insecure employments in that the latter appear to them as a consequence of their free individual choice. The authors' listed examples and biographies do not indicate any rupture or transversal, "immanent" alterations – right in the sense of Deleuze/Guattari or Negri/Hardt they repeatedly refer to – of neoliberal market logics. As Deleuze famously put it, one form to resist is flight, or the art of tracing a line of flight: "fleeing, but throughout my

---

7   "If the logic of *virar* leads to idiosyncratic arrangements, which enable to get to circumstantial self-sufficiency and to 'carry it off', it is also a phenomenon many times tied to a broader, new and more situational design of professional life, in which the career as thought of in terms of a totality gives way to an autonomy of the fragment: in every project, it is possible to change your position, your activity, and 'to learn by doing', incorporating new skills. 'Nobody is any longer but one thing alone' decrees the easygoing columnist Tom Leão in an article about the *slash generation*, published in *O Globo* newspaper on September 9, 2010."

flight, I am *searching* for *a weapon"* (Deleuze and Parnet 1996: 47). While there is, in truth, an improvising and learning-by-doing aspect of whatever practice directed to put up with a given situation of precariousness, an impulse to flee, that is, a preliminary tracing of a potential exodus (Lorey 2012: 133) remains an indispensable force – that might prevent one from contributing to the logic of eternal (personal and economic) growth.

Quite different social classes and employment groups, as we have indicated, may incorporate the latter logic. However, this should not lead us to conclude that these groups would also be affected by the same consequences, if one quits or loses a job or if one fails to put up with the demands of contemporary employments. Young service workers I encountered during my research at *Visibly Hot* may have clearly less leeway in stages of unemployment or more limited contracts than the socially privileged groups as studied by Almeida and Eugenio (2011). The former do not have parents with social networks in business or in the arts as the latter do; neither can they count on friendships made at federal or private elite universities. Their opportunities are rather similar to how Souza characterizes those of the allegedly emerging "strugglers" within Brazilian society: they continue to imply painful experiences, and what is more, they are subjected to social scrutiny that dispose of their disqualification (Souza 2012: 67). If, at *Visibly Hot,* an employee raises suspicion of no longer incorporating the cool way of "ser diferente" or simply does not hit the sales targets, she or he can be promptly dismissed. The salesclerks' experience of the discharge thus means not only to be put in a situation conditioned by the sector-specific labor market (most employees either stay unemployed for a while or find a contract for another sales job), but very often also an individual setback in self-esteem and recognition.

5.1.2 Incorporating individual performance and beauty

The tensions and fears of failure that emanate from the imperative of personal-economic growth are actually not restricted to career planning or job opportunities. As I have suggested in chapter two, brands and media discourse are today heavily taking part in directing fashionable or desirable subjectivities through the body, equally propagating the need for self-optimization. Depending on the purposes of the marketing project, they may either diminish or neutralize differences of social class or, conversely, emphasize them in particular ways in order to put in scene the allegedly unlimited material possibilities as unfolding through capitalist markets and its subjects. The human body is a decisive means to this goal; in other words, it is the performance of beauty that exemplifies success and self-perfection. At this juncture, class difference is commonly articulated in a mediated form, that is, in ways of representing specific racial traits and gender identities.

Quite explicitly, we have encountered this phenomenon with the example of Leidiane in chapter three (3.4.3): resident and native of Rocinha, where she had felt unattractive, she changed her ways of experiencing her black raced femininity through *Visibly Hot*, namely from the moment a customer called her stylish and beautiful. Similarly, branch manager Andrea, who identifies with the sexy white girl from the brand's advertisement (see 3.4.2), has proved to be characteristic of the sales workers' drive for social recognition through body performance. Hereto, Edmonds (2010) has suggested to consider beauty as subjective expressions of aspired "cultural citizenship". In Brazil, the spread of beauty industries and neoliberal logics – which he broadly grasps as a regionally specific historical period "beginning in the mid-1980s" and delineating "the expansion of a market logic into new realms of social and biological experience" (Edmonds 2010: 106) – were supported by both "savage capitalism" in Brazil's favelas and the expansion of public hospitals' services. Plastic surgeries, the author shows, have turned into popular beauty practices among indigent and other groups with a strong willingness for social upward mobility. But far from representing a vulgarization of the social elite's aesthetics, these beauty practices needed to be understood as "tactic", hence

"physical beauty often impetuously disregards social hierarchy. It is quite obvious that the elite are not always good-looking, even when their privilege thoroughly pervades other aspects of their social person, from taste in photography to table manners. Beauty hierarchies do not simply mirror other hierarchies of wealth or status. Rather, it is precisely the gap between aesthetic and other scales of social position that makes attractiveness such an essential form of value and all-too-often imaginary vehicle of ascent for those blocked from more formal routes of social mobility. While beauty is unfair in that it appears to be 'awarded' to the morally undeserving, it can also grant power to those excluded from other systems of privilege based in wealth, pedigree, or education." (Edmonds 2010: 20)

As I will show in what follows (5.1.3-5.1.5), Edmond's suggested cultural inner logic of beauty is salient in *Visibly Hot* employees' modes of self-staging. Particularly in the fashion sales business, people continuously negotiate who – and for what specific physical traits or innovative ideas of self-perfection – deserves (or not) the title of being beautiful. The need for beauty thus exposes both constraining and potentially empowering forces. In the example of Pedro, the two aspects merge due to his biographical background. At the beginning of his job engagement, he enthused about the brand *Visibly Hot* because he thought that it helped him to overcome the disqualifications of beauty he had suffered as a child and adolescent. However, after a while at work, he realized that there were still forces which questioned or rejected his individual notion of beauty. Narcissism and being directed towards sales targets, Pedro critiques now, may have oppressive effects; the models of the market were far from being open-minded and finally used only "standardized" looks.

Conceiving beauty as being directed towards "cultural citizenship" (Edmonds 2010), *Visibly Hot*'s promises for being fashionably different appear in a less surprising light. Actually, the brand draws on already existing articulations of beauty claims among Brazilian society. Jarrín (2010), whose argumentation is close to Edmond's, has termed these claims as pertaining to "cosmetic citizenship": he holds that the search for cosmetic surgery in public hospitals would further the belief in the potency of one's individual body, finally its capacity to "sew" the wounds of social exclusion. The affective involvement of patients from the popular classes in the beauty industry, so the author reflected, a hypermodern and technological self, based on inseparable forms of being and consuming (Jarrín 2010:24). Beauty tactics however reveal a double-sided face. As Edmonds makes clear, their inherent aspirations for social recognition remain mostly imaginary. Thus in his view, beauty is entangled in modernity's contradictions

"between new freedoms and desires unleashed in consumer capitalism and the constraints on freedom experienced by 'liberated' subjects as they are exposed to the hazards of generalized exchange." (Edmonds 2010: 33)

Beauty is thus a precarious affair. It depends not only on the recognition by the taste of other social groups or friends, but also on the moods of the market.

It is my argument that *Visibly Hot* engineers personal affects of its employees based on the logics of "cultural citizenship" directed towards beauty. Workers' vanity to incorporate the fashionable difference bundles a highly motivating ardor, but the same is constantly exposed to cause personal frustrations. Salesclerks like Pedro may experience higher individual recognition through the brand than they did before, that is, outside the workplace. But since the aspirations for beauty and style remain attached to their sales performance, even a short period of low work motivation can immediately cause sanctions and deny the newly gained recognition.

Terming the service employment in question as precarious is thus twofold: first, it refers to (timely and materially) limited contracts and structural insecurities, and second, it names the hazards of (whatever different) beauty ideals employees subject themselves to. Especially this second aspect, as I assert further, implements again the objective of work under the "pharmacopornographic" reigns: overall excitement instead of satisfaction (Preciado 2008: 185). To be someone attractively and sexually different – in consumable ways and equally connoted by citizenship – is a ceaseless process and often remains imaginary; this is not to say that utopias were fruitless for political change. The problem lies rather in the belief of individual growth, which for the foreseeable future turns the singular into an exchangeable product. Workers at *Visibly Hot* often experience this after one or two years of employment. Their aspired goals dissolve, and frustration is articulated not only on a professional level, but also, if not foremost, immediately through feelings directed to relations of friendship and commitment that failed.

5.1.3 Limited freedom, new controls: Pedro's emphatic criticism

Pedro, whom I met twice during my fieldwork, is an example of a salesclerk whose emotional attachment to the brand after a while suffered an incisive rupture – an alienation from his employment that would change his life course and set free a range of critical worldviews. At the moment of our first encounter, in 2012, he had recently begun working for *Visibly*

Hot. He then was excited by the brand and talked about the advantages compared to other fashion companies like C&A, where he used to work before. At *Visibly Hot*, he wouldn't need to wear a formal uniform and he could behave in accordance with his own different style. Even the fact that it took him at least three attempts until he finally got accepted in the job interview could diminish neither his admiration nor identification with the brand. Pedro liked the permissive and easy-going lifestyle and his rhapsodies for the brand were highly due to his beauty aspirations. In his account, he expressed a different style by his allusions to US Afro American music and aesthetics, something "quite Brooklyn", as he put it. He used to hang out with his friends from the shop; they went out partying on the weekends or met at the enterprise's activities. In sum, he felt completely "à vontade" – at ease with himself and with the immediate world around him. And Pedro's related, high work motivation even made him one of Rio de Janeiro's most awarded salesclerks during months.

When I met Pedro again at the end of 2014, his opinion about *Visibly Hot* had radically changed. "Dei a louca, fui pro mundo"[8], as he commented. He had resigned a couple of months before, then without any plans for another job or engagement. In the meantime, Pedro became an artist. He got to realize performance projects for a community based NGO in Olaria, his neighbourhood in the Northern Zone of Rio de Janeiro. He had to get along with a small grant instead of a salary, but he liked it a lot, since he could work with a theater professional (the project coordinator) and also because he saw a need in teaching arts to young people from his neighborhood. In contrast, he had only negative feelings left for his formerly idolized enterprise. Particularly the logics of money and its consequences for one's personality is what Pedro most criticizes in the service employment offered by *Visibly Hot*.

"Eu mudei porque, na verdade, trabalhar em loja é uma coisa muito escravizante. Você fica escravo do dinheiro. É uma merda. Porque, por exemplo, você tem meta. Somos cinco vendedores. [imita voz de gerente] Vamos lá gente, tem um prêmio aqui – o primeiro lugar, eu vou dar R$ 100 no final de semana, e o segundo lugar, eu vou dar R$ 30. Então, acaba que você trabalha em função do dinheiro. E assim, você trabalhar em loja, é muito ego. Então assim, você fica com um ego muito in-

---

8   "I went nuts, I went into the world"

flável. Porque, ah, tem prêmio ali, ah, é melhor vendedor, melhor vendedor [Pedro], seiôquê. Então, tudo acaba que você se acha melhor. Então, assim, eles fazem uma lavagem cerebral na sua cabeça. E acaba que você se torna uma pessoa vazia. Porque se você ficar numa loja a sua vida inteira, está com dinheiro, ego, prêmios, torna você uma pessoa vazia. Nisso – quando eu estava na [*Visibly Hot*], eu conheci uma galera, saia muito – por quê? É um saco. Você trabalha no shopping de domingo a domingo, você só quer extravasar."[9] (Pedro, 23, former salesclerk at *Visibly Hot*)

For Pedro, *Visibly Hot*'s promise for recognition has finally taken shape as something that is driven by money (what even leads him to compare it to slave work) and that finds its only objective in heightening the salesclerk's self-esteem. In our conversation, he underlined that he got uncomfortable when he realized that he himself was becoming more and more egocentric. And indeed, my own observation notes also related to that impression. Even in our conversation, I found striking how he used to heavily emphasize "Eu, Pedro" [Me, Pedro] when starting a sentence. As we could conclude from this, the brand's incentives for one to live her/his authentic individuality left its traces. They seem to get incorporated up to a level, which in the case of Pedro instructed his way of making him stand out from his neighbours, his family, from other artists, and most tellingly from other salesclerks.

---

9 "I changed [job] because, in fact, working in a shop is something that is very enslaving. Because you turn into a slave for money. It's shit. For example, you have a target. We are five salesclerks. [imitating his boss] Guys, we have these premiums here – for the first place, I will give you an extra payment of R$ 100 at the weekend, for the second place R$ 30. So, everything makes you work under the rule of money. And, you know, to work in a shop is very ego. You get a very inflatable ego. Because, ah, there is a premium here, ah, you are the best vendor, best vendor [Pedro], whatever. So, everything makes that you feel yourself better. Actually, hmm, they brainwash you. And, well, this turns you into an empty person. Imagine if you stay at a shop your whole life, you have money, ego, premiums, but you are an empty person. With that- when I was working for [*Visibly Hot*], I got to know a nice crowd, I went clubbing a lot– why? It's crap. Because you work in a shopping center from Sunday to Sunday, you only want to get wasted."

When he is talking about *Visibly Hot*'s motivation arguments today, Pedro's discourse is rather close to the classical critical theory of capitalist ideology. People are getting "empty", as it were a natural consequence of being directed towards money. In retrospect, Pedro describes his personal development over the former two years as a process of recognizing another reality. For a time, he thought that his work was really cool. He enjoyed knowing the *Visibly Hot* crowd, to spend his money right in the shopping centre where he worked, a "very consumerist life". Above all, he says, at 20 years of age R$ 1500 was really a lot of money to him. But then he changed his mind. Profits and egocentrism, he realized, were only directed at serving the enterprise's proper benefits. "They tap you out" [*sugam*], he revolts, and one could not find any time to study or read books. Today, Pedro thinks that even the brand's conventions are stupid, because they were only about premiums and they did not transmit any ideals. Work, he substantiated, should be either enriching for oneself or beneficial for society.

Pedro's political positioning also transpires when we are talking about identity. He disidentifies with categories of either being "gay" or being "heterosexual" in favour of believing in the forces of affectivity [*afetividade*], and more generally, in favour of being an open-minded artist with both a religion and a racial consciousness. The neopagan religion Wicca lately caught his attention in spiritual terms and feminists of and around the Black Panther movement, as he says, helped him to better understand racism against black people. He especially referred to a Brazilian activist who travelled to New York in the 70s, soon returning to her country with the political insight that blacks in Brazil were lacking the sense of recognizing themselves as blacks within society. Pedro sees her analysis as still highly valuable for the present-day situation, as the polemics around racial quota in higher education would prove. Beneath his stance for broader social recognition of Afro-religious belief and practice like *candomblé*, his political idea is also attached to appearance. He had suffered open racial prejudice by his Portuguese grandparents since he was a child, the reason why at times he thought that his lips, his nose and his hair were altogether unsightly. Only years after he would have learnt to like himself.

It was part of my first impressions that both black consciousness [*consciência negra*] and a drive to being-seen as a young, beautiful and fashionable guy had to do with Pedro's former admiration for the brand. Consequently, at the second encounter I reminded him of our first conversation and the fact that he had once highly valued *Visibly Hot* for its open-mindedness towards different identities. Now, he specified:

"É aberto até um certo ponto. Eu sou muito revolucionário. [...] Chegou um momento que eu deixei a barba crescer, usava calça rasgada; eu acho o estilo da rua mais despojado, mais lindo. Mas aí eles começaram a brigar comigo. Porque a barba ficou um pouquinho maior. O cabelo ficou maior. Aí, eles falaram para mim, cara, você não quer usar turbante?! Eu, não, eu não quero usar turbante. Isso já começou a me incomodar, sabe. [...] Começaram também dizer que tinha que cortar a barba. [...] Às vezes eram raios mínimos, mas eles queriam que eu usasse um padrão."[10] (Pedro, 23, former salesclerk at *Visibly Hot*)

Pedro stated that the negative reactions to his changing visual style even worsened after a while. Some of his teammates commented that he had an untidy appearance, bad smell and dirty hair. He felt injured and rejected in his beauty ideals, especially by people like his direct supervisor, whom he had helped a lot in terms of professional success of the sales point and whom he had considered as a friend.

The critique Pedro started to outline about the logics of monetary profit is now shading off into an open critique on *Visibly Hot*'s diversity politics. "They tell you a lot of marvelous stories when you get there, but they are actually not that open-minded". This would also be the case with respect to sexuality. At his sales point, Pedro said, "there were always a lot of gays". And at some point, the team leader commented that it was getting to be too much, that it could not turn into such a "colorful, lesbian thing". Pedro reacted outraged to his team leader's directives. "There is a moment when the masks fall off", he cynically denoted. He now thought that most of his colleagues at *Visibly Hot* were hanger-ons and had even

---

10 "Open-minded up to a certain point. [...] There came a time when I grew out my beard, I wore ripped trousers; because I think that the real street style is cooler, more beautiful. But then they started to argue with me. Because the beard was a bit longer, my hair also was longer. They said, hey, couldn't you wear a headscarf?! I said no, I don't! This already bothered me, you know. [...] They also told me to cut my beard. [...] Sometimes, it was only softer teasing, but they wanted me to get into the norm [*padrão*]."

agreed to segregation. "Two years in the company, and then there is someone who tells me that the place was getting too colorful! And what if I am gay?" Pedro also gave an example of how supervisors and team leaders tried to instruct Enilson, one of his sales colleagues.

"Tinha um garoto lá na loja, que era o [Enilson]. Ele era muito, muito gay, muito veado. Ele vendia horrores. Mas aí, a gerente falou que ele tinha que tomar cuidado quando ele estava atendendo homem. Porque eles poderiam não gostar."[11] (Pedro, 23, former salesclerk at *Visibly Hot*)

"But so what?", Pedro asked himself. If the customer knew that *Visibly Hot* was a company in which a lot of the salesclerks were crazy, that it was a "shop with faggots", he, the customer, needed to adapt himself, and not the other way round.

The restrictions Pedro (and also some of his teammates) encountered are pointing to the limits of *Visibly Hot*'s promises for "different" lifestyles and emancipation. His critique thus resembles that of critical inquiries about whether the so called diversity management was mere rhetoric (see chapter two), a somewhat "genius trick", as some feminist voices argue, of combining the promise for more justice and inclusion with the guarantee for more sales (Purtschert 2007:91). On one hand, *Visibly Hot* is mobilizing different subjects: young people that bear the prospect of offering a kind of affective outbreak from the monotony of everyday life to the customer public. But on the other hand, it guards the borders of how "different" these young people can present themselves. For it must be a notion of diversity that can securely be consumed, celebrated and result in surplus, to use Sara Ahmed's terms, it must function as "feel good" politics (Ahmed 2012:69). Salesclerks who are troubling the heteronormative order too much or whose body styling is too experimental are apparently disturbing because they could eventually affect customers in unpredictable

---

11 "There was this guy, Enilson. He was very much a faggot, very gay, very queen. He was selling [sunglasses] like hot cakes. But then the shop manager told him to take care when he was attending to men. Because these men may not like it."

and "bad" ways. In the words of vendor Larissa, a *Visibly Hot* salesclerk "tem que ser louco, mas não para assustar".[12]

Pedro's feeling of disappointment, arisen by the failures of the diversity politics he encountered at his workplace, refers not simply to an institutional, somewhat abstract origin. Beyond his delineated critique of the capitalist logic of profit, he shows himself frustrated by the disproportion between how much he personally invested in the job and, nevertheless, got to a point where his friends from work no longer accepted him in the style he had designed for himself. As a consequence, he closed literally all friendships he maintained at *Visibly Hot*. Since he left the company, he reports, he would not have any more contact with his teammates. For his part, he explains this rupture by pointing out that almost all these former friends were "conservative" and "full of prejudice" [*preconceituosos*]. Most upsetting he finds the case of his direct boss, someone he not only liked very much at the beginning, but whom he helped in terms of innumerable extra hours in order to make their sales point win a premium. According to both the professional responsibilities he assumed and the cordial relation he had with her, Pedro was expecting a sort of corresponding recognition of him as a person. He finally left because this recognition was denied and because resistance – his attempts to convince his boss of the general inconveniences as well as unfulfilled promises he found in the employment at *Visibly Hot* – did not prosper.

5.1.4 Carol's unbroken passion

The elaborated critique of Pedro is quite distant from how Carol experiences her sales employment. When I meet her almost three years after our first encounter in 2012, she is again thoroughly happy for what she is doing. After several interruptions, she has returned to *Visibly Hot* at the end of 2014 and also returned to the same shopping center she had already worked at in the past. Christmas sale had come off so well for her that she was awarded a range of prizes and thus promoted to the position of a deputy branch manager. As I am approaching the shop, Carol is dedicated to instructing her sales team how to unwrap and sort the newly arrived collection of sunglasses. I hesitate until one of the salesclerks approaches me

---

12 "has to be crazy, but not to scare [anyone]"

by starting the usual sales performance. Dismissing with a smile, I directly approach Carol and we immediately start our conversation. First, I address the topic of her awards I had known of through Facebook. Carol responds proudly:

"Ganhei, de melhor vendedora da rede no Rio de Janeiro! Eu tenho uma plaquinha em casa aqui, tenho uma foto que depois eu posso te mostrar. Eu ganhei de melhor vendedora da rede pelas mãos do [ênfase] dono da [*Visibly Hot*] mesmo, do [Diogo], do presidente. Ele veio, me deu a placa. Legal, né? É reconhecimento, cara."[13] (Carol, 24, salesclerk at *Visibly Hot*)

Similarly to Pedro, Carol is quite ostensibly looking for recognition at her workplace. The latter need is not restricted to her sales performance. It includes an overall expectation in being confirmed as a person, in seeing herself reflected as a cool and successful individual: a mode of recognition, which in the present case comes about as an amalgam of both submission under an explicit logic of competition for money and an enthusiastic consent to the dominion of the enterprise's "president". Since the brand's founder is very successful in promoting himself as an icon of style as well as of a cordial, nonhierarchical and extraordinarily successful corporate management (see the discussion in section 2.3), Carol can expect to find herself within the same coordinates of representation. At least, this seems to be her intention when she enthuses about Diogo's presence at her award ceremony.

Given the long way Carol took until she finally was promoted in comparison to other cases like Bruna or Jéssica, who became branch managers after but a couple of months holding the position of an ordinary salesclerk, our conversation comes soon to a point where she seems to feel compelled to explain her delay. In general terms, Carol observes that at times she was immature and that only through her latest personal transformation she would now be serious enough to get a chance for promotion.

---

13   "Yes, I won, for being the best salesclerk of the network in Rio de Janeiro! I have a medal at home, I have a photo of it I can show you later. I won the prize of best salesclerk in the network, personally handed over by the [emphasizing] owner of [*Visibly Hot*] himself, [Diogo], the president. He came, gave me the medal. That's cool, isn't' it? That's recognition, you know."

"Foi, assim, crescimento pessoal também. Porque eu tenho quatro anos na [*Visibly Hot*], e nunca tinha subido de cargo, assim. Só como vendedora mesmo. Essa vez que eu voltei, eu- assim, as coisas caminharam para isso. Parece que eu cresci pessoalmente, esse descanso deu uma outra cabeça, séria; então, as coisas caminharam para que eu fosse mesmo. E continuam andando para que eu me torne gerente."[14] (Carol, 24, salesclerk at *Visibly Hot*)

Carol explains her process of becoming a better professional with reference to a longer work break that changed her thoughts and that implicitly prescribed her overdue promotion. But what had actually happened over the past three years? After one and a half years at *Visibly Hot* in Rio, Carol had left the shop in 2013. She returned to her home city, Belo Horizonte, where she got a job in another store that sold sunglasses. But it would not last long before she returned to the brand, because she was re-hired at the shop floor: "Eles foram lá para o quiosque para me chamar para voltar para a [*Visibly Hot*]. Aí, eu super adorei, porque é uma coisa que eu já sei fazer, né?".[15] Carol was obviously pleased that her former employer called her back from business competitors. Consequently, she would stay in Belo Horizonte as a *Visibly Hot* salesclerk for eight months until she quit again. This time, she felt tired of the job and remained several months unemployed, "curtindo a família. Um tempo para mim, sabe, sem condição. Porque a galera na [*Visibly Hot*]- suga mais a gente, um pouco, né?"[16] After that break, she decided to return to Rio, where she rapidly got a job at another competing brand for sunglasses, Lupalupa. But as she didn't like the style, she would again return to *Visibly Hot*, which was easier at that

---

14 "It was like personal growth, too. Because I am here at [*Visibly Hot*] for four years, and I've never been promoted, you know. Only as a proper salesclerk. This time I returned, I- you know, things were designed to work out. It seems that I grew personally, this rest gave me another perspective, a serious one; so, things were designed for me to work out. And so they continue, so that I become a branch manager."

15 "They went right to the kiosk in order to invite me to return to [*Visibly Hot*]. Well, I really loved that, because it's something I already know, right?"

16 "enjoying family. Some time just for me, you know, without any constraints. Because people at [*Visibly Hot*]- they tap you out a little bit, right?"

moment because in the face of Christmas sales they were in need of extra employees.

As the sensation of being a victim of *sugar* – also mentioned by her colleague Pedro – and the resultant exhaustion that had once made her leave the job was the only thoroughly negative aspect Carol reported to in her speech, I asked her to specify that feeling.

"É- venda em si cansa mesmo. Acho assim, é dom, sabe. Acho que não são tantas pessoas que aguentam trabalhar com vendas; a pressão a que se submetem- é um emprego que se trabalha de domingo a domingo, se tem uma folga na semana. Por exemplo, o meu horário é até às 16h aqui, agora estamos 19.15. Então- mas não é nem que a empresa obriga. Eu fico, por exemplo, primeiro por que eu preciso vender, eu preciso de dinheiro; segundo é que estar na [*Visibly Hot*] me faz bem, sabe, eu não vejo a hora passar. Então, assim, é- esse tempo em BH que eu descansei, que eu parei para descansar, eu- estava exausta, eu não conseguia atender cliente igual ao que eu atendo. Aí, eu resolvi tirar esse tempo para mim, entendeu? Para descansar a cabeça, para descansar o corpo. Eu fiquei de janeiro até agosto sem trabalhar e tudo. Só descansando. E depois eu voltei com tudo."[17] (Carol, 24, salesclerk at *Visibly Hot*)

Carol specifies that sales employment is a hard job. There would be a lot of pressure stemming from intense conditions, such as the single day off per week and the additional fact that employees were routinely doing (uncompensated) overtime. However, it seems important to her to underline

---

17 "It's- sales as such are really tiring. I think it's a given, you know. I think that there are few people who really sustain working with sales; the pressure to which they subject themselves- it's an employment for which you work from Sunday to Sunday, you have one day off. For example, my work schedule ends at 16h here, now it's 19.15h. So- but it's not even that the enterprise would make me. I stay, for example, first because I need to sell, I need money; and second, because being here at [*Visibly Hot*] makes me feel good, you know, time flies by. So, it's like- that time I relaxed in Belo Horizonte, I paused to get some rest- I was exhausted, I was unable to attend customers the way I normally do. Therefore, I decided to take this time out for me, you know? To get some rest for my head, to relax my body. From January to August I was without work or anything. Only resting. Afterwards I came back with all energy."

that this was not a critique directed at *Visibly Hot*. Right at the moment of talking about the difficulties in sales she managed to confront, Carol stresses that the enterprise would not force anyone to work overtime. Quite the contrary, she goes on, it was her free and decided will, first, to making money she needs, and second, to spending time at that place – the shop – where she would feel fully at ease and where time would fly.

Still, fatigue is what Carol "mentally and physically" felt when she left the company the last time. I reply that several other salesclerks reported that their exhaustion was tied to the loss of their initial enthusiasm [*paixão*] for the brand. How would she think about the subjective transformation of that passionate relation to the brand so many people talked about?

"O meu caso é muito específico. Eu entrei na [*Visibly Hot*] apaixonada. Eu entrei porque eu já queria aquilo. Eu tinha 18 anos, e eu passava lá nos quiosques. Eu via as pessoas. Era diferente dos outros trabalhos. Tem muita loja que você passa e tem pessoas trabalhando com uma expressão horrível. Sabe, descansada... acho que cliente não quer isso. Eu sou cliente mesmo sendo vendedora. Então, se eu entro em uma loja e a pessoa vai me atender mal, eu não vou comprar. Aqui a gente tem um atendimento diferente. Aqui a gente tem uma pegada diferente, tem uma energia diferente. Aí, eu me apaixonei. E assim, é claro que a gente tem as nossas saciações. Depois no dia a dia, nada é perfeito. Eu tive as minhas saciações na [*Visibly Hot*], houve momento em que eu me cansei. E quando eu me cansei, eu preferi sair do que tratar outros mal, não trocar ideias- contaminar as outras pessoas. E é isso, cara, eu continuo me apaixonando pela [*Visibly Hot*]. O dono da marca faz isso. Ele, por exemplo, deu um cruzeiro para os melhores vendedores. Eu fui, fiquei quatro dias lá. E a gente descansa, querendo ou não, e a gente volta com uma energia total de vender mais e, assim, fazer acontecer."[18] (Carol, 24, salesclerk at *Visibly Hot*)

---

18 "I am a very specific case. I started passionately at [*Visibly Hot*]. I went there because I had already wanted that. I was 18 and I passed by the shops. And I saw those people. It was different from other jobs. There are a lot of shops where you are passing by and people are working with a horrible [facial] expression. Lazy, you know...I think the customer doesn't want that. I am a customer even while being a salesclerk. So, if I enter a shop and the person does not know how to attend to me, I won't buy anything. Here we have a different

Carol self-confidently relates that she is very authentic in her relation to the brand: her individual passion was not only unbroken and furthery developable, but it was already there before she started working for *Visibly Hot* (another proof for this she had shown me by her tattoo of the brand's logo at our first encounter, to what I referred to in section 3.3). Passion, to Carol, is not only personal, but also describes the (high) degree of professionalism of the company's outstanding service work. She measures this by identifying herself as a customer, too. This again heightens her energetic self-control, because she supposedly mirrors her own standards of how she wants to be prompted to buy something when she enters a shop.

What is of critical interest here is the extent to which several salesclerks experience and incorporate the unidirectional, compulsive economic logics of growth (Rosa et al. 2014: 43). If we look at the passage above from a socio-linguistically inspired perspective, it is noticeable that Carol uses expressions that are mistakable for *Visibly Hot*'s official doctrine. The very notion of passion she mobilizes, but also the advertisement-like statements of "total energy" and "make things happen", completely converge with the dominant managerial jargon. This goes even as far as she tends to assert that her individually taken decision to leave the company was due to avoiding her teammates' "contamination" – as if having personal conflicts at the workplace was a dangerous virus that had to be curtailed.[19] Furthermore, she also explains her fatigue as a state to be individ-

---

attendance. Here we have a different drive, a different energy. So, I fell in love. And, you know, for sure we have our satiations. In daily life, nothing is perfect. I had my satiations at [*Visibly Hot*], there was a moment I got tired. And when I got tired, I preferred to leave than to mistreat others, to stop touching base with them- contaminate the others. And that's it, you know, I continue falling in love with [*Visibly Hot*]. The brand's owner does this. For example, he gave a cruise ship to the best vendors. I was there; I stayed four days. And we relax, like it or not, and we come back with total energy focused on selling more, and like that, on making things happen."

19 Carol also pointed out that this quitting happened because of conflicts she had with a colleague at work. Differently from former conflictive situations she had gone through at *Visibly Hot* and in which she stayed in order to "show that I was stronger than the other person", that time she would have preferred to "retreat" [*me retirar*]. Today, in the position as a deputy branch manager, she felt

ually overcome by a rest in order to collect one's strength for an even more energetic comeback to sales work. Carol is convinced of *Visibly Hot*'s rapid economic growth and unhesitatingly translates this into her individual need for "personal growth". The latter, so goes the logic, would lead to more mature behavior, which again increases one's chances and job opportunities within the company.

Speaking about conflicts, I confront Carol with the case of Pedro, since I know that they worked in the same sales team three years ago and I presuppose that she must have accompanied the dispute via the enterprise's close social networks. Actually, she is contrary to Pedro's arguments regarding *Visibly Hot*'s deficient diversity politics and she sees his demission in the light of his stubborn behavior related to his beard.

"Essa- assim, eu discordo. Eu estava; eu peguei essa época quando ele estava saindo. E ele, na verdade, estava muito cansado e ele juntou tudo. Eu acho que a [*Visibly Hot*] pode abraçar qualquer tipo de pessoa, de religião e raça. Mas, a questão de higiene pessoal, você tem que ter na vida, entendeu? A [*Visibly Hot*] tem regras, como qualquer outra empresa. Tem uniforme, tem jeito de cortar cabelo e deixar a barba. Então, assim, é – ninguém pode ir trabalhar com uma barba enorme, nenhuma empresa ia deixar. Foi o caso dele. Mas essa questão de abominar ele, ah eu não vou mais trabalhar com homossexual, isso não existiu não, não é verdade. Eu conheço bem as épocas da [*Visibly Hot*] e isso jamais existiu. Cara, você pode falar que 70% da [*Visibly Hot*], pelo menos no Rio e em BH, são gays e lésbicas. Ou é bi. É assim, é sério, nunca teve isso. É bom trabalhar com homossexual. Essa questão do sexual não existiu, mas a coisa da barba é- porque ele levou pro lado pessoal. Mas não era. Era só aparar, sabe."[20] (Carol, salesclerk at *Visibly Hot*)

---

more mature, as she says, and she would even teach her team that it was not worthwhile arguing because of a pair of sunglasses: at the end, this would only trouble [*atrapalhar*] customers and hence compromise one's commission rate.

20 "This- you know, I disagree. I was there; I was present when he was leaving. And actually, he was very tired and he put it all together. I think that [*Visibly Hot*] can embrace every kind of person, of religion and race. But the question of hygiene, you've got to have that for your life, right? [*Visibly Hot*] has its rules, like any other enterprise. There's a uniform, there's a way to cut your hair and adjust your beard. So, you know- no one can go to work with a huge beard, neither enterprise would let you do that. That was his case. But that

Carol cannot understand Pedro's harsh critique; she thinks that he overreacted because he was generally tired of the job. Racism or religious prejudice, she defends, were absolutely out of question at *Visibly Hot*. Salesclerks at Dubai would work wearing a burka, "é super maneiro".[21] According to Carol, the only problem with Pedro was that he would disrespect common norms of hygiene; that is, of well-tended beard and hair. She thus disconnects the sphere of individual hygiene from Pedro's political concern regarding the brand's marginalization of unforeseen articulations of body aesthetics.

About sexual orientation, Carol equally defends the brand's official diversity discourse. She had never experienced or seen what Pedro believed to hear from his boss with respect to a threatening "homosexualization" of the sales team. Quite the contrary, the mere fact that more than half of all employees were gays or lesbians would prove that homophobia was inexistent. To her view, what circulated in social media about *Visibly Hot* as representing a "gay brand" is another funny piece of evidence of the brand's gay friendliness.

"Primeiramente, eu acho engraçado. Porque existe mesmo, essa brincadeirinha. A gente brinca. Ah, primeiro dia da pessoa- é sapatão? Ah não é? Então vai sair logo [risos]. A gente brinca. Na verdade, é porque a [*Visibly Hot*] abraça qualquer tipo de gênero, raça, religião, se você é ateu. [...] Então, as pessoas se sentem com maior vontade de chegar e pedir emprego na [*Visibly Hot*]. Por medo de outras empresas, acontece, de não aceitar uma pessoa negra, uma pessoa lésbica, uma pessoa gay. Por isso que virou isso, né?"[22] (Carol, 24, salesclerk at *Visibly Hot*)

> thing of abominating him, ah, I won't work any longer with homosexuals, no, that didn't exist, that's not true. I know the different periods of [*Visibly Hot*] very well, and that never existed. Man, you can say that 70% of [*Visibly Hot*], at least in Rio de Janeiro and Belo Horizonte, consists of gays, lesbians. Or they are bisexual. That's how it is, really, there was never such a thing. It's good to work with homosexuals. That thing of the sexual didn't exist, but the thing with his beard- because he took it personally. But it wasn't. He should only trim it, you know."

21 "that's really cool."
22 "First of all, I think it's funny. Because it really exists, that joke. We ourselves joke about that. Ah, it's her first working day- is she a lesbian? No she isn't?

5.1.5 Keeping a safe distance: Juliano

Juliano has not only worked in the same sales team as Pedro, but he also left the company at exactly the same moment and without a job prospect. I meet him about one and a half years after his exit from *Visibly Hot*. In the meantime, he has been experiencing both shorter job engagements, like as a call center agent for a graphic enterprise, and unemployed periods. Since two months ago, he is working as an employee in a furniture store in the district of Madureira. Juliano sees his actual job as transitional. In the near future he plans to become engaged with his girlfriend and to study history or literature at the university, for which he has saved money. When our conversation moves on to the case of Carol, whom he also knew right at the beginning of his employment at *Visibly Hot*, he smilingly affirms what Carol says about herself: "Ela é um caso à parte. Ela é louca, apaixonada pela marca."[23] He has heard of her comeback to the company and in general terms thinks that Carol might be one of the most persistent fans of *Visibly Hot*.

> "Eu- hoje, não conheço ninguém que está igual apaixonada pela marca como ela. Nem o franqueado é tão apaixonado como ela."[24] (Juliano, 24, former salesclerk at *Visibly Hot*)

Consequently, Juliano does not find it surprising that the company, in Belo Horizonte, called her back. Carol, in his eyes, would know the demanded sales job very well. However, Juliano distances himself from her story. Albeit in a lighter version, he specifies that he had considerably changed his mind with respect to *Visibly Hot*, in a similar way as Pedro did.

> Ah, so she'll leave very soon [laughing]. We joke about that. Actually, it's because [*Visibly Hot*] embraces all type of gender, race, religion, or if you're an atheist. [...] So, people feel much more comfortable in looking for work at [*Visibly Hot*]. For fear of other enterprises, it happens, that they don't accept a black person, a lesbian or a gay person. That's why it turned out like that, right?"

23 "She's a special case. She's crazy, passionate about the brand."
24 "I- today, I don't know anyone who would be as passionate about the brand as her. Not even the franchisees are that passionate."

"Eu achava uma coisa. E hoje eu acho completamente o oposto do que eu imaginei- ou do que eles passam. Eles passam por algum comercial, por TV ou alguma mídia em áudio. Passam que é bem livre, que ali você pode ser quem você quiser- o que [sorriso] não é bem assim. Não é. Engana muito. Quem entrar na [*Visibly Hot*], achando que pode ser quem quiser- [risos] não é, não é bem assim mesmo."[25] (Juliano, 24, former salesclerk at *Visibly Hot*)

Juliano openly criticizes the brand's promise for being outstandingly liberal, foremost with respect to its suggestive slogan "you can be whoever you are". In his view today, the company would not fulfill this; its selection criterion – "being eclectic" – would rather resemble a fine net of norms and demands than a truly open-minded policy. Against expectation, Juliano says, he now feels freer at the furniture shop than at times at *Visibly Hot*.

"Na [*Visibly Hot*], se diz que tem que ser eclético. Tipo você tinha que fazer barba, tinha que fazer cabelo, porque tem uma regra, assim- e lá, onde parecia ser mais formal, mas não. Te deixam bem livre. Me surpreendeu."[26] (Juliano, 24, former salesclerk at *Visibly Hot*)

---

25 "I thought about it in a certain way. And today, I think just the opposite of what I had imagined or of what they transmit. They propagate it by advertising, on TV or on audio media. They propagate that it's very free, that there you could be whoever you want to be- what is [laughs] really not the case. It isn't. Very deceiving. Those who enter [*Visibly Hot*] thinking that they could be whoever they want- [laughs] no, it's really not like that."

26 "At [*Visibly Hot*], the saying goes that one has to be eclectic. Like, you had to trim your beard, you had to style your hair, because there are rules, you know- and there [at the furniture shop], where it looks like it's much more formal, but no. They let you be free. I was surprised."

Juliano relates that he didn't trim his beard for more than a month, something that would have been impossible at the sunglasses company. *Visibly Hot*'s subtle restrictions were further not only of physical nature, but also encompassed salesclerks' overall behavior. Juliano at first hand references the experiences and polemic rebellions of Pedro he witnessed from immediate proximity.

"Ele [o Pedro] era o principal alvo disso. [...] É, porque a [*Visibly Hot*] não é tão eclética, não. Tem que fazer a barba, tem que se manter numa linha, padrãozinho. [...] O [Pedro] era bem comprado nisso, tanto na aparência como no comportamento."[27] (Juliano, 24, former salesclerk at *Visibly Hot*)

In Juliano's view, Pedro turned into a sort of prime target of the corporate identity's policing as given shape by several team colleagues and superiors. In his opinion, he asserts, he wouldn't know exactly why, but Pedro definitely suffered more style restrictions (or even mocking) than other salesclerks. And this, Juliano continues, also partly explains why his friend felt that personally attacked and disrespected. Commenting the moment of Pedro's (and his own) demission, Juliano adds that there was also the former's wide frustration about the annual convention. Although Pedro was undoubtedly the most successful and committed salesclerk at that time, his branch manager would have opted for another crewmember to accompany her to the brand's party island.[28] According to Juliano, these disappointments made Pedro really feel sad, since he thought that "mesmo fazendo tudo, ninguém olhava, ninguém via o que ele estava fazendo."[29]

Juliano himself did not have such drastic or personally affecting experiences. He left the company foremost because, at that moment, the shop

---

27 "He [Pedro] was the main target of it. [...] This is because [*Visibly Hot*] is not that eclectic, no. You have to trim the beard, you have to keep to a line, the chicanery of standards. [...] [Pedro] was very reprimanded to that respect, both in appearance and behavior."

28 It is usual within the company that free entrance and travel costs for the participation in the annual convention are given to best-selling salesclerks, whereas the final decision is in the hands of the respective branch manager.

29 "even doing everything possible, nobody noticed, nobody saw what he was performing."

he worked at seemed to him a mess [*confusão*]. Besides the conflict around Pedro's daring style, he reports that there were several cases of theft – not by customers, which was also quite common in the shopping center – but by employees. A pair of sunglasses, for example, disappeared out of one's bag, later appeared again somewhere else. The internal ambience of mistrust and mutual accusation actually meant that the whole team except the branch manager would have left the store. Finally, it was under these circumstances that Juliano came to the conclusion that he could no longer work at that place. "Foi nessa confusão que- eu estava já mais ou menos três anos aqui- estava de saco cheio."[30] In addition to this corrupted atmosphere, Juliano was also requested to do more and more overtime, to the extent that there was no time left for any other activities. "Chegou uma hora que não dava mais. Aí, eu saí."[31]

With respect to Pedro's unease about *Visibly Hot*'s questionable sexual diversity politics, Juliano prefers not to interfere too much. In general terms, he thinks that his colleague's conflict was more of an interpersonal nature. In his view, Pedro had a complex and somewhat competitive relation to Enilson; although the latter also used tight shorts and was "more feminine [*afeminado*] than Pedro", he was hardly sanctioned, neither by the branch manager nor by the supervisor. Furthermore, Juliano underlines that the two guys' sales strategies were different: while Pedro explicitly chatted up with the male customers he liked, Enilson would have acted more unobtrusively. "Mas o Pedro achou sempre que ele estava certo, que ele poderia fazer"[32], Juliano comments, adding that he was not sure whether this was right or not. However, within the enterprise's codes of conduct, he strictly distinguishes homophobia and style restrictions. Although he agrees with Pedro that *Visibly Hot* was not that free as they said it to be, he contradicts the latter's reproach of LGBT-hostile stances.

"Eu lembrei dele falando isso. Mas eu acho que não- não em relação à opção sexual. Mas no sentido do estilo, moda. Ele queria usar um shortinho. [...] Não

---

30 "It was at that mess- I was already more or less three years there- I was fed up"
31 "At one point, I couldn't stand it any longer. So, I quit."
32 "But Pedro always thought that he was right, that he could do that"

deixaram. Isso deixou ele mais chateado."³³ (Juliano, 24, former salesclerk at *Visibly Hot*)

For Juliano, wearing tight shorts is a question of style, which is why he explains Pedro's frustration as the result of superiors hindering him in the creation of his authentic style. Since Juliano sees himself as less eclectic, he says that he was surprised about the fact that after both had resigned from *Visibly Hot*, he and Pedro became friends, close friends [*amigo mesmo*]. Formerly, he thought that Pedro was totally crazy and somewhat strange. Pedro in turn thought that Juliano was a jerk [*babacão*] and they were not that close during the time at the shop. While their common frustrations and critique of *Visibly Hot* led them to create a sort of affective solidarity (Hemmings 2012), transcending their differing identity claims, former friendships seem to have dissolved. Juliano completely lost contact with other people from *Visibly Hot*. Somewhat wearily, he clarifies: "Talvez achávamos que todos fossemos amigos ali. E fomos- se separou e ninguém mais procurou o outro. Não seguiu a amizade. Só eu e o Pedro mesmo."³⁴

5.2 PRECARIOUS RECOGNITION IN MOTION

Particularly Juliano and Pedro experienced frustrations at *Visibly Hot* as a matter of failed social relations. They thought they had made friends with teammates (the sensation of family, as the managerial discourse goes), but these friendships turned out to be restricted to their engagement for the company. Since service work is heavily based on social bonds like friendships, work as a sphere of life is obviously extending its significance for intimate processes of social (de)recognition³⁵. This process is more than

---

33 "I remember that he said that. But I think that's not the case- not in relation to sexual orientation. But in the sense of style, of fashion. He wanted to wear very tight shorts. [...] They didn't let him do that. This made him more upset."
34 "Maybe we thought that we were all friends there. And we left- separated and nobody kept in touch. Friendship didn't continue. Only me and Pedro."
35 In the context of financial accounting, *derecognition* means the "removal of a previously recognized financial asset or liability from an entity's balance sheet"

remarkable, hence it points to the contradictory nature of the work relations in question. While beauty and cool behavior are being articulated in ways which are both indistinguishable and inseparable from the belief in individual growth, they are equally expected to be validated, that is, recognized by forms of social collectivity and feelings of friendship that are opposite to the idea of competition. The mutual entanglement of both aspects as well as the speed of their enunciation may thus reflect the challenges so many working people are facing in order to maintain their status. If we temporarily follow the theses of Rosa (2005), this is not least a consequence of the spiral-like acceleration performance of capitalism, which encompasses subjects worldwide.

"In the 21st century, people have the feeling that they must always run faster to keep their place." (Rosa et al. 2014: 36)

Investments in the body, in affective labor as well as in the pretended free will in doing overtime – as we have seen in the example of Carol – can be addressed as such attempts to keep or improve one's position.

As I have argued earlier, neoliberal interpellations to the subject, which are today central to capitalist logics of growth, unfold a character that traverses virtually all social classes. Guattari (2007), when travelling through Brazil in the 1980s in search of leftist uprisings that would disrupt, from within, the chains of both colonialism and cold war, had already called attention to the related intensifying production of subjectivities by what he called "International World Capitalism (IWC)". The "social forces that administer capitalism today", he then said,

"understand that the production of subjectivity is possibly more important than any kind of production, more essential than the production of petroleum and energy." (Guattari and Rolnik 2007: 36)

(Bragg 2015). In this sense, the term embraces quite aptly the precarious aspect of social recognition in an entrepreneurial, identity-based setting: recognition is subjected to financial "liability", that is, its constant need to submit proof of its usability in economically profitable ways.

Capitalist forces would proceed in deterritorialized modes, they abandoned territorialized machines like those of ethnic groups, castes or professional associations (Guattari and Rolnik 2007: 35): its global governance transcended both continental borders and former oppositions of social class. Production was thus no longer restricted to social and productive relations, but equally embraced "a modernization of behavior, sensibility, perception, memory, social relations, sexual relations, imaginary phantoms etc." (Guattari and Rolnik 2007: 39). Furthermore, this process led to an entanglement of moveable ideological role reversals, a conflation of the exploited and the exploiter, which – at least for the time being – hindered the effervescence of broader movements against exploitation[36].

Contemporary self-staging of beauty and individual growth within the realm of service work and consumption is emblematic for such complex dependencies as well as deterritorialized contributions to the economic order. Carol, who substantiates that the brand *Visibly Hot* supported her in confronting her vulnerability as a young lesbian, is being urged to individually respond to political struggles about sexuality as a part of her affective labor that includes a sophisticated styling of her body. Her longing is thus characterized by the will of growing in a social position, which is at the same time affected by outer threats of homophobia and inner promises for recognition through individual work performance. Neither unruly to consumerist promises nor compliant to hegemonic social constraints concerning sexual orientation, Carol literally incorporates the precarious contradictions of how recognition is being articulated in an era of economic and social acceleration.

Interestingly, Carol's notion of recognition is hardly different from the notions put forward by recognition theorists like Honneth (2011). The latter presuppose that, first, a normative framework is indispensable for recognition finding its completion, and second, that such recognition is necessarily equivalent to freedom. Queer and feminist perspectives have deeply questioned such concepts of recognition as reciprocal dyad because

---

36 Guattari specifies: "What gives strength to capitalistic subjectivity is that it is produced both by the oppressors and by the oppressed. [...] A kind of relation of complementarity and dependence is established between the various social categories, which ultimately dismantles class alliances and social alliances" (Guattari and Rolnik 2007: 60).

the same led to a normative and hence always socially exclusionary standpoint. Butler (2005) develops her approach on the basis of her critique of the subject and processes of subject formation under historically specific power relations. Against an ontological notion of recognition, she writes:

"The norms by which I recognize another or, indeed, myself are not mine alone. They function to the extent that they are social, exceeding every dyadic exchange that they condition." (Butler 2005: 24)

Certainly, Butler utters the supposition that the idea of recognition's need for a normative setting was not thoroughly wrong. But to her, the consequences of possibly reinstalling exclusionary norms are more drastic. Consequently, her point consists in showing how the points of reference for recognition, of both our selves and of others, are structurally permeated by social norms. And therefore, they are not simply of a bilateral and reciprocal nature, as Hegel had assumed (Butler 2005: 31).

In *Visibly Hot*'s and other related neoliberal promises of difference lies what Butler addresses as the problem of arrogance within the hegemonic logics of recognition. Agents of these logics assume that they could "see" how the other actually "is" (Simmons 2006:87). In our case, this means that the enterprise in question has a very clear (and normative) plan of how lesbian, gay, black and further "different" identities "are" and how they are subsequently recognized – for the sake of freedom – through the brand. For Butler, such a notion of recognition obscures the singularity of the very heterogeneous others, which is to say that their singularity remains unrecognizable. As discussed in section 3.4, such subjects are not recognized with equal rights in their very difference (Maihofer 2013). New normative constraints spread over the stylized self. *Visibly Hot*'s appeal for combating racist and heterosexual norms hence appears as highly ironic, given that it even includes the request for the workers' individual investments in their personal becomings and changeable identities.

According to Engel (2009), such a design of difference is nothing but a globally operative, neoliberal calculation: profit-oriented forces would grant "concessions of recognition" (Engel 2009: 227) of divergent modes of existence in order to ensure consent to the economic order. In the latter, anyone is hailed to proceed as a virtuosic entrepreneur of the (own) self, shaping a life of self-determination and authenticity. This observation further leads the author to draw attention to the overlap with emancipatory sexual politics. For neoliberal discourse recurs – in very similar ways as queer discourse – on the constructed, processual, and performative character of subjectivity; yet even the emphasis on ongoing processes of becoming could be found in both discourses (Engel 2009: 152). Consequently, Engel is concerned with examining the difficult question of how to rescue, under such conditions, queer critique – a queer critique, which would enable one to equally challenge heteronormativity *and* capitalism.

Unfortunately, Engel's suggestions remain rather vague because she methodologically restricts her inquiry to the perception and production of art and mass media images. In her view, queer politics needed to insist on the paradoxes and radical heterogeneity (Engel 2009: 157), which naturally unfold in the production of subjectivity. With reference to Phelan (2001), Engel suggests to articulate this concern as "politics of strangeness", that is, the production and perception of images, in which human differences are depicted as inextricably strange, estranging and untamable. It remains unclear, however, how such politics can or should be performed by people in everyday life, that is, beyond the artistic or mass media production sites, and to what extent this effectively questioned both heteronormativity and capitalism. Other sexual dissident voices from the Global South have hereto critically explored the limits of the political will for strangeness. Argentinian activist and poet Silvestri (2014) does not only scrutinize the language based, imperial bias of queer, which in her view is about to lose its critical potential and to be absorbed more easily by pop marketing when referred to in romance language areas such as Latin America. With respect to her personal experiences from living with Crohn's disease, she also asks the uncomfortable question of if anyone intentionally wanted to be sick. This form of somatic strangeness, she holds, is hardly subsumable under the queer (just as under capital), since it would be difficult to imagine someone playfully striving to transcend the regulatory ideal of the healthy body (Silvestri and Staunsager 2015).

Pain, bad feelings or unproductive bodies indeed seem to draw the outskirts of neoliberally digestible difference. Guattari, albeit not dealing with the limits of queer politics, already expressed the same unease as Engel about capitalism's globally absorbing incorporation of subjectivities. Now, close to Silvestri, he identified an absence of existential sensitivity as intrinsic to "capitalistic" subjectivity (Guattari 1990).

"The appropriation of the production of subjectivity by the IWC [International World Capitalism] is draining all knowledge of singularity. It is a subjectivity that does not know the essential dimensions of existence such as death, pain, loneliness, silence, or the relation with the cosmos and time. Feelings such as anger are surprising and scandalous." (Guattari and Rolnik 2007: 58)

In Guattari's view, IWC effects a serial production of subjectivity, which "drains" singularity, that is, it factors out existential dimensions of human feeling; namely the painful or negative ones that are not worthy or convenient for profit seeking performances. However, the author also insists that under the conditions imposed by IWC, processes of capitalist "individuation" and potentially emancipatory "singularization" are deeply intertwined. There is, in other words, an immanence of both resistance and reproduction. Guattari thus advocates to generally focus the question of how a "molecular revolution" or "micropolitics of singular processes"[37], which pertain to the realm of desires and "frustrated", at best resisted the serial production of IWC, could be articulated within the reigning processes of individuation (Guattari and Rolnik 2007: 52).

Differently from the convictions of the sociology of work, such micropolitics of singularization do not only take place within political economy or in industrial plants, but literally in all production facilities of subjectivity. We have encountered emblematic "frustrating" and "estranging" articulations – right in the double sense, as both individual and structural – in the case of Pedro. In fact, he describes situations he experienced at *Visibly Hot*, in which both the mode and the limits of otherness (being different) were subject to rigid contestation. They can be read as struggles on what kind of bodies and selves are in- and outside the consumable norm of freedom. Pedro goes through a becoming-minoritarian in the sense of Guattari, transcending the capitalistically "drained" singularity: the beard, the hair, and not least his direct confrontation with the logics of ongoing growth are disclosing the restrictions of *Visibly Hot*'s promises for freedom and individual recognition.

---

37 Guattari declares that the term as such was not of high importance to him, and that the notion of becoming minoritarian he and Deleuze used elsewhere (Deleuze and Guattari 1980) would express the same political concern (Guattari and Rolnik 2007: 61).

Admittedly, Pedro's dissident cartography, as we have also known through his experience, has turned out to be misconceived. Due to a broad consent to the managerial notion of diversity, his commitment for another fashionable strangeness (his individual style and body display) is deemed to fail. Despite Pedro's direct interventions, he does not succeed in persuading his superiors and colleagues to rethink their position, neither in dislocating their normative references. His frustration, compound of personal, amicable as well as professional aspects, ends in flight. As Lorenz and Kuster (2007: 153) remind us: sexual labor often denies the alternatives of resistance and reproduction. It mobilizes laborers to rework or participate in conflicting social polemics, but it disclaims any form of responsibility or shelter for the eventual unproductive outcomes. This again explains why so many workers at *Visibly Hot* skillfully inhabit the precarious positions of their being different, obviously aware of running the risk of facing sanctions. Joe, salesclerk and one of the innumerous initiators of *Visibly Hot* videos on Youtube, is a young black guy, who wears an Afro big hair hairstyle, sunglasses and skinny short jeans. His video portrays him, as the title suggests, in a "moment of fun", performing the song *End of Time* of pop singer Beyoncé, also known as one of the most famous gay idols worldwide. It is as if Joe communicated his version of being different through his accomplished movements, commenting both his amusement and the exhausting challenges imposed by the need for recognition. However, he may probably fail as much as his colleagues in creating and multiplying that kind of social places that would provide safe shelter from capital's normative program of diversity.

The articulations of difference encountered at *Visibly Hot* can in sum be described as precarious, in other words, as ensnared in the precariousness that unfolds in the normative, and consumable notion of recognition. According to the perspectives on precariousness and precarization stemming from the field of queer and feminist studies (Motakef 2015), finding oneself in a precarious position is not to be reduced to a male and Western centered fear of slipping off the normality of welfare state's public assistance benefits[38]. Under the influence of Butler's political essays against

---

38 This is, in general terms, the main objective by feminist critiques of common sociological debates on precarity such as represented by Castel (1995) and Dörre (2006).

violence (Butler 2004), being precarious generally refers to the question of when a life is worth grieving, primarily in political and social terms. It describes thus a situation which we can all get into. Although there is evidently no equality amongst the multiplicity of precarious positions, for Butler the precariousness of life must not be seen as a threat but as the very point of departure for new alliances. As also the notion of sexual labor (Lorenz and Kuster 2007) suggests, not only the subjects are produced and reworked within contemporary employment, but also their relations and positions. Articulations of salesclerks like Pedro, Juliano and Carol give proof of how the relation of recognition as a market subject and recognition as a subject of civil society (the "LGBT subject" or the "black subject") are being worked on. Recognition, as we could say then, is subject to moving relations and hence always conditioned by hegemonic struggles, negotiations, and future meaning.

In what follows, I want to further illustrate the ambivalences that emerge from rapidly moving meaning of the precarious in the urban Brazilian context. On one hand, capitalist contributions to modernity's acceleration seem to affect individual feeling of contemporary service workers. On the other hand, high speed of consumption incentives and flexible identity switchovers entail modes of (over)identification that have not been foreseen by economic "normality". Especially groups from peripheral positions – youth gatherings in shopping centers, the *rolezinhos*, and funk MCs – are openly challenging the prerogative of explanation regarding consumer society's morals and logics of recognition.

5.2.1 The fatigue of self-inventions

The remodeling of the very relation between work and identity (du Gay 1996) demands a high degree of adaptation to new rhythms of service employees. Supervisor Ana, who is in charge of maintaining the norms, regulations and procedures of *Visibly Hot* at the shop floor, says that she is happy with her job because it allowed her to sell a professional attitude, which is linked to an anti-discrimination policy. Particularly, she likes the challenge to "fazer este ponto de venda funcionar, mesmo quando eu não estou aqui"[39]. Holding the position of a supervisor, Ana explains, was like

---

39 "to get this sales point working, even in the moments when I am not there."

assuming the role of the shop's "shadow". Hardly she would directly approach a salesclerk. Her primary mission consisted in monitoring the branch managers so that the latter continually developed their critical eye towards their sales staff. Consequently, she only exceptionally intervened and critically evaluated a salesclerk's performance after a given sales situation, in order to sharpen the branch manager's perception. Echoing her own speech, she would both reprimand and compliment the employees:

"Poxa, faltou você adicionar um relógio! Ou aqui nessa hora, você viu que o cliente desistiu dessa peça, eu percebi porque ele desistiu, por que você falou nisso, nisso, nisso. Assim como eu também vou estar elogiando, diretamente para ele, quando eu estiver visualizando a situação."[40] (Ana, 32, supervisor at *Visibly Hot*)

Ana outlines that pushing the sales teams was an interesting task because she had to "make things happen" without playing an executive role. Nevertheless, she also admits to have difficulty with the high turning rates in retail. Ana expresses the feeling of never arriving at the target. Success in retail work was always of momentary appreciation, and new goals would urge her to creatively start again and again.

"Um grande desafio para o supervisor é que o varejo é muito rápido. As coisas- a gente não para nunca. Acaba uma meta, começa outra. Acaba um dia, ai você já tem o outro- é nosso trabalho, ele é muito- eu acho que acontece isso com todas as profissões. Mas a gente não para nunca, né? Se aquela loja está indo bem, a gente está de parabéns um dia, mas o outro dia já tem que começar cobrar uma nova meta. E como a gente depende- é um trabalho que depende, o meu resultado depende de outras pessoas, eu tenho que sempre re-inventando a forma de acessar aquele funcionário."[41] (Ana, 32, supervisor at *Visibly Hot*)

---

40 "Man, you missed adding a watch! Or in that other moment, you saw that the client renounced this piece, I realized that he renounced because you said this and this and that. But I would also directly compliment him, when I see the situation."

41 "One of the biggest challenges for the supervisor is the fact that retail is very fast. The things- we never stop. If one target is reached, there comes another. One day is over, and there you've already got to- that's our work, it's very- I think that this is happening with all professions. But we never stop, right? If

Emblematically, Ana links her permanent need of reinventing her motivation strategies directed at the sales staff to her very personal commitment in changing her identity.

"O tempo todo eu tenho que estar me reinventando de novo, porque se não, eu não motivo ninguém fazendo todos os dias as mesmas coisas."[42] (Ana, 32, supervisor at *Visibly Hot*)

Ana emphasizes that it was both interesting and very bad that, as a retail professional, one could succeed in maintaining the same quality of labor, but the results would not necessarily be stable. Sales professionals depended on economic variables, on fluctuations and specificities of each shopping center. Consequently, it was insufficient to recycle old strategies; she had to keep on with discovering new forms of (motivation) work. Ana states that this awareness frequently shocked her, because daily reinventions of her self were highly exhausting. "Às vezes é muito chato. Você não pode entrar em uma rotina de trabalho."[43]

The absence of stability and routine, which Ana bemoans, are part of a development in working relations Deleuze (1992) had observed with the emergence of control society in the early 1990s. Differently from what Foucault had so accurately illustrated with the device of disciplining power in institutions (Foucault 1977), the deployment of control such as within marketing logics produced, as he argued, a mode of power, which is of short-term and obligations of rapid rotation, but at the same time of a continuous and unlimited impetus. Regarding the subject, Deleuze sees incisive self-subordinating effects: "Man is no longer man enclosed, but man in debt" (Deleuze 1992:6). Coercion is not adjusted here by an oppressive exteriority, but by engineering the feeling of owing something to the enterprise. At *Visibly Hot*, supervisors like Ana may be most affected of this

---

    that shop is doing well, we are praised one day, but the other day we already need to meet a new target. And as we depend- it's a work that depends, my result depends on other persons, I always need to re-invent the mode of accessing that employee."

42 "All the time I have to reinvent myself, because if I don't, I won't motivate anyone to do the same things day after day."

43 "Sometimes, it really sucks. You cannot establish a work routine."

trend, because she is under higher pressure than the salesclerks; she needs to pass on their personal feeling and creative ideas to a number of other employees. The continually changing self-inventions she mentions are emblematic of the debt: as the brand's rhetoric of creativity, self-realization and anti-discriminatory policies discursively unfold in the idea of freedom, Ana is asked to express her gratitude to the enterprise.

Similar conflicts reveal the cultural diagnosis of "acceleration" by Rosa (2005). For the German sociologist, the crux lies in increasing speed: the acceleration of all spheres of human existence was, as in Simmel (1903), a consequence of modernity. In his view, late modernity provides new horizons of opportunities – technological progress allows faster and location-independent communication of people via Internet, let alone a generally experienced, greater extent of freedoms. However, the expectations directed to these horizons are provoking new constraints; such as the economic appeal that one had to act as a "gambler", moving through life in highly dynamic and flexible states of existence and work. According to Rosa, our *Being-In-The-World* is actually a question of time, that is, its subjective and social experience, which is a product of historical constellations. Central to his understanding is his argument, that as subjects we had scarcely "qualities" of time at our disposal: we could hardly co-decide about, nor evade its horizons, structures, speed rates and rhythms (Rosa 2005:15).

Rosa diagnoses the present's "time crisis", so to speak, the crisis-ridden character of "relations on the horizon of (late) modernity" (Rosa 2005:173), to which capitalism has contributed to a large extent. Particularly identities, the author continues, degenerated to situational self-relations:

"identification with spaces, with fixed communication partners and reference groups, and with things takes on a temporally delimited and contingent character. The person is compelled to distance or emancipate herself from them to the extent that she can withstand a change (whether voluntary or forced) without a loss of self." (Rosa 2013: 106)

Rosa thus sees a coercion directed towards the contingent, which would finally cause "placeless" subjects, forged as "devoid of identity and history". This phenomenon, he holds, indicated most clearly late modernity's break with "classic" modernity (Rosa 2005: 237). The shrinking of identity in its classical terms was closely linked to capitalist logics of market growth, awarding

"flexibility and a willingness to change in contrast to inertia and continuity: subjects must either conceive themselves from the very beginning as open, flexible and eager to change or run the danger of suffering permanent frustration when their projected identities are threatened with failure by a quickly changing environment." (Rosa 2013: 148)

In concordance with what was discussed above with the question of precariousness and recognition, I do not share Rosa's standpoint. Although the author's diagnosis of social acceleration is providing important impetus to contemporary critical theory, Rosa tends to reduce the question of "placeless" and "frustrated" identity by implicitly contrasting it to a romanticizing notion of an allegedly former, "classic", coherent subject. In so doing, he misses the chance to reflect his own normative understanding of what and which kind of identities are actually meant by that and why the same are promising freedom (or not). When it comes to gender, sexual or racial identity – as I tried to show through my own work – capitalist forces may displace or multiply its meanings, but to no extent do they do away with "classic" Western identity logics. Affected people like service workers are not threatened by seeing their identities shrinking away; rather, their frustration stems from very existential needs of having to put up with new labor regimes, which seduce them into precarious positions.

Ana's pursuit of recognition is especially directed towards being valued as a professional in sales supervision. Her expectations are indeed disappointed in the ways in which Rosa strives to analyze the effects of social acceleration. Once Ana gets to the point of having reached the target, market forces undo or redefine the targets: "another project and another task. That means there is no horizon" (Rosa et al. 2014: 29). Ana, as we have seen, is aware of the fact that her work does not include a stable performance benchmark and that this provokes both an economically insecure and pressurized situation. Nevertheless, and therein affected by the same feeling as the salesclerks, she opts for the employment because of the brand's attractive diversity politics and dynamics. It is hardly attestable though that Ana sees her need to "reinvent" herself in the face of a threatening "loss of self", as Rosa's argument (2013: 106) suggests.

The point is that through the present labor regimes, which are waving in people's manifold identity aspirations, the very notion of recognition is affected as well. Rosa's approach (2005) is here very close to the shortcomings of Honneth's recognition theory (Honneth 2011). According to McQueen (2015), recognition theorists are attached to the conviction that a stable and coherent identity led to a universally valid sense of freedom. With the case study of transgender, the author shows that the question of recognition is however much more complex. First, it becomes clear that not everyone has the same means of choice; transgender people are often subject to high social pressure and suffering, stemming directly from the hegemonic male-female binary that normalizes both coherence and stability of gender identity. Second, some transgender do have the important question of whether they want to subject themselves to these dominant logics of recognition. For particularly legal and medical recognition of transgender identities

"can be a normalising, disciplinary form of power even as it works to protect transgender identities and thus respond to the issues of exclusion and oppression that they are subject to." (McQueen 2015: 156)

Referring to Butler (2005), McQueen does not want to see the concept of recognition as completely abandoned. Rather, he calls for highlighting its ambivalences as well as the need for analyzing the ongoing struggles over its meaning. Accordingly, new appropriations of recognition could lead to incisive challenges (and possibly shifts) of meaning.

"Being recognised can often initiate a whole new set of struggles over one's sense of self and the different, often incompatible, ways that one is recognized." (McQueen 2015: 4)

Results and effects of these struggles are things we can neither exactly predict nor control. But what they reveal is that recognition, as hegemony, is precarious in that it is conflictive and movable, and thus potentially open for reappropriation.

5.2.2 *Rolezinhos* and celebrating capitalism – "um tapa na cara da sociedade"[44]

In recent years, several Brazilian urban metropolises, and especially São Paulo, have become the stage of a new phenomenon of youth gatherings. Reaching a momentary climax at the beginning of 2014, hundreds of mainly black teenagers of the poor neighborhoods in the urban peripheries meet for so called *rolezinhos* in shopping centers. Translatable as "little excursions or outings" (Assis 2014), *rolezinhos* are somewhat spontaneous, but thoroughly and publically organized through social networks. Asked in interviews made by newspaper journalists, the adolescents say they host *rolezinhos* "para curtir, tirar umas fotos, pegar umas meninas, comer uns lanches"[45] (Macedo and Toledo Piza 2014). But their strolling movements in the shopping centers apparently brought the integrity of these both public and private spaces into utter confusion. The teenagers playfully mobilized sudden group running in the corridors, they eventually hindered the escalators' usual functioning by clustering together, or they simply populated the seats of the food court areas and listened to their music. Being afraid of robbery, many shops decided to close. Furthermore, security agents and police forces started to deny the teenager's entrance in the shopping centers, until they finally started to arrest them. What followed in the media was an explosion of sudden social panic and political concerns. Who were these young people from the peripheries? Did they demand entrance to the world of consumption from the middle classes? How could the public commercial spaces restrict the teenagers' entry in the name of racist exclusion and socioeconomic marginalization? And finally, how should justice speak for the sake of security and simultaneously of equality?

I do not pretend to give answers to these questions. Rather, they should serve to picture the contemporary discursive conduct of diversity in Brazilian commercial spaces, namely related to shopping centers. The emphatic emotional reactions in the media towards the *rolezinhos*, dating from January and February of 2014, are emblematic for the existing gulf between the neoliberal incentives for introducing consumption into all areas of so-

---

44 "a slap in society's face"
45 "to have fun, take some pictures, hit on some girls, have some snacks"

ciety and the still strong social stereotype saying that consumers were both white and from middle classes. What turned out at that very moment was that the old hegemony of consolidated consumers had suddenly become challenged, affected by the fear of being menaced by unexpected, although so economically incentivized, subjects.

Capitalizing poor neighborhoods and its residents is part of the accelerating process of projective integration equally experienced by other minoritized social groups. Above state interventions, especially private investors have ultimately recognized the urban peripheries as new markets. After the so called pacification of the *Complexo do Alemão*, for example, the state's military invasion of one of the biggest shantytown areas of Rio de Janeiro in 2011, a large-scale investor announced the construction of a new shopping center right in this area (Nogueira 2013): *Favela Shopping* is the name of this project launched in 2013. Celso Athayde, one of its public promoters and co-founder of the *Central Union of Slums* (CUFA) emphasized that they would count with the financial help of the Inter-American Development Bank (IDB) and that five more shopping centers of this model were planned (Carvalho 2013). Athayde is a cultural producer for hip-hop music and sports that originate from the urban shantytowns. Together with musicians such as *NegaGizza*, a black female rapper from Rio, he has promoted a series of events and programs mainly aimed at creating spaces for black adolescents (CUFA 2015).

For Elias Tergilene, the main entrepreneur of the *Favela Shopping* project, Athayde has certainly been a welcomed partner. The favela population, countrywide comprising around 12 million people made it to one of the economically most "interesting" groups for investment. First, they are supposed to assure (or to be the new motor of) the market economy through their consumer practices. And second, their purchases help to sustain the discourse about the emergence of a supposed new middle class (Neri 2008)[46]. The example of *Favela Shopping* shows very clearly that contemporary market forces have long dissociated themselves from former social models, which excluded low-income earners and the poor. Rather, the opposite is the case: these forces now strive to embrace ever more the market-distant groups through monumental projects, micro credits and

---

46 For a critique of this discourse see the anthology *A nova classe média no Brasil como conceito e projeto político* (Bartelt 2013).

paying by installments[47]. The objective is not exclusion, as some sociologists like Padilha (2006) hold, but the realization of complete inclusion of the indigent groups into the sphere of the consumer market.

Against the backdrop of this already real-existing, visible extension of the market sphere, it is surprising that the *rolezinhos* are generally interpreted as these adolescents' urgent need for recognition and social belonging in consumption (see for example Leblon 2014). The young people in question are actually already representing one of the groups that comparatively spends most money on consumer goods like sports shoes, sunglasses or clothes. What is more, they intrinsically express their appraisal of branded products and fashion labels. Accurately, Assis (2014) points to the importance of *funk de ostentação*, a recent, popular funk music style from São Paulo, for the *rolezinho* members. *Funk de ostentação* [ostentation funk] emerged in the urban peripheries and is today enjoying great success in the commercial music industry. The lyrics, which broad groups that participate in the *rolezinhos* may identify with, speak of the ways people from the outskirts amounted to costly material goods, praising their ambitions. They mainly include fancy cars, brand fashion, pool parties and bosomy girls. As one of the founding songs of *funk de ostentação*, MCs Backdi and Bio G3's *Bonde da Juliet* from 2008 celebrates the American sunglasses brand Oakley and explicitly aims for making a show of high-priced status symbols as a form of sarcastic self-affirmation and social affront.

"Eles gostam de desfilar por aí
com um tênis que custa mais de 500 reais
óculos que custam mais de 1500 reais
E correntes de ouro no pescoço
Essa pouca vergonha que nós vimos agora
É um tapa na cara da sociedade

É o bonde da Juju
É o bonde da Juju
Porque água de bandido
É whisky Red Bull"[48] (Backdi and BioG3 2008)

---

47 For the question of debt overload of small consumers, see Hennigen (2012).

In this short extract of the song, the MCs are not only referring to the gang's highly expensive body ornaments, but also to their political concern. A gangster not being ashamed in showing off his precious property, they suggest, is a "slap in society's face". What they have in common with the *rolezinhos* is that they radically articulate a claim for visibility, that is, for a proper place within neoliberal consumerism's promises and temptations.

It would be misleading, however, to explain these articulations with the only reference to that hegemonic idea of recognition, which irradiates from society's elite. In other words, the "slap in society's face" hardly combines with the theory that the *rolezinho* adolescents were about to ask politely for admission into the club of middle class consumption practices. As also the anthropological perspectives on beauty citizenship carve out (Edmonds 2010), indigent groups of the urban peripheries continue to be excluded from a broad range of access to education, health and dignified housing, but not from consumption. Particularly the beauty industries have consolidated an enormous market in the shantytown areas (Machado-Borges 2009). But also clothing and overall fashion products are heavily circulating goods. Brands such as *Visibly Hot*, Oakley or Nike now heavily depend on the low-income earners. As the observations of salesclerk Juliano further attests: "quem mais compra aqui é quem menos tem"[49]. Incorporating the promises in consumption is, however, no guarantee for one being recognized in the elite's terms. Poor black adolescents' performance in shopping centers using 500 Reais sneakers are causing fear, which easily spills over into racist based security precautions and openly pronounced social exclusion.

Therein lies the political aspect of the *rolezinhos*. The precarious possibilities and resources of the youth gatherings for being recognized are directly challenging – be it intentionally or not – the pillars of colonially composed social domination. This is not about glorifying these young

---

48 "They like to parade around here; with sneakers that cost more than 500 Reais; sunglasses that cost more than 1500 Reais; and gold chains around the neck; this little shame we have seen right now; it's a slap in society's face; it's Juju's gang; it's Juju's gang; because the water of the gangsters; is whisky and Red Bull."

49 "who buys the most here is who has the least [money]"

people from the urban peripheries as revolutionaries. As Assis (2014) rightly notes, the often openly sexist and misogynous performances of masculinity, which is omnipresent in *funk de ostentação*, is far from corresponding to an understanding of difference as dedicated to an aspiration for a more egalitarian society. However, what remains is the destabilizing, challenging character of the adolescents' interventions with respect to the dominant notion of recognition.

"The *rolezinhos* constitute the moment when black and brown teenagers decide to collectively occupy sanitized and disciplined spaces of consumption – a consumption which in the first place was not meant for them – in order to make of it a locus of enjoyment and fun in their own terms – a form of leisure, linked to a lifestyle much celebrated by 'ostentatious funk', so far segregated and misrecognized." (Assis 2014)

Shopping centers as well as objects for consumption thus turn out to be potential arenas of struggle over the very highness of market citizenship and hence also over the realization claim of modern consumer society's promise of difference. When it comes to the articulation of proper aesthetics and identity claims, however, the questions of, first, what kind and notion of recognition young people are aspiring for, and second, by whom this recognition should be conceded, remain widely open to future negotiations. Celebrating capitalism in the name of liberation from social norms and exclusions – which appears to be the case with both the *Visibly Hot* sales workers and the *rolezinho* adolescents – does not automatically do away with the crux of difference. Whether economic growth-driven modes of existence are at all capable of providing shelter to the precarious still needs to be proven.

6. Conclusion

In the 21st century, affective labor is a major channel, through which promises and aspirations for recognition of difference – be that of sexually, racially or other minoritized content – are articulated. As I historically traced back in chapter two, contemporary modes of commercial (self)government are connected to the emergence of brands and evolving branding strategies on the eve of the 20th century. Taking on globally advancing procedures during decades, people's desires have increasingly become production sites of both profits and sociality (Arvidsson 2006). Front-line employees in retail since the 1990s have been increasingly facing the requirement of molding their singular identities as a part of their labor (du Gay 1996). Retail is then also one of the sectors where corporate branding in the name of *diversity management* has lately had a crucial impact. According to this model, sexual as well as racial/ethnic diversity is to be exploited and celebrated as welcomed social capital (Purtschert 2007). Service employees are asked to give shape to their deviance from cultural norms in playful and creative ways. Depending on the context and sales situation, they may even need to further perform their peculiar identities in order to acquire an eventually still unanticipated emancipatory advantage for their enterprise in comparison to other brands and institutions. Fancy black hairstyles and queer desires are suddenly promoted as the expression of both libertarian and pragmatic success.

Pointing to the transformation of work in its subjectivating effects, I showed that the advancing importance of brands and diversity strategies is momentous. The latter act not only as landmarks for selfhood and subjectivity of young service workers, but also as strategies to sell products. Branding purposely mixes and continually deterritorializes what is for sale and what is at stake for the employee's temporary life goals. With the example of the Brazilian fashion enterprise *Visibly Hot*, it became clear that service labor is charging the vitality of employees' bodies: it mobilizes corporeal techniques, such as fashionable styling of hair and of skin via tattoos or piercings, of behavioral moods and "attitudes", as well as of affective strategies like inducing flirting, amicable, emphatic or sexually loaded emotional ambiences. It belongs both to the requirements as well as to the direct effects of this work that the very separation of private and public, leisure and labor dissolves. Many salesclerks say that they feel intimate bonds to their teammates, to a degree that the team represented their "family". Moreover, this family eventually embraces customers. As sales techniques strive to engineer emotional proximity, relations to customers are of informal, amicable and even amorous nature. After all, work in many situations ceases to be experienced as work. It playfully integrates what a salesclerk personally wants to achieve in life and leisure.

By insisting on the cultural conditions and contradictions that cooperate in commercial (self)government, I argued that the Brazilian case is embedded in the cultural politics of cordiality (subsection 4.3). On one hand, this refers to the controversial myth of the *homem cordial* (Holanda 2014). Engaging Brazilian intellectuals since the 1930s, the highly informal and amicable work relations, Brazilians' supposedly "overflowing" affectivity, were seen as either the cause or the potential overcoming of the country's delay in (European styled) modernization. On the other hand, cordiality is what deeply characterizes contemporary relations in domestic work, mediating hierarchy in often subtle, because of officially amicable rules and affections (Vidal 2007). Both aspects proved to be of importance to the articulations of *Visibly Hot* sales staff. As part of their daily labor, sales employees' affective experiences through language or the body do not match with socially distanced and rationalized work ethics. Rather, it turns out that their allegiance to the brand and the sensation of pertaining to a "family" is intertwined with the logics of cordiality in that it rhetorically undoes hierarchy and heightens a broad volition for social recognition, which is aspired to take place at work.

The aspect of recognition through labor also led my critical appraisal of Hochschild's famous notion of emotional work (Hochschild 2003). As outlined throughout chapter four, sales techniques and techniques of self-government found at *Visibly Hot* can be compared to the latter author's study on flight attendants. Both employments are strongly molded by staff training, where service workers are taught the codes of conduct, that is, of specific posture and emotional behavior. Differently, however, from the example of Delta Airlines, salesclerks in the present study are neither asked nor willing to take off their uniform, as it were, the resulting moods and personalities after official hours. On the contrary, their stories show that lessons learnt at sales trainings are equally perceived as life's essential skills, referring directly to "personal growth" and highlighting one's singular authenticity. At the level of the individual, the idea of diversity even intrudes into the (sales) strategies of the affective. As discussed with the example of salesclerk João, although trainings are transmitting a sort of model or template, the same needs to be adapted by each employee in her or his very authentic personality; it entirely unfolds in the diversity spirit of "não importa se você é estranho, não importa se você é gay".[1]

Consequently, I argued that we deal with a kind of affective labor, which on an everyday level knits together individual bodies with identity and power. In the words of Lorenz and Kuster (2007), this is sexual labor: it demands efforts of workers to submit themselves to sexual norms in given moments, while in other situations workers are urged to actively shift or displace these norms, "working on" them through their very bodies and emotions. The example of Pedro's sales strategies indicates how he mobilizes images and sexual fantasies, which describe such efforts. With those male customers he assumes a drive for sex appeal to be confirmed by women, he elicits the character of the heartthrob in his counterparts. With other men, however, Pedro starts flirting. In doing so, he ensures that his identity referred to black power and street style comes to the fore; identifications he sees as belonging neither to mainstream nor to hegemonic norms of the body.

Affective labor actually demands efforts that both emanate from and are directed towards multiple social constraints. These are however not necessarily restricted to the realm of sexuality and heteronormativity, as the notion of Kuster and Lorenz (2007) implies. The point is that affectivity often simultaneously unfolds in cultural norms such as whiteness or trends of youthful fashion. With and above Lorenz and Kuster, I therefore suggested the term affective labor to embrace two dimensions. On one

---

1 "no matter if you are strange, no matter if you are gay"

hand, it refers to the immediate excitement of customers in interaction, it is literally about affecting customers: flirts, affective plays and the establishing of emotional proximity. On the other hand, affective labor equally comprises identity work, which is directed towards longer time frames and which transcends the sphere of the workplace: it is about general work on the self.

The latter dimension has been the topic of chapter three, where I extensively examined the aspirations of salesclerks. With the aim to understand the ways of how these young people actively participate in the brand's propagated diversity politics, the aspect of individual authenticity turned out to be crucial. Salesclerks enthusiastically receive the slogan "ser diferente", *Visibly Hot*'s central promise; they experience it as a question of style and beauty, but also of a specific consciousness to inhabit the different, like foremost being gay, lesbian, black or alternative. Most of them rave about this opportunity: "Here I can be the way I really am". Young employees see here their individual gain in freedom, even though they realize that there are a couple of rules determining how that freedom is to be achieved. Many of them think that one needs a minimum of identification with the brand, but not an adherence to standardized guidelines. If one is recognized as a similar in the basic concept of "ser diferente", their conviction goes, she or he has the license to fill this being different with content in a mode of individual authenticity. Whether one already "is" or still "becomes" authentic at work is secondary. What the examples of Larissa and Leidiane show is that the bigger creative changes in style and beauty practices, the better are the chances for someone to turn into a new role model for the brand.

The individual processes in affective labor helped us to understand that marketing and corporate branding alone cannot implement the model of celebrated diversity. To use the words of Hall (1996), it needs the workers to "suture" the interpellations via identification. The example of Carol is impressive, but not only because she tattooed the brand's symbol on her forearm. On one hand, it is notable that she constantly contributes to the norm of the right working attitude and "ser diferente" through her somatic practices and explications, even if she repeatedly fails on this path, leaving no doubt about the fact that she will never completely and at all times reach that target. On the other hand, we should not reduce her active collaboration in diversity management to an imprudent act, that is, a thorough fall into the tentacles of market and mass consumption. According to Carol's own account, it is her "vulnerability" due to her being a lesbian that is best taken care of at *Visibly Hot* compared to other, more "conventional companies." Her identity claims are not de facto a commodity. Neither her identity aspirations, nor her feelings have been assigned an exact price. Carol's claims are rather to be seen as a part of her personhood, an articulation that can never be fully absorbed by market logics nor substituted by money, albeit it unfolds in a thoroughly marketable fashion.

Nonetheless, the problem remains of how far individual economic potential and the right to be different are intertwined, but not at all equivalent. As depicted in chapter five, the salesclerks' very concrete experiences are pointing to symptoms of fatigue, which also stem from this incongruity. Although most of the employees are evaluating their job in positive terms, my research has found that the enthusiasm for the brand is limited to one or two years of employment. As in the case of Pedro, frustration derives from *Visibly Hot´s* normative enclosure of how "different" one's style or sexuality finally could be, but also from the ways in which worker selves are inexorably subjected to the logics of sales. Like his colleague Juliano, he articulates a thorough critique on the brand's diversity policies, saying that the latter was not as open-minded as it promised and that it made one turn into a premium-directed narcissist. He went through sanctions and bullying that referred to his beard, hair, smell and tight clothing. Style emancipation was largely limited to sales success. Pedro's disappointment however points to precarious (if not failed) recognition he expected to get from the brand and the amicable relations he maintained at the workplace.

The precarious – this is what I elaborated taking into account the related debates in queer and feminist studies (Lorenz 2007b; Muñoz 2007; Lorey 2012; Motakef 2015) – does not solely refer to contractual shortcomings like flexible salaries, commission targets, extra hours or insecure and short-time engagements in the sphere of employment. These factors are one part of precarious work. Referring to the question about difference and diversity, another part of the precarious however points to the additional efforts of those affective workers who are not lucky enough to match fancy, approved cultural norms and identities as of the beginning. If we again compare the example of Andrea with that of Leidiane, Pedro or Carol, it becomes clear that they are facing very different demands to work on their selves as well as on cultural norms of recognition. Andrea's proximity to the image of the sexy white girl grants her a certain security: first, because she is enabled to move through nationally and internationally circulating beauty ideals; and second, because she can directly relate to the role model of that sexual attracting, which appears in official *Visibly Hot* advertising. Pedro, Leidiane and Carol in contrast need to invest much more effort, if they are interested in receiving a moderately comparable social recognition at the workplace. There is a range of contradictions and social conflicts that they need to creatively address in order to be considered a beautiful black person, or in order to be looked at as a cool and prestigious young adult "although" lesbian or gay.

Inhabiting precarious positions is what the young salesclerks are being taught and motivated to do by the brand's instructions. Sales supervisor Ana distinguishes that *Visibly Hot* does not only like, but also highly esteems those black people who "valorize" their race. As affective laborers, sales employees are urged to fill categories such as those of race, sexual orientation or gender with fashionable (old or new) content. Yet the shifts taking place have ambivalent effects. Workers often sustain problematic regimes of masculinity and femininity when reiterating sexist imagery of the brand's advertisement or when mobilizing fantasies in consumer interaction. At the same time, they help to ensure that homosexual desire and black skin are woven into sales as so-called positive assets. Starting from precarious positions always means that changes are possible, eventually even those that were not anticipated by the brand strategies. Pedro has experimented corporeally as well as emotionally with such counter strategies and found at least an individual line of flight. However, his example also shows that his room for maneuver remained highly restricted within the brand, that he was confronted with sanctions until a point when he left the company.

The limits of *Visibly Hot*'s promise of difference lie finally not only in the fact that the aspired individual authenticity is restricted to a relatively short job engagement. My analysis of advertising, marketing strategies and foremost of self-assessments made by salesclerks shows that the pluralization of valorized identities at the workplace – namely those of lesbians, gays and blacks – do not result in a fundamental questioning, but rather in a continuation of the modern Western idea of equality (Maihofer 2009). Diversity strategies apply a policy, as it were, of sorting young people's differences into small packets that are all productively lined up and assembled into a colorful "family". The capitalistically marketed difference in subjects does not know pain and has no negatively conspicuous attributes. Furthermore, diversity's difference remains the difference of others; it is not conceived as a thing that all humans do carry with them. At *Visibly Hot*, controversies about the "valorization" of gays indicate this quite clearly. While some employees say that it is "good to work with homosexuals" and that the brand embraces them with ardor, other sales workers stick to stereotypes like "homossexuais não gostam de esporte"[2] or preferred to diminish all excessively "faggotish" behavior at the sales point.

The promise of difference as analyzed with the example of *Visibly Hot* is thus not to be reduced to a pure phenomenon of political economy. As above argued with the emergence of brands and branding government, the relationship of cultural-economic processes and modes of subjectivity are today probably as inseparable as ever before. In the present book, I tried to formulate a cultural and social critique that strives to understand how subjectivity feels like when sexual liberation and racial emancipation are eventually experienced as a part of labor as well as of markets and hence of a globally unbroken belief in neoliberal logics of growth. While early brands were deployed to strengthen colonial projects and to legitimize unequal treatment of the sexes as well as of the races from above (McClintock 1995), contemporary brands seem to unfold in young people's aspirations literally from within. For the sales employees in question, it has thus become increasingly difficult to articulate oneself in the midst of cultural interpellations and political expectations. It is not enough for one to be nice, good-looking and productive. One has to simultaneously prove her or his authenticity, furthermore reworking on emancipatory goals that convert blacks and LGBTs into cool subjects as a part of daily labor.

Finally, not only are product markets globally entangled, but they are also current cultural logics of difference in that they circulate faster and in more place-independent digital channels. Identifications and images of the self as articulated by *Visibly Hot* sales staff are thus at the same time embedded in national political contexts and globally circulating discourse of emancipation. For this I have put forward the preliminary thesis that Bra-

---

2   "homosexuals do not like sports"

zil's hegemonic state narrative provides a fertile ground for the concept of diversity. Firstly, corporate branding mixes the latter with the discourse of racial democracy. And secondly, entrepreneurial diversity is linked here to the establishment of a specific "Gays, Lesbians and Sympathizers" (GLS) market segment in the 1990s. In the case of *Visibly Hot*, both of these reference points surprisingly evoke the "family" as the emblematic form of a culturally desirable social collective, through which each individual's recognition in "being different" is to be concealed. The fatiguing efforts of the brand's salesclerks however show that recognition is often a frustrating business, since they rarely arrive or maintain themselves at their aspired social places. In the midst of new excitements and constraints, sexual as well as racial liberation remain highly contested; to date, they are neither socially consensual nor do they embrace a secure shelter of equal rights in difference.

Bibliography

Abercrombie & Fitch (2013): "Life as a Greeter – Episode 2", https://http://www.youtube.com/watch?v=kWtG7_OGF9s&sns=tw, accessed 18.02.2013.

Abreu, Nuno Cesar Pereira De (2002): Boca do Lixo: cinema e classes populares, Ph.D. thesis, Universidade Estadual de Campinas.

Abu-Lughod, Lila (1993): Writing Women's Worlds: Bedouin Stories, Berkeley: University of California Press.

Acker, Joan (1990): "Hierarchies, Jobs, Bodies: A Theory of Gendered Organizations", in: Gender & Society 4(2), p. 139-158.

Acker, Joan (2006): "Inequality Regimes: Gender, Class, and Race in Organizations", in: Gender & Society 20(4), p. 441-464.

Ahmed, Sara (2004a): "Collective Feelings: Or, the Impressions Left by Others", in: Theory Culture Society 21(25), p. 25-42.

Ahmed, Sara (2004b): The Cultural Politics of Emotion, Edinburgh: Edinburgh University Press.

Ahmed, Sara (2010): "Happy Objects", in: Melissa Gregg/Gregory Seigworth (Org.), The Affect Theory Reader, London & Durham: Duke University Press, p. 29-51.

Ahmed, Sara (2012): On Being Included. Racism and Diversity in Institutional Life, London/Durham: Duke University Press.

Almeida, Maria Isabel Mendes de (2009): "Juventude e Empreendedorismo: uma abordagem das novas 'subjetividades executivas'", in: Desigualdade & diversidade (PUCRJ) 3, p. 5-15.

Almeida, Maria Isabel Mendes de/Eugenio, Fernanda (2011): "Autonomías táticas: Criatividade, liberação e inserção profissional juvenil no Rio de Janeiro", in: Política & Trabalho 35, p. 11-28.

Almeida, Maria Isabel Mendes de/Tracy, Kátia Maria de Almeida (2003): Noites nômades. Espaço e subjetividade nas culturas jovens contemporâneas, Rio de Janeiro: Rocco.

Althusser, Louis (1976): "Idéologie et appareils idéologiques d'État (Notes pour une recherche)", in: Louis Althusser (Org.), POSITIONS (1964-1975), Paris: Les Éditions sociales, p. 67-125.

Amit, Vered (2008): "Introduction. Constructing the field", in: Vered Amit (Org.), Constructing the Field: Ethnographic Fieldwork in the Contemporary World, London/New York: Routledge, p. 1-18.

Anderson, Benedict (1991): Imagined Communities: reflections on the origin and spread of nationalism, London: Verso.

Antunes, Ricardo/Druck, Graça (2013): "A terceirização como regra?", in: Revista TST 79(4), p. 214-231.

Anzaldúa, Gloria (2007): Borderlands/La Frontera. The New Mestiza, San Francisco: Aunt Lute Books.

Arango, Luz Gabriela Gaviria (2013): "Emociones, saberes y condiciones de trabajo en los servicios: manicuristas en Colombia y Brasil", in: Revista Latino-americana de Estudos do Trabalho 30(18), p. 103-132.

Arango, Luz Gabriela Gaviria/Molinier, Pascale (Org.)(2011): El trabajo y la ética del cuidado, Medellín: Carreta Editores.

Ariès, Philippe (1960): L'Enfant et la vie familiale sous l'Ancien Régime, Paris: Plon.

Arvidsson, Adam (2006): Brands. Meaning and value in media culture. London/New York: Routledge.

Assis, Mariana (2014): "Rolezinho: Politics in Brazil's Shopping Malls?", in: Public Seminar, http://www.publicseminar.org/2014/01/rolezinho-politics-in-brazils-shoppingmalls/#.WBd_q3qZnXs, accessed 12.10. 2015.

Backdi/Biog3 (2008): "Bonde da Juliet", http://letras.mus.br/backdi-biog3/1548816/, accessed 21.10.15.

Bailey, Michael/Oberschneider, Michael (1997): "Sexual Orientation and Professional Dance", in: Archives of Sexual Behavior 26(4), p. 433-444.

Bartelt, Dawid Danilo (Org.) (2013): A "nova classe media" no Brasil como conceito e projeto politico, Rio de Janeiro: Fundação Heinrich Böll.

Beck, Ulrich (1999): Schöne neue Arbeitswelt, Frankfurt am Main: Campus.

Beleli, Iara (2007): "Corpo e identidade na propaganda", in: Estudos Feministas 15, p. 193-215.

Beleli, Iara (2009): "'Eles[as] parecem normais': visibilidade de gays e lésbicas na mídia", Bagoas 4, p. 113-130.

Benjamin, Walter (1996): Das Kunstwerk im Zeitalter seiner technischen Reproduzierbarkeit, Frankfurt am Main: Suhrkamp.

Bezerra, Elvia (2005): "Ribeiro Couto e o homem cordial", Revista Brasileira 44, p. 123-130.

Bischoff, Daniel/Grzenia, Dennis/Wollner, Sven (2011): "The Evolution of Moving Pictures", in: BLINK 2, p. 6-17.

Boltanski, Luc/Chiapello, Eve (2005): The New Spirit of Capitalism, London/New York: Verso.

Boltanski, Luc; Thévenot, Laurent (1999): "The Sociology of Critical Capacity", in: European Journal of Social Theory 2 (3), p. 359-377.

Bonfim, Mirele Cardoso Do/Gondim, Sônia Maria Guedes (2010): Trabalho emocional: demandas afetivas no exercício profissional, Salvador: EDUFBA.

Bourdieu, Pierre (1979): La distinction. Critique sociale du jugement, Paris: Les Éditions de Minuit.

Bourdieu, Pierre (2002): La domination masculine, Paris: Seuil.

Braga, Ruy (2006): "Uma sociologia da condição proletária contemporânea", Tempo Social 18(1), p. 33-152.

Braga, Ruy (2012): A política do precariado: do populismo à hegemonia lulista, São Paulo: Boitempo.

Bragg, Steven (2015): "Accounting Tools: Dictionary/Derecognition", http://www.accountingtools.com/dictionary-derecognition, accessed 19.10.2015.

Braz, Camilo (2014): "De Goiânia a 'Gayânia': notas sobre o surgimento do mercado 'GLS' na capital do cerrado", in: Estudos Feministas 22, p. 277-296.

Brites, Jurema (2007): "Afeto e desigualdade: gênero, geração e classe entre empregadas domésticas e seus empregadores", in: cadernos pagu 29, p. 91-109.

Bröckling, Ulrich (2013): Das unternehmerische Selbst. Soziologie einer Subjektivierungsform, Frankfurt am Main: Suhrkamp.

Burawoy, Michael (1979): Manufacturing Consent: Changes in the Labor Process Under Monopoly Capitalism, Chicago: University of Chicago Press.
Butler, Judith (1990): Gender trouble: feminism and the subversion of identity, New York/London: Routledge.
Butler, Judith (1993): Bodies that matter. On the discursive limits of "sex", New York/London: Routledge.
Butler, Judith (2004): Precarious Life: The Powers of Mourning and Violence, London: Verso.
Butler, Judith (2005): Giving an Account of Oneself, New York: Fordham University Press.
Cardoso, Alberto (2013): "Juventude, trabalho e desenvolvimento: elementos para uma agenda de investigação", in: Caderno CRH 26(68), p. 293-314.
Carls, Kristin (2007): "Affective Labour in Milanese Large Scale Retailing: Labour Control and Employees' Coping Strategies", in: ephemera 7(1), p. 46-59.
Carrara, Sérgio (2013): "Négocier les frontières, négocier aux frontières: l'anthropologie et le processus de 'citoyennisation' de l'homosexualité au Brésil", in: Brésil(s) 4, p. 103-123.
Carrara, Sérgio/Simões, Júlio Assis (2007): "Sexualidade, cultura e política: a trajetória da identidade homossexual masculina na antropologia brasileira", in: cadernos pagu 28, p. 65-99.
Carvalhal, Andre (2014): A moda imita a vida: como construir uma marca de moda, São Paulo: Estção das Letras e Cores.
Carvalho, Pedro (2013): "Shopping no Alemão já tem 61 franquias 'acordadas', diz Celso Athayde", in: IG São Paulo 06.07.2013, http://economia.ig.com.br/2013-06-07/shopping-no-alemao-ja-tem-61-franquias-acordadas- diz-celso-athayde.html, accessed 30.10.2015.
Castel, Robert (1995): Les métamorphoses de la question sociale: une chronique du salariat, Paris: Fayard.
Castillo, Mayarí Gallardo/Maldonado, Claudia Graus (Org.)(2015): Desigualdades. Tolerancia, legitimación y conflicto en las sociedades latinoamericanas, Santiago de Chile: RiL Editores.
Chakrabarty, Dipesh (2002): "Europa provinzialisieren. Postkolonialität und die Kritik der Geschichte", in: Sebastian Conrad/Shalini Randeria (Org.), Jenseits des Eurozentrismus. Postkoloniale Perspektiven in den

Geschichts- und Kulturwissenschaften, Frankfurt/New York: Campus, p. 283-312.

Clifford, James/Marcus, George (1986): Writing Culture: The Poetics and Politics of Ethnography, Berkeley: University of California Press.

Clough, Patricia Ticineto (2007): "Introduction", in: Patricia Ticineto Clough (Org.), The Affective Turn. Theorizing the Social, London/ Durham: Duke University Press, p. 1-33.

Collier, John/Collier, Malcolm (1986): Visual Anthropology. Photography as a Research Method, Albuquerque: University of New Mexico Press.

Colling, Leandro (2007): "Homoerotismo nas telenovelas da Rede Globo e a cultura", conference paper, Anais do III Encontro de Estudos Multidisciplinares em Cultura, Salvador da Bahia.

Comaroff, John/Comaroff, Jean (2009): Ethnicity, Inc., Chicago/London: The University of Chicago Press.

Coppa, Francesca (2006): "A brief history of media fandom", in: Karen Hellekson/Kristina Busse (Org.), Fan Fiction and Fan Communities in the Age of the Internet, Jefferson NC: McFarland, p. 41-60.

Corrêa, Mariza (1996): "Sobre a invenção da mulata", in: cadernos pagu, 6-7, p. 35-50.

Costa, Sérgio (2007): Vom Nordatlantik zum "Black Atlantic". Postkoloniale Konfigurationen und Paradoxien transnationaler Politik, Bielefeld: transcript.

Costa, Sérgio (2014): "O Brasil de Sérgio Buarque de Holanda", in : Revista Sociedade e Estado 29(3), p. 823-839.

Crenshaw, Kimberlé Williams (1989): "Demarginalizing the Intersection of Race and Sex: A Black Feminist Critique of Antidiscrimination Doctrine", in: Feminist Theory and Antiracist Politics 140(1), p. 139-167.

CUFA (2015): "Sobre a Cufa", http://www.cufa.org.br/sobre-cufa.php-slide-2, accessed 30.10.2015.

Dalla Costa, Mariarosa (2004): "Capitalism and Reproduction", in: The Commoner 8, p. 1-12.

Davis, Angela (1982): Rassismus und Sexismus. Schwarze Frauen und Klassenkampf in den USA, Berlin: Elefanten Press.

Deleuze, Gilles (1992): "Postscript on the Societies of Control", in: October 59, p. 3-7.

Deleuze, Gilles/Guattari, Félix (1980): Mille Plateaux, Paris: Les Éditions de Minuit.
Deleuze, Gilles/Parnet, Claire (1996): Dialogues, Paris: Flammarion.
Deliovsky, Kathy (2008): "Normative White Femininity: Race, Gender and the Politics of Beauty", in: Atlantis 33(1), p. 49-59.
Demirović, Alex (2008): "Critique and Truth. For a New Mode of Critique", in: eipcp/europäisches institut für progressive kulturpolitik 04-2008, http://eipcp.net/transversal/0808/demirovic/en, accessed 19.11.2015.
Dornelas, José (2013): "Entrevista com Caito Maia, da Chilli Beans", http://www.josedornelas.com.br/caito-trechos/, accessed 14.01.2015.
Dörre, Klaus. "Prekäre Arbeit. Unsichere Beschäftigungsverhältnisse und ihre sozialen Folgen", in: Arbeit 1(15), p. 181-193.
du Gay, Paul (1996): Consumption and Identity at Work, Lodon/Thousand Oaks/New Delhi: SAGE.
Dubar, Claude (2005): A socialização: construção das identidades sociais e profissionais, São Paulo: Martins Fontes.
Economia Baiana (2012): "Brasil terá 474 shopping centers até o final deste ano", http://economiabaiana.com.br/2012/05/08/brasil-tera-474-shopping-centers-ate-o-final-deste- ano/, accessed 22.01.2014.
Edmonds, Alexander (2010): Pretty Modern. Beauty, sex, and plastic surgery in Brazil, Durham/London: Duke University Press.
Elias, Norbert (1978): Über den Prozess der Zivilisation. Soziogenetische und psychogenetische Untersuchungen. Erster Band: Wandlungen des Verhaltens in den westlichen Oberschichten des Abendlandes, Frankfurt am Main: Suhrkamp.
Elliott, John Hall (2011): "Social-scientific criticism: Perspective, process and payoff. Evil eye accusation at Galatia as illustration of the method", in: HTS Teologiese Studies, 67(1), p. 1-10.
Engel, Antke (2009): Bilder von Sexualität und Ökonomie. Queere kulturelle Politiken im Neoliberalismus, Bielefeld: transcript.
Erel, Umut/Haritaworn, Jin/Gutiérrez Rodríguez, Encarnación/Klesse, Christian (2010): "On the Depoliticisation of Intersectionality Talk. Conceptualising Multiple Oppressions in Critical Sexuality Studies", in: Yvette Taylor/Sally Hines/Mark Casey (Org.), Theorizing Intersectionality and Sexuality, Basingstoke: Palgrave Macmillan, p. 56–77.

Federici, Silvia (2012): "The Reproduction of Labor Power in the Global Economy and the Unfinished Feminist Revolution", in: Silvia Federici (Org.), Revolution at Point Zero: Housework, Reproduction, and Feminist Struggle, Oakland CA: PM Press, p. 91- 114.

Fleury, Maria Tereza Leme (2000): "Gerenciando a diversidade cultural: experiências de empresas brasileiras", in: RAE - Revista de Administração de Empresas 40(3), p. 18-25.

Flick, Uwe/Kardorff, Ernst Von/Steinke, Ines (2008): "Was ist qualitative Forschung? Einleitung und Überblick", in: Uwe Flick/Ernst von Kardorff/Ines Steinke (Org.), Qualitative Forschung. Ein Handbuch, Reinbek bei Hamburg: Rowohlt, p. 13-29.

Foltin, Robert (2002): "Immaterielle Arbeit, Empire, Multitude. Neue Begrifflichkeiten in der linken Diskussion. Zur Hardt/Negris 'Empire'", in: grundrisse – zeitschrift für linke theorie & debatte 2(1), p. 6-20.

Fontes, Olivia de Almeida/Borelli, Fernanda Chagas/Casotti, Leticia Moreira (2012): "Como ser homem e ser belo? Um estudo exploratório sobre a relação entre masculinidade e o consumo de beleza", in: Revista Eletrônica de Administração 72(2), p. 400-432.

Foster, Robert J. (2007): "The Work of the New Economy: Consumers, Brands, and Value Creation", in: Cultural Anthropology 22(4), p. 707-731.

Foucault, Michel (1977): Überwachen und Strafen. Die Geburt des Gefängnisses, Frankfurt am Main: Suhrkamp.

Foucault, Michel (1987): Sexualität und Wahrheit: Der Wille zum Wissen, Frankfurt am Main: Suhrkamp.

Foucault, Michel (1991): "Governmentality", in: Graham Burchell/Colin Gordon/Peter Miller (Org.), The Foucault Effect. Studies in Governmentality, Chicago: University of Chicago Press, p. 87–104.

Foucault, Michel (2008): Nascimento da Biopolítica, São Paulo: Martins Fontes.

França, Isadora Lins (2006): Cercas e pontes: o movimento GLBT e o mercado GLS na cidade de São Paulo, MA thesis, Universidade de São Paulo.

França, Isadora Lins (2007): "Identidades coletivas, consumo e política: a aproximação entre mercado GLS e movimento GLBT em São Paulo", in: Horizontes Antropológicos 13(28) 2007, p. 289- 311.

França, Isadora Lins (2012): Consumindo lugares, consumindo nos lugares: homossexualidade, consumo e subjetividades na cidade de São Paulo, Rio de Janeiro: EdUERJ.
Gardnier, Ruy (2001): "A rica fauna da pornochanchada", in: Contracampo Revista de Cinema 36(1), http://www.contracampo.com.br/36/frames.htm, accessed 14.11.2014.
Gaudio, Rudolf (2003): "Coffeetalk: StarbucksTM and the commercialization of casual conversation", in: Language in Society 32(5), p. 659-691.
Giles, Judy (2004): The parlour and the suburb: domestic identities, class, femininity and modernity, Oxford/New York: Berg.
Gill, Rosalind (2009): "Supersexualize Me!: Advertising and the 'Midriffs'", in: Feona Attwood (Org.), Mainstreaming Sex. The Sexualization of Western Culture, London/New York: I.B.Tauris, p. 93-110.
Gilroy, Paul (1995): The black Atlantic: modernity and double-consciousness, Cambridge MA: Harvard University Press.
Glaser, Barney/Strauss, Anselm (1967): The Discovery of Grounded Theory, Chicago: Aldine.
Glauser, Christoph (2001): Einfach blitzsauber. Die Geschichte des Staubsaugers, Zürich: Orell Füssli.
Globo TV (2014): "Como a Chilli Beans se transformou em uma rede com 600 pontos de venda", http://globotv.globo.com/editora-globo/revista-pegn/v/como-a-chilli-beans-se-transformou-em-uma-rede-com-600-pontos-de-venda/3606280/, accessed 20.11.2014.
Goffman, Erving (1979): Gender Advertisements, New York: Harper and Row.
Gomes, Luciani (2012): "Brazil's continuing franchising boom", BBC News 27.05.2012, http://www.bbc.com/news/business-18143355, accessed 15.12.2014.
Gomes, Nilma (2003): "Corpo e cabelo como símbolos da identidade negra", II Seminário Rizoma, Florianópolis.
Gonçalves, Adriana Inhudes da Cruz/Hoelz, Antonio Marcos Ambrozio/Pimentel, Fernando Puga/Lage, Filipe de Sousa/Machado, Marcelo Nascimento (Org.)(2012): "A economia brasileira: conquistas dos últimos dez anos e perspectivas para o future", in: Banco Nacional de Desenvolvimento Econômico e Social (Brasil) (Org.), BNDES 60 anos: perspectivas setoriais, Rio de Janeiro: BNDES, p. 12-41.

Gonzaga, Gustavo (1998): "Rotatividade e qualidade do emprego no Brasil", in: Revista de Economia e Política 18(1), p. 120-140.

Gregori, Maria Filomena (2004): "Prazer e perigo: notas sobre feminismo, sex-shops e S/M", in: Adriana Piscitelli/Maria Filomena Gregori/Sérgio Carrara (Org.), Sexualidade e saberes: convenções e fronteiras, Rio de Janeiro: Garamond, p. 235-256.

Gregori, Maria Filomena (2006): "Relações de Violência e Erotismo", in: Adriana Piscitelli/Hildete de Melo Pereira/Sônia Maluf Weidner/Vera Lucia Puga (Org.), Olhares Feministas, Brasília: UNESCO, p. 255-280.

Gregori, Maria Filomena (2012): "Erotismo, mercado e gênero. Uma etnografia dos sex shops de São Paulo", in: cadernos pagu 38, p. 53-97.

Grossberg, Lawrence (Org.) (1992): Cultural Studies, New York/London: Routledge.

Grossberg, Lawrence (1997): "Cultural Studies: What's in a Name? (One More Time)", in: Lawrence Grossberg (Org.), Bringing It All Back Home: Essays on Cultural Studies, Durham: Duke University Press, p. 245-271.

Guattari, Félix (1990): As três ecologias, Campinas: Papirus.

Guattari, Félix/Rolnik, Suely (2007): Molecular Revolution in Brazil. Los Angeles: Semiotext(e).

Gubrium, Jaber/Holstein, James (2013): "Analytic Inspiration in Ethnographic Fieldwork", in: Uwe Flick (Org.), The SAGE Handbook of Qualitative Data Analysis, Los Angeles/London/New Delhi: SAGE Publications, p. 35-48.

Gutiérrez Rodríguez, Encarnación (2010): Migration, domestic work and affect: a decolonial approach on value and the feminization of labor, New York/Abingdon UK: Routledge.

Hall, Stuart (1996): "Introduction: Who Needs 'Identity'?", in: Stuart Hall/Paul Du Gay (Org.), Questions of Cultural Identity, London/Thousand Oaks/New Delhi: SAGE, p. 1-17.

Hardt, Michael (1996): "Introduction: Laboratory Italy", in: Paolo Virno/Michael Hardt (Org.), Radical Thought in Italy: a potential politics, Minneapolis MN: University of Minnesota Press, p. 1-11.

Hardt, Michael (1999): "Affective Labor", boundary 26(2), p. 89-100.

Hardt, Michael/Negri, Antonio (2000): Empire, Cambridge MA/London: Harvard University Press.

Hark, Sabine/Laufenberg, Mike (2013): Sexualität in der Krise. Heteronormativität im Neoliberalismus, in: Erna Appelt/Brigitte Aulenbacher/Angelika Wetterer (Org.), Gesellschaft. Feministische Krisendiagnosen, Münster: Westfälisches Dampfboot, p. 227-245.

Hartewig, Karin (2009): Der verhüllte Blick: Kleine Kulturgeschichte der Sonnenbrille, Marburg: Jonas Verlag.

Heilborn, Maria Luiza (2006): "Entre as tramas da sexualidade brasileira", in: Estudos Feministas 14, p. 43-59.

Heilborn, Maria Luiza/Sorj, Bila (1999): "Estudos de gênero no Brasil", in: Sérgio Miceli (Org.), O que ler na ciência social brasileira (1970-1995), ANPOCS/CAPES, São Paulo: Editora Sumaré, p. 183-221.

Hemmings, Claire (2012): "Affective solidarity: Feminist reflexivity and political transformation", in: Feminist Theory 13(2), p. 147-161.

Hennigen, Inês (2012): "O lado avesso do sistema consumo-crédito: (super)endividamento do consumidor", VI Econtro Nacional de Estudos do Consumo, Rio de Janeiro.

Hirata, Helena/Guimarães, Nadya Araújo (Org.)(2012): Cuidado e cuidadoras: as várias faces do trabalho do care, São Paulo: Atlas.

Hochschild, Arlie Russell (2003): The Managed Heart: Commercialization of Human Feeling, Berkeley/Los Angeles/London: University of California Press.

Hochschild, Arlie Russell (2013): "Foreword", in: Alicia Grandey/James Diefendorff/Deborah Rupp (Org.), Emotional Labor in the 21st Century. Diverse Perspectives on Emotion Regulation at Work, New York/Hove UK: Routledge, p. xiii.

Hofmann, Susanne (2010): "Corporeal Entrepreneurialism and Neoliberal Agency in the Sex Trade at US-Mexican Border", in: Women's Studies Quarterly 38(3/4), p. 233-256.

Holanda, Sérgio Buarque de (2012): Roots of Brazil, Notre Dame IN: University of Notre Dame Press.

Holanda, Sérgio Buarque de (2014): Raízes do Brasil, São Paulo: Companhia das Letras.

Holt, Douglas (2002): "Why Do Brands Cause Trouble? A Dialectical Theory of Consumer Culture and Branding", in: Journal of Consumer Research 29(1), p. 70-90.

Honneth, Axel (2011): Das Recht der Freiheit – Grundriß einer demokratischen Sittlichkeit, Berlin: Suhrkamp.
hooks, bell (1994): Black Looks. Popkultur – Medien – Rassismus, Berlin: Orlanda Frauenverlag.
Horkheimer, Max/Adorno, Theodor W.(1969): Dialektik der Aufklärung. Philosophische Fragmente. Mit einem Nachwort von Jürgen Habermas, Frankfurt am Main: S. Fischer Verlag.
Hörning, Karl H./Winter, Rainer (1999): "Einleitung", in: Karl H. Hörning;/Rainer Winter (Org.), Widerspenstige Kulturen. Cultural Studies als Herausforderung, Frankfurt am Main: Suhrkamp, p. 7-12.
Hughes, Jason (2010): "Emotional Intelligence: Elias, Foucault, and the Reflexive Emotional Self", in: Foucault Studies 8(1), p. 28-52.
Illouz, Eva (1997): Consuming the romantic utopia: love and the cultural contradictions of capitalism, Berkeley/Los Angeles: University of California Press.
Indeed (2014): "Avaliações – Chilli Beans", http://www.indeed.com.br/cmp/Chilli-Beans?from=SERP, accessed 05.05.2014.
Jarrín, Alvaro (2010): Cosmetic Citizenship: Beauty, Affect and Inequality in Southeastern Brazil, Ph.D. thesis, Duke University, Durham.
Kirkham, Pat (Org.)(1996): The gendered object, Manchester/New York: Manchester University Press.
Kneidinger, Bernadette (2010): Facebook und Co. Eine soziologische Analyse von Interaktionsformen in Online Social Networks, Wiesbaden: VS Verlag für Sozialwissenschaften.
Kögler, Hans-Herbert (1999): "Kritische Hermeneutik des Subjekts. Culural Studies als Erbe der Kritischen Theorie", in: Karl H. Hörning/Rainer Winter (Org.), Widerspenstige Kulturen. Cultural Studies als Herausforderung, Frankfurt am Main: Suhrkamp, p. 196-237.
Kornblum, William (2012): Sociology in a Changing World, Belmont CA: Wadsworth.
Kozinets, Robert V./Dolbec, Pierre-Yann/Earley, Amanda (2013): "Netnographic Analysis: Understanding Culture through Social Media Data", in: Uwe Flick (Org.), The SAGE Handbook of Qualitative Data Analysis, London/Thousand Oaks/New Delhi/: SAGE, p. 262-276.
Krell, Gertraude/Sieben, Barbara (2007): "Diversity Management und Personalforschung", in: Gertraude Krell/Barbara Riedmüller/Barbara Sie-

ben/Dagmar Vinz (Org.), Diversity Studies. Grundlagen und disziplinäre Ansätze, Frankfurt a.M./New York: Campus, p. 235-254.

Laclau, Ernesto/Mouffe, Chantal (1985): Hegemony and Socialist Strategy. Towards a Radical Democratic Politics, London: Verso.

Lakoff, Robin Tolmach (2006): "Identity à la carte: you are what you eat", in: Anna De Fina/Deborah Schiffrin/Michael Bamberg (Org.), Discourse and Identity, Cambridge UK/New York: Cambridge University Press, p. 142-165.

Lamont, Michèle (1992): Money, Morals, and Manners. The Culture of the French and the American Upper-Middle Class, Chicago: University of Chicago Press.

Latour, Bruno (2014): "On some of the affects of capitalism", http://www.bruno-latour.fr/sites/default/files/136-AFFECTS-OF-KCOPENHAGUE.pdf, accessed 07.07.2015.

Lauretis, Teresa de (1987): Technologies of gender. Essays on Theory, Film, and Fiction, Bloomington/Indianapolis: Indiana University Press.

Lazzarato, Maurizio (1996): "Immaterial Labor", in: Paolo Virno/Michael Hardt (Org.), Radical Thought in Italy: A Potential Politics, Minneapolis/London: University of Minnesota Press, p. 133-147.

Lazzarato, Maurizio (2007): "The Misfortunes of the 'Artistic Critique' and of Cultural Employment", in: eipcp/europäisches institut für progressive kulturpolitik 02-2007, http://eipcp.net/transversal/0207/lazzarato/en, accessed 19.11.2015.

Lazzarato, Maurizio/Negri, Antonio (2001): Trabalho imaterial: formas de vida e produção de subjetividade, Rio de Janeiro: DP&A Editora.

Leblon, Saul (2014): "Rolezinhos: os pobres estão afrontando sua invisibilidade", Carta Maior 18.01.2014, http://www.cartamaior.com.br/?%2FEditoria%2FCidades%2FRolezinhos-os-pobres-estao-afrontando-sua-invisibilidade%2F38%2F30039, accessed 30.10.2015.

Lima, Ari (2002): "Black or Brau: Music and Subjectivity in a Global Context", in: Charles Perrone/Christopher Dunn (Org.), Brazilian Popular Music and Globalization, New York/London: Routledge, p. 220-232.

Lopes, Moisés (2003): "A 'intoxicação sexual' do novo mundo: sexualidade e permissividade no livro Casa-Grande & Senzala", in: Revista Mediações 8(2), p. 171-189.

Lorenz, Renate (2007a): "Long working hours of normal love. Hannah Cullwick's photographs and diaries", in: Lorenz (Org.), NORMAL LOVE, Berlin: b_books, p. 104-124.

Lorenz, Renate (Org.) (2007b): NORMAL LOVE. precarious sex, precarious work. Katalog zur Ausstellung/exhibition catalog, Berlin: b_books.

Lorenz, Renate (2009): Aufwändige Durchquerungen. Subjektivität als sexuelle Arbeit, Bielefeld: transcript.

Lorenz, Renate/Kuster, Brigitta (2007): Sexuell Arbeiten: Eine queere Perspektive auf Arbeit und prekäres Leben, Berlin: b_books.

Lorey, Isabell (2008): "Kritik und Kategorie. Zur Begrenzung politischer Praxis durch neuere Theoreme der Intersektionalität, Interdependenz und Kritischen Weißseinsforschung", in: eipcp/europäisches institut für progressive kulturpolitik 10/2008, http://eipcp.net/transversal/0806/lorey/de, accessed 01.03.2014.

Lorey, Isabell (2012): Die Regierung der Prekären. Mit einem Vorwort von Judith Butler, Wien: Turia + Kant.

Lury, Celia. Brands (2004): The logos of the global economy, London & New York: Routledge.

Macedo, Leticia/Toledo Piza, Paulo (2014): "'Rolezinho' nas palavras de quem vai", G1 São Paulo 15.01.2014, http://g1.globo.com/sao-paulo/noticia/2014/01/rolezinho-nas-palavras-de-quem-vai.html, accessed 15.05.2014.

Machado-Borges, Thaïs (2009): "Producing Beauty in Brazil. Vanity, Visibility and Social Inequality", in: vibrant 6(1), p. 208-237.

Maia, Caito/Araújo, Rodolfo (2012): E se colocar pimenta? A história da marca mais quente do Brasil, sem cortes, Rio de Janeiro: Elsevier.

Maia, Suzana (2012): "Identificação e branquidade inominada: corpo, raça e nação nas representações sobre Gisele Bündchen na mídia transnacional", in: cadernos pagu 38, p. 309-341.

Maihofer, Andrea (2009): "Dialektik der Aufklärung – Die Entstehung der modernen Gleichheitsidee, des Diskurses der qualitativen Geschlechterdifferenz und der Rassentheorien", in: Zeitschrift für Menschenrechte 1(FrauenMenschenrechte), p. 20-36.

Maihofer, Andrea (2013): "Geschlechterdifferenz – eine obsolete Kategorie?", in: Dominique Grisard/Ulle Jäger/Tomke Könige (Org.), Verschieden sein. Nachdenken über Geschlecht und Differenz, Sulzbach/Taunus: Ulrike Helmer Verlag, p. 27-48.

Maihofer, Andrea (2014): "Sara Ahmed: Kollektive Gefühle – Elemente des westlichen hegemonialen Gefühlsregimes", in: Angelika Baier/ Christa Binswanger/Jana Häberlein/Yv Eveline Nay/Andrea Zimmermann (Org.), Affekt und Geschlecht. Eine einführende Anthologie, Wien: Zaglossus, p. 253-272.

Manning, Paul (2010): "The Semiotics of Brand", in: Annual Review of Anthropology 39, p. 33-49.

Marcuse, Herbert (2004): Der eindimensionale Mensch. Studien zur Ideologie der fortgeschrittenen Industriegesellschaft, Springe: zu Klampen Verlag.

Marinho, Isabela (2013): "Aluna passa em 2° lugar em mestrado com projeto sobre Valesca Popozuda", G1 Rio de Janeiro 18.04.2013, http://g1.globo.com/rio-de-janeiro/noticia/2013/04/aluna-passa-em-1-lugar-em-mestrado-com-projeto-sobre-valesca-popozuda.html, accessed 30.11.2014.

Martins Filho, Júlio (2012): "Raça e consumo: a identidade do negro na nova realidade do negro na nova realidade do mercado e dos meios de comunicação do Brasil", in: Cadernos Zygmunt Bauman 2(4), p. 162-201.

Marx, Karl (1957): Das Kapital: Kritik der politischen Ökonomie, Stuttgart: Kröner.

Mcclintock, Anne (1995): Imperial Leather: Race, Gender and Sexuality in the Colonial Contest, New York: Routledge.

Mcdowell, Linda (2009): Working Bodies. Interactive Service Employment and Workplace Identities, Chichester: Wiley & Blackwell.

McQueen, Paddy (2015): Subjectivity, Gender and the Struggle for Recognition, Houndmills/New York: Palgrave Macmillan.

Mcrobbie, Angela (2009): The Aftermath of Feminism. Gender, Culture and Social Change. London/Thousand Oaks/New Delhi/Singapore: SAGE.

MDIC Ministério Do Desenvolvimento, Indústria E Comércio Exterior (2014): Importância do Setor Terciário, http://www.mdic.gov.br/sitio/interna/interna.php?area=4&menu=4485, accessed 12.07.2015.

Mennel, Birgit/Salzmann, Andrea (2008): "Buchbesprechung zu Sexuell Arbeiten. Eine queere Perspektive auf Arbeit und prekäres Leben", in: grundrisse – zeitschrift für linke theorie & debatte 25, http://www.

grundrisse.net/buchbesprechungen/brigitta_kuster_und_renate_lorenz. htm, accessed 18.08.2015.

Mesquita, Sushila (2011): Ban Marriage! Ambivalenzen der Normalisierung aus queer-feministischer Perspektive. Wien: Zaglossus.

Middleton, Richard (1990): Studying popular music, Buckingham: Open University Press.

Miller, Michael B. (1981): The Bon Marché: Bourgeois Culture and the Department Store, 1869-1920, Princeton/Chichester: Princeton University Press.

Miller, Peter/Rose, Nikolas (2008): Governing the Present. Administering Economic, Social and Persoanl Life, Cambridge UK/Malden MA: Polity.

Moebius, Stephan (2009): Kultur, Bielefeld: transcript.

Motakef, Mona (2015): Prekarisierung, Bielefeld: transcript.

Muñoz, José Esteban (2007): "Queerness's labor, or, the work of disidentification", in: Renate Lorenz (Org.), NORMAL LOVE, Berlin: b_books, p. 126-133.

Nahoum, André Vereta (2013): Selling "cultures": The Traffic of Cultural Representations from the Yawanawa, Ph.D. thesis, Universidade de São Paulo.

Nava, Mica (1997): "Modernity's Disavowal: Women, the City and the Department Store", in: Pasi Falks/Colin Campbell (Org.), The Shopping Experience, London/Thousand Oaks/New Delhi: SAGE, p. 56-91.

Neri, Marcelo (2008): A Nova Classe Média, Rio de Janeiro: CPS/FGV.

Nogueira, Danielle (2013): "Alemão terá shopping com 100% de mão de obra local. Dois anos após ocupação, grupo mineiro investirá R$ 17 milhões em complexo de lojas", O Globo 12.02.2013, http://oglobo. globo.com/economia/alemao-tera-shopping-com-100-de-mao-de-obra-local-7554804, accessed 18.12.2014.

Oliveira, Graziele (2014): "Valesca Popozuda: 'Ser vadia é ser livre'", O Globo Época 12.04.2014, http://epoca.globo.com/ideias/noticia/2014/ 04/bvalesca-popozudabser-vadia-e-ser-livre.html, accessed 9.11.2014.

Ong, Aiwa (2007): "Neoliberalism as a mobile technology", in: Transactions of the Institute of British Geographers 32(1), p. 3-8.

Padilha, Valquíria (2006): Shopping center: a catedral das mercadorias, São Paulo: Boitempo.

Pendergrast, Mark (2000): For God, Country and Coca-Cola: The Definitive History of the Great American Soft Drink and the Company that Makes it, New York: Basic Books.

Pernau, Margrit (2015): "A transnational history of emotions. Forschungsbericht 2015", http://www.mpg.de/9008445/MPIB_JB_2015, accessed 13.09.2015.

Phelan, Shane (2001): Sexual Strangers: Gays, Lesbians, and Dilemmas of Citizenship, Philadelphia: Temple University Press.

Pillow, Wanda/Mayo, Cris (2007): "Toward Understandings of Feminist Ethnography", in: Sharlene Nagy Hesse-Biber (Org.), Handbook of Feminist Research, Thousand Oaks: Sage Publications, p. 155-171.

Pinho, Osmundo/Rocha, Eduardo (2011): "Racionais MC's: Cultura Afro-Brasileira Contemporânea como Política Cultural", in: Afro-Hispanic Review 30(2), p. 101- 114.

Piscitelli, Adriana (2007): "Corporalidade em confronto: Brasileiras na indústria do sexo na Espanha", in: Revista Brasileira de Ciências Sociais 22(64), p. 17-32.

Piscitelli, Adriana (2009): "As fronteiras da transgressão: a demanda por brasileiras na indústria do sexo na Espanha", in: Sexualidad, Salud y Sociedad 1, p. 177-201.

Portal Educação (2013): "Técnicas de Rapport", http://www.portaleducacao.com.br/administracao/artigos/33461/tecnicas-de-rapport, accessed 30.11.2013.

Preciado, Beatriz (2008): Testo Yonqui, Madrid: Espasa.

Pringle, Rosemary (2013): "Bureaucracy, Rationality and Sexuality: The Case of Secretaries", in: Ursula Müller/Birgit Riegraf/Sylvia Wilz (Org.), Geschlecht und Organisation, Wiesbaden: Springer VS, p. 65-85.

Programa Expressão (2012): "Navio Chili Beans – Convenção 2012" https://http://www.youtube.com/watch?v=p6-CB-BAHkU, accessed 16.10.2013.

Purtschert, Patricia (2007): "Diversity Management: Mehr Gewinn durch weniger Diskriminierung? Von der Differenz im Umgang mit Differenzen", in: Femina Politica 1, p. 88-96.

Purtschert, Patricia/Meyer, Katrin (2010): "Die Macht der Kategorien. Kritische Überlegungen zur Intersektionalität", in: Feministische Studien. Zeitschrift für interdisziplinäre Frauen-und Geschlechterforschung 1(28), p. 130-142.

Rabinow, Paul (1977): Reflections on Fieldwork in Morocco, Berkeley: University of California Press.

Ramalho, José Ricardo (2013): "Trabalho e os desafios da pesquisa sociológica", in: Revista Brasileira de Sociologia 1(1), p. 89-105.

Rancière, Jacques (1987): Le maître ignorant, Paris: Fayard.

Rancière, Jacques (2008): Le spectateur émancipé, Paris: La Fabrique.

Raposo, Otávio (2013): "Planeta B-Boy. Novos capitais culturais pela dança", in: Lígia Ferro/Otávio Raposo/Pedro Abrantes (Org.), Urban Culture in Action: Politics, Practices and Lifestyles, Lisboa: Second International Conference of Young Urban Researchers, p. 35-54.

Redação/G1 (2015): "Propaganda de O Boticário com gays gera polêmica e chega ao Conar", G1 São Paulo 02.06.2015, http://g1.globo.com/economia/midia-e-marketing/noticia/2015/06/comercial-de-oboticario-com-casais-gays-gera-polemica-e-chega-ao-conar.html, accessed 06.11.2015.

Redação/ON (2013): "Esclarecendo dúvidas sobre o vale-alimentação", O Nacional 03.06.2013, http://www.onacional.com.br/geral/38126/esclarecendo+duvidas+sobre+o+vale-alimentacao, accessed 04.11.2015.

Redação/Terra (2014): "Dribles na falta de dinheiro marcam sucesso da Chilli Beans", Terra 26.06.2014, http://economia.terra.com.br/vida-de-empresario/dribles-na-falta-de-dinheiro-marcam-sucesso-da-chilli-beans,3e57737bb24d6410VgnVCM10000098cceb0aRCRD.html, acessed 13.01.2015.

Redação/WSCOM (2013): "Shopping no Alemão já tem 61 franquias", WSCOM 07.06.2013, http://www.wscom.com.br/noticia/economia/SHOPPING+NO+ALEMAO+JA+TEM+61+FR ANQUIAS+-151061, accessed 14.01.2015.

Rezende, Claudia Barcellos (2009): Retratos do estrangeiro: identidade brasileira, subjetividade e emoção, Rio de Janeiro: Editora FGV.

Rodrigues, Tatiane Cosentino/Abramowicz, Anete (2013): "O debate contemporâneo sobre a diversidade e a diferença nas políticas e pesquisas em educação", in: Educação e Pesquisa 39(1), p. 15-30.

Rosa, Hartmut (2005): Beschleunigung. Die Veränderung der Zeitstrukturen in der Moderne, Frankfurt am Main: Suhrkamp.

Rosa, Hartmut (2013): Social acceleration: a new theory of modernity, New York: Columbia University Press.

Rosa, Hartmut/Lessenich, Stephan/Kennedy, Margrit/Waigel, Theo (Org.) (2014): Weil Kapitalismus sich ändern muss. Im Gespräch mit Hartmut Rosa, Stephan Lessenich, Margrit Kennedy, Theo Waigel. Mit einem Vorwort von Elmar Altvater, Wiesbaden: Springer VS.

Rose, Nikolas (2004): Powers of Freedom. Refraiming Political Thought, Cambridge UK: Cambridge University Press.

Saraiva, Luiz Alex Silva/Irigaray, Hélio Arthur dos Reis (2009): "Políticas de diversidade nas organizações: uma questão de discurso?", in: RAE 49(3), p. 337-348.

Sauer, Birgit/Penz, Otto (2013): "Editorial", in: Österreichische Zeitschrift für Soziologie 38(Themenheft: Kommodifizierung von Gefühlen und Gefühlsarbeit), p. 129-129.

Sauer, Birgit/Penz, Otto (2014): "Affektive Subjektivierung: Arbeit und Geschlecht", in: Freiburger Zeitschrift für GeschlechterStudien 20(2), p. 79-94.

Saukko, Paula (2003): Doing Research in Cultural Studies. An introduction to classical and new methodological approaches, London/Thousand Oaks/New Delhi: SAGE.

Schmitz, Sigrid/Ahmed, Sara (2014): "Affect/Emotion: Orientation Matters. A Conversation between Sigrid Schmitz and Sara Ahmed", in: Freiburger Zeitschrift für GeschlechterStudien 20(2), p. 97-108.

Shaw, Lisa/Dennison, Stephanie (2007): Brazilian National Cinema, Abingdon/New York: Routledge.

Silverman, Kaja (1992): Male Subjectivity at the Margins, New York: Routledge.

Silverman, Kaja (1997): "Dem Blickregime begegnen", in: Christian Kravagna (Org.), Privileg Blick. Kritik der visuellen Kultur, Berlin: Edition ID-Archiv, p. 41-64.

Silvestri, Leonor (2014): "Queer – Precio y desprecio de un valor. Taller de Leo Silvestri. Primer encuentro turno jueves noviembre 2014", https://http://www.youtube.com/watch?v=5l-MwlNVST8, accessed 21.10.2015.

Silvestri, Leonor/Staunsager, Mai (2015): "Games of Crohn. Documental sobre Leonor Silvestri y su vida con Crohn", https://www.youtube.com/watch?v=oTgv-3K9mg4, accessed 01.10.2015.

Simmel, Georg (1903): "Die Großstädte und das Geistesleben", in: Theodor Petermann (Org.), Die Großstadt. Vorträge und Aufsätze zur Städteausstellung, Dresden: Gehe-Stiftung, p. 185-206.

Simmons, Aaron (2006): "Giving an Account on Oneself", Journal for Cultural and Religious Theory 7(2), p. 85-90.

Singer, André (2012): Os sentidos do lulismo. Reforma gradual e pacto conservador, São Paulo: Companhia das Letras.

Soares, Angelo (2000): "Interactions et violences dans les supermarchés: une comparaison Brésil – Québec", in: Cahiers du Genre 28, p. 97-115.

Souza, Ildembergue Leite de/Souza Leão, André Luiz Maranhão de (2013): "Dionísio Usa Chilli Beans? – Análise Mitológica da Publicidade da 'Marca da Pimenta'", in: RAC Revista de Administração Contemporânea 17(5), p. 574-597.

Souza, Jessé (2012): Os batalhadores brasileiros: nova classe média ou nova classe trabalhadora?, Belo Horizonte: Editora UFMG.

Sproll, Martina (2013): "Precarization, Genderization and Neotaylorist Work. How Global Value Chain Restructuring Affects Banking Sector Workers in Brazil", in: desiguALdades.net Working Paper Series 44, http://www.desigualdades.net/Resources/Working_Paper/44_WP_Sproll_Online_revised.pdf, accessed 22.10.15.

Sussekind, Arnaldo (2005): "O salário-comissão e sua alteração", in: Revista TRT 30(55), p. 47-51.

Targetjobs (2015): "Ten skills you'll gain from working in part-time retail jobs", https://targetjobs.co.uk/internships/275105-ten-skills-youll-gain-from-working-in-part-time-retail-jobs, accessed 22.05.2015

Tavares, Andrea (2013): "Caito Maia", View Edição 127, http://www.viewmagazine.com.br/opiniao/entrevista?edition=127, accessed 22.09.2013.

Taylor, Timothy (2012): The Sounds of Capitalism. Advertising, Music, and the Conquest of Culture, Chicago: The University of Chicago Press.

Thornberg, Robert/Charmaz, Kathy (2013): "Grounded Theory and Theoretical Coding", in: Uwe Flick (Org.), The SAGE Handbook of Qualitative Data Analysis, London/Thousand Oaks/New Delhi/Singapore: SAGE, p. 153-169.

Trabalhista, Guia (2015): "Tabela dos valores nominais do salário mínimo", http://www.guiatrabalhista.com.br/guia/salario_minimo.htm, accessed 21.01.2015.

Tsianos, Vassilis/Karakayali, Serhat (2010): "Transnational Migration and the Emergence of the European Border Regime: An Ethnographic Analysis", in: European Journal of Sociology 13(3), p. 373-387.

Tsianos, Vassilis/Papadopoulos, Dimitris (2006): "Precarity: A Savage Journey to the Heart of Embodied Capitalism", in: eipcp/europäisches institut für progressive kulturpolitik 10/2006, http://eipcp.net/transversal/1106/tsianospapadopoulos/en, accessed 16.07.2015.

TV Estadão (2012): "Consumidor infantil está na mira da Chilli Beans", http://economia.estadao.com.br/videos/videos,consumidor-infantil-esta-na-mira-da-chilli-beans,186625,,0.htm?pagina=5, accessed 25.11.2014.

Tyler, Melissa/Hancock, Philip (2001): "Flight Attendants and the Management of Gendered 'Organizational Bodies'", in: Kathryn Backett-Milburn/Linda Mckie (Org.), Constructing Gendered Bodies, Basingstoke: Palgrave, p. 25-38.

Vidal, Dominique (2007): Les bonnes de Rio. Emploi domestique et société démocratique au Brésil, Villeneneuve d'Ascq: Septentrion.

Warner, Michael (1993): "Introduction", in: Michael Warner (Org.), Fear of a queer planet: queer politics and social theory, Minneapolis: The University of Minnesota Press, p. vii-xxxi.

Weber, Max (2005[1904]): Die protestantische Ethik und der Geist des Kapitalismus, Stuttgart: Reclam.

Wei, Junhow (2014): "Mass media and the localization of emotional display: The case of China's Next Top Model", in: American Journal of Cultural Sociology 2(2), p. 197-220.

Wolkowitz, Carol (2006): Bodies at Work, London/Thousand Oaks/New Delhi: SAGE.

Wuggenig, Ulf (2008): "Paradoxical Critique", in: eipcp/europäisches institut für progressive kulturpolitik 04-2008, http://eipcp.net/transversal/0808/wuggenig/en, accessed 19.11.2015.

Zelizer, Viviana (2005): The Purchase of Intimacy, Princeton: Princeton University Press.

Zola, Émile (1980[1883]): Au Bonheur des Dames, Paris: Éditions Gallimard.

Social Sciences

Maik Fielitz, Laura Lotte Laloire (eds.)
Trouble on the Far Right
Contemporary Right-Wing Strategies and Practices in Europe

2016, 208 p., 19,99 € (DE),
ISBN 978-3-8376-3720-5
E-Book: 17,99 € (DE), ISBN 978-3-8394-3720-9
EPUB: 17,99 € (DE), ISBN 978-3-7328-3720-5

Andréa Belliger, David J. Krieger
Organizing Networks
An Actor-Network Theory of Organizations

2016, 272 p., 34,99 € (DE),
ISBN 978-3-8376-3616-1
E-Book: 34,99 € (DE), ISBN 978-3-8394-3616-5

Julia Sattler (ed.)
Urban Transformations in the U.S.A.
Spaces, Communities, Representations

2016, 426 p., 39,99 € (DE),
ISBN 978-3-8376-3111-1
E-Book: 39,99 € (DE), ISBN 978-3-8394-3111-5

All print, e-book and open access versions of the titels in our entire list are available in our online shop www.transcript-verlag.de/en!

Social Sciences

Frank Eckardt, Javier Ruiz Sánchez (eds.)
City of Crisis
The Multiple Contestation
of Southern European Cities

2015, 264 p., 29,99 € (DE),
ISBN 978-3-8376-2842-5
available as free open access publication
E-Book: ISBN 978-3-8394-2842-9

Derya Özkan (ed.)
Cool Istanbul
Urban Enclosures and Resistances

2014, 172 p., 29,99 € (DE),
ISBN 978-3-8376-2763-3
E-Book: 26,99 € (DE), ISBN 978-3-8394-2763-7

Michael Friedman, Samo Tomsic (eds.)
Psychoanalysis: Topological Perspectives
New Conceptions of Geometry and Space
in Freud and Lacan

2016, 256 p., 34,99 € (DE),
ISBN 978-3-8376-3440-2
E-Book: 34,99 € (DE), ISBN 978-3-8394-3440-6

All print, e-book and open access versions of the titels in our entire list
are available in our online shop www.transcript-verlag.de/en!